Martha Franks:
One Link in God's Chain

Martha, Chefoo, 1926

MARTHA FRANKS:
One Link in God's Chain
by
J. Donald McManus

TAXAHAW PUBLICATIONS
Lancaster, South Carolina

To Judie, Jay, and Lee

Acknowledgments

To my wife, Judie, who introduced me to Martha Franks and who, when I proposed to write this story, encouraged me. She has carefully combed my writing, suggesting ways to improve the text and supplying punctuation which I have often neglected.

To my son, Jay, who so carefully and eagerly transferred the whole from my writing on scores of legal pads to computer disks, all of which remains something of a bewilderment to me.

To my son, Lee, who often passed through the room where I wrote, asking, "How's the writing going, Poppy?"

To the Kelford and Menola Baptist Churches where as a pastor I was first introduced to Miss Franks.

To the Lawtonville Baptist Church where the friendship ripened.

To the First Baptist Church of Kershaw, whom I pastored when the dream was born.

To Cornerstone Baptist Church of Camden, South Carolina, who gave me a year's liberty to write the text and listened eagerly and patiently to my tri-weekly reportings.

Special thanks to

— Dr. Betty Hodges, Professor of English, University of South Carolina, Lancaster, for her helpful suggestions concerning the writing.

— Esther and Mary Ada Jenkins who read and listened to my tales.

— Nell Blakeney who read the text and who has often enthusiastically encouraged me to continue writing

and most of all to Martha.

A Note

on Illustrations, Proverbs and Letters:

The exquisite illustrations on the cover, and scattered throughout this book, are photocopies of Chinese paper cutouts. Someone cut each by hand with the crudest pair of scissors. I chose these from handbound, silk-covered autograph books which formerly sold in China for a few pennies.

Every language has its proverbs. China's have an especial appeal to me. I selected each one for its relevance to the story. They are obviously intended to mark changes of time, place and tempo.

Rather than Chapter headings or numbers, I divided the book with samples from Martha Franks' great volume of handwritten letters. Only two were not written by her. The first, from her father, was selected for its warm, fatherly touch; the other was that dictated by Martha to a young student who wrote the letter in Chinese.

Introduction

The Best Memory . . .
Not so firm
As faded ink

I remember vividly the day the idea first came to me to write this story. Martha Franks stood in my pulpit and I, after having introduced her, sat in the pew to listen. I do not remember how many times I had heard her before, perhaps a dozen.

Each time she spoke, I felt something real in her words and manner. She was deadly serious, but with a sense of humor and self-depreciation that made me comfortable.

That morning I sat back to enjoy, for she often spoke the same words. But on that particular morning, I thought that someone needed to write Martha's story. I could hardly wait until lunch. As we sat at the table, I said, "Miss Martha, someone needs to write your story and I'd like to be the one to do it." Her immediate response was, "I'd like you to."

I was taken aback. I don't know what I had expected, but I had never really thought about writing a biography before. I didn't know where to begin.

On that occasion of our initial conversation concerning the writing of this text, I asked, "Martha, why did you go to China? What did you have to offer God?" Her immediate response was, "I was just one link in the chain." I rejoined, "That's it! That would make a good title: *Martha Franks: One Link in God's Chain.*" She liked it, too.

I soon learned that Martha's family and friends had saved hundreds of letters written from China over a period of forty years. When they came into my possession, they were in folders by year of writing. Upon reading some of the letters, I discovered that in addition to being a wonderful chronicle of those tumultous times in China (and the world), they told the story of a life lived in commitment to God and the people of China. Martha wrote warm, passionate, humorous, informing letters. They were sometimes written so as to conceal from her family the danger and deep sense of loneliness she felt. Others, written to intimate friends show how very human she really was and how many of those feelings, common to the lot of us, were her experience, too.

The letters reveal a woman who grew into a servant of God, one step at the time. She did not arrive in China full-blown. Her beginning was all enthusiasm for something she did not even begin to comprehend.

When I began the writing in 1985, two people who gave me a bit of the portrait of Martha which would only be blank spaces on the canvas otherwise were Martha's sister Rosalie who died in 1988 at the age of 98, and Bertha Smith, who might have been an asset to Joshua at Jericho or Ai or anywhere else he chose to fight. She too died in 1988 at the age of 99. And then the effort came to a halt until January, 1989. Each Monday I traveled to Laurens to read what Martha had written. She listened to my writing from the letters and added words of correction or explanation. Little by little, the two came together. In the process, Matsu Crawford, a grade-school friend, gave me a picture of Martha as a student in public school and at college. Martha's dear friend, Olive Lawton, gave another view as she spoke of their friendship now spanning almost three quarters of this century.

In the process, I have viewed a life up-close, almost intimately. Martha and I have shared ourselves with each the other in a manner that is rare. Few holds have been barred; little turf has been marked out of bounds. The experience has been unique and wonderfully exciting. We became friends.

Foreword

Soon after I joined the staff of the Foreign Mission board, Martha Franks became my friend and mentor. I have considered her my "special friend" for forty years. Always ready with a warm heart and listening ear, she knows at once how to encourage and challenge to a deeper commitment to faith in the Lord.

The author of this biography has captured the many facets of her personality. She never fit anyone's mold. Possessing a strong will, she was willing to make any sacrifice if convinced of God's leading. It took courage for a young woman in her twenties to leave the security of family for a distant China.

Upon her arrival in China, she began a never-ending love affair with the land and its people. When she went to teach kindergarten in Hwanghsien, she was in the land of Lottie Moon. Some have said that the two women had many traits in common.

Martha adapted readily, working with all ages. From kindergarten in Hwanghsien to village work in Tsining, she, like Lottie Moon only a few years before, saw great response to the sharing of God's Word. When the invitation came to teach in the theological seminary in Hwanghsien, she reluctantly left village evangelism. For the remainder of her career, she found great joy in teaching. She has often quipped, "I went to China to teach kindergarten children, and ended up teaching preachers. But there wasn't much difference!" Her keen sense of humor and ready wit sometimes got her into trouble, but made life more interesting for those who knew her.

She has always had a rare appreciation for all things beautiful, whether clothing or the artifacts of ancient China. Along with her love of beauty, she retains a keen sense of the ugliness of suffering in the world and the determination to make a difference. I recall a Sunday morning in Taipei as I followed her around a dormitory for deaf and blind children. Making the rounds, Martha washed a dirty face, buttoned a shirt, tied shoes and helped the children into the van and drove them to Sunday School where she and a Chinese woman taught them of God's love. This biography reveals her sensitivity to the needs of people and her great gift of inspiring others to help in meeting those needs.

When the time came for retirement, Martha might well have settled in to enjoy her new home in Laurens. Instead, she began to put feet on her dream of a retirement home where old Christians might end their days. Even as she criss-crossed the country leading prayer retreats and speaking to a variety of audiences, every spare moment was given to making the dream real. Once again, her gift for inspiring others led the people of Laurens to join in the efforts at fund-raising through the "Thrift and Gift Shop" which brought in many thousands of dollars. The dream came true in 1985 when Martha and a host of others moved into the *Martha Franks Retirement Center.*

In July 1990, I visited Martha in that lovely place which reflects her love of beauty. The home is filled with pieces from China purchased over half a lifetime.

As we visited, I recalled sitting on her porch, eighteen years before, as she spoke of her dream of this home. Martha Franks dreams dreams, works hard, trusts God, and inspires others to make the dreams come true. She has lived out her faith across the world.

From small towns of South Carolina to the villages and great cities of China, countless lives have been changed through the efforts of this one woman who gave her life in service to God.

Edna Francis Dawkins
Richmond, Virginia
October 1, 1990

Contents

Acknowledgments / *vii*
Introduction / *ix*
Foreword / *xii*

Little Orphant Annie Goes To Church,
   Laurens / *5*

God Has a Plan for her Life,
   Winthrop, Schoolfield, Southern Seminary / *25*

"I *Will* Learn This Language!"
   Peking, Hwanghsien / *41*

A Young Missionary Experiences the *Great Revival,*
   Tsining / *94*

"Someone has to be in charge . . ."
   Hwanghsien under the Japanese / *163*

"The Old Order Changeth . . ."
   Shanghai / *183*

". . . Yielding Place to the New,"
   Taiwan / *196*

Old Women Dream Dreams (and work hard),
   Laurens and everywhere / *230*

". . . And God Fulfills Himself in Many Ways."
   the world / *243*

A bar of iron
Continually ground . . .
A needle

Mid-summer's day, August 14, 1989, dawned beautiful and clear. It was a Saturday, day of graduation for several hundred students at Clemson University. President and Mrs. Max Lennon were hosting a breakfast and lunch for those being presented with honorary degrees.

The honorees were two men and a woman. The men were both giants in their fields of business. They were good men, hard-working, successful, honorable men both. They were of that variety of men whose ability, financial and otherwise, carried weight at Clemson as they might have carried weight anywhere.

But what of the woman in white, this "all-white" woman, as one little Chinese girl had dubbed her long ago? Who was she and what did she have to do with Clemson University? There must have been several in that room who wondered who she was.

Dr. Martha Linda Franks receives congratulations from Dr. Max Lennon of Clemson University

Sitting in the corner of the room, this old woman dressed in a white suit was every bit as regal as Helen Hayes playing the Queen Victoria. For a fact, she bore a striking resemblance to Helen Hayes. Her snow white hair pulled back into a French twist gave her an air of elegance that somehow exuded at once a confidence and humility that were impressive. Her face showed determination, but softened by what must be an inner peace and joy long cultivated. It was a pretty and kind face, not done overnight, but a face eighty-eight years in the making. There were no traces of sadness, no regret, nor fear, nor sorrow on that face — all those had been absorbed a long time ago in other ways; they did not dare intrude themselves upon that face.

As she spoke, her voice was soft and gentle. It bespoke a kindness born out of a self-assurance that recognizes no superiority in itself other than to be and to do as a single person among the great and wonderfully mixed bag which is the cacophony of humankind. She was little Martha Linda Franks of Laurens, South Carolina, and for almost half her years, of China.

Laurens is not so far from Clemson in miles. But for Martha Franks, born in 1901 in that little county-seat town, it is worlds away from this day. At a time when many of her contemporaries traveled little, she has literally been around the world several times. She has traversed this continent more times than she could readily number. She spent two-thirds of her adult life, before retirement, in a vast land, surrounded by what most in the group that day might have referred to as "foreigners." They were no strangers to this little woman. She might have easily echoed the words of Ruth from the Bible, "Your people shall be my people." As different as they were, they became for more than forty years, "her people," and she spent her energies sharing with them "her God." The God she shared was a God of love and compassion for a poor, oppressed people who often struggled to exist on the thin rough edges of disaster and despair. Her faith and her manner had often inspired them to faith in her God.

Why would Clemson University honor such a life? Or why not? In an age worshipping often at the shrines of wealth and power, it was refreshing to see it attend the shrine of a life given "in service to humanity" and to humanity's God.

As the processional began, the officials marched in, dressed in all the varieties of the symbols of their fields of endeavor. Along with them, slowly, but surely and stately, Martha Linda Franks. The thoughts crowding her head said, "Who, me? Who would have ever believed it of Marnie? What in the world would Mama and Poppa have said? Mama never thought I'd make it when I was a little girl. Well, old girl, you've arrived; you're going to be Doctor Franks."

And soon she was. President Max Lennon upon introducing her, read from the program:

> Miss Martha Franks, retired Baptist missionary, has lived a life devoted to serving others. "Miss Martha," as she is affectionately known, retired in 1966 to her hometown of Laurens after a forty-one-year career in China and Taiwan.
>
> Youngest of six children in a church-going family, her interest in becoming a missionary began to develop as a child in the Sunbeam Band, a Baptist organization for children, at First Baptist Church of Laurens. She made her commitment to foreign mission work while a student at Winthrop College, where she majored in education with emphasis on kindergarten work and earned a B.A. degree.
>
> Miss Franks taught kindergarten in Virginia for two years, and then went to Louisville, Kentucky, to study at the Woman's Missionary Union Training School (now merged with Southern Baptist Theological Seminary) for a year. In 1925, she was appointed by the Foreign Mission Board and sailed for China.
>
> Upon retirement, Miss Franks had given more than forty years of service among the Chinese. She had lived through their wars and revolutions and was twice interned by hostile armies. She had witnessed their sufferings under the repressive regimes of the Japanese and the Communists and had felt the effects of the great social and political upheaval which has to alter profoundly the old China she had known.
>
> Her last overseas post was Hsinchu, Taiwan, where she worked in a church for a year before her return to the States in 1965. Previously she was dean of women at Baptist theological seminaries in Taipei, Taiwan, and Shanghai and Hwanghsien, China, and educational and evangelistic worker in Hwanghsien and Tsining, China.

JOHN A. FRANKS

Seed and Feed
Heavy Groceries, Plantation Supplies
Wagons and Harness

Laurens, S.C.   December 30, 1936

Miss Martha Linda Franks
Hwanghsien Shantung China

Dear Kid,

Seated in my nice new easy Chair, the best one I have ever owned. I am dropping you a few lines to let you know how much I appreciate it. I thank you. Well I am feeling fine. My general health is good. Dr. Teague says I may be here when you come home if I take care of myself and I am trying to do that.

We had dinner with May Bramlet today and it was a good one. You know she is a good cook. Bee Ducket sent us a gallon of nice oysters for Christmas and we have enjoyed them very much. The rashions this Christmas have been extra good.

Johnny is spending part of his vacation at home. He is looking well. My business this year has not been very good on account of a short crop. I see from the papers that the soldiers are getting into North China close to you. Don't let them trap you. Are you getting the Advertiser regularly? I will see the editor and tell him to see to it.

I almost forgot to tell you about my horse. I have the best one I have ever owned, but he is getting a little too frisky these cool days. Guess I will have to change him for a gentle one.

This is the first letter I have tried to write since writing you last. I am writing with pencil because my hand is so wobbly I can't write with pen and ink. Well I will have to stop, its my bed time.

Much love from
Dad
Thanks for the chair.

There are many stories about her warmth, wit, persistence, and versatility. She played the accordion for street meetings in Taipei, attracting crowds from which came the nucleus of True Light Baptist Church. She taught a seven-year-old blind boy to read by forming Chinese characters for him with marbles placed in a tray of sand. And she drove a panel truck from Laurens to San Francisco so she could take it to Taiwan for use in Baptist work.

Since returning home, she has directed her energies toward the establishment in Laurens of a Christian retirement center for retirees from all faiths. Ground was broken in 1983, and today, the Martha Franks Baptist Retirement Center is among the finest in the state. But Miss Franks' work in her "retirement" years has not been limited to her concerns for the aging.

She began a new ministry among her own people, driving to places throughout the Carolinas and Georgia to fulfill a heavy schedule of speaking engagements, mostly to high school students, to tell them first-hand about the oppressions of Communism.

It has been said of her that, "Wherever Martha Franks goes, she leaves a trail of sunshine." Others have said, "In joy, sadness, illness, despair, disappointment, or triumph, she always knows exactly what to say, when to say it, and how to say it."

Clemson University is honored to recognize and salute the life's work of a great humanitarian, Miss Martha Franks, through the presentation of this honorary doctoral degree.

The hood was placed over her head and carefully draped down her back, and the deed was done. She was now Martha Linda Franks, Doctor of Humane Letters. All else is addenda, but what a preceding!

Happy people
Never count
Hours as they pass

Had they only known, someone might well have announced to the town of Laurens and to China the day Martha Linda Franks was born. That roly-poly squirming little bundle of energy let everyone know of her presence from the beginning.

The Franks family: John, Sallie, Martha, Rosalie, Alleene, Henry, Clyde, Charles

It had been eleven years since a girl had been born to John and Sallie Franks, and adjustments had to be made in everyone's life in the Franks' house on South Harper Street. Martha demanded and got attention from everyone from the first day. What consternation there was as she grew! The family didn't know quite what to make of this assertive, inquisitive, determined little girl who had invaded their presence. She would not go away; she would only go her own way. They had either to adjust or be left standing wide-eyed as she cut her own path. That is not to say that Martha was deliberately disobedient or bad; behavior of that ilk would never have been tolerated. Martha was so different from the others and so much younger that even as she and the family looked at the same things, they could not help seeing them as different as red and green. When they added a column, they came up with different results every time. Martha never understood why they could not see things her way. Sometimes it seemed that they were all in a conspiracy to either stifle or snuff out altogether any hope of joy she might entertain.

They were a happy family. There was none of that hollow, raucous laughter that is too often mistaken for joy. There was rather a pervasive and deep sense of wholeness which resulted in happiness from being and doing as a family. There was a reserve about them that to an outsider might have left the impression that they were not close or that there was little joy among them. Even at the age of eighty-eight, Martha remembered the lack of touching and hugging and remarked that it had left a void in her experience which she felt even in her old age. Perhaps it was the circumstances and the times which caused many families of that late Victorian age to make little outward show of affection. As it happened, that trait of reserve would serve her well years later in her relationship with the people of China; but as a child she needed the touching and show of affection and seldom got it.

John Franks was a product of the post-Civil War South. His own father had been killed in that war, and he had been left as a two-year-old to be reared by his mother. The years of his childhood were difficult ones for the South. There was little time or money for formal education as opposed to those of his class who had been educated before the war's devastation. As with so many others, they were left with little more than their pride and an adherence to a strict code of conduct often exaggerated to the extreme. As Martha recalled the days when Grandmother Franks Downey lived with the family, until her death just before the First World War, she understood much better the man who was her father. Mrs. Downey's dress and manner were always correct, and she expected the same from each member of the family. Despite that upbringing without a father which left him reserved, he loved Martha dearly and she knew it.

While he was quiet and restrained in manner, he was a good man. His family knew it and the community knew it. Admiral McGowan, a Laurens native who had risen to that rank in the United States Navy, once addressed a letter to the "Best Man in Laurens;" it was delivered to John Franks. He was what was called then an excellent provider: He made a good living. His family lacked for nothing. His farm supply business prospered, and he was respected in the community, both for his business acumen, and for his judgment as a leader in the affairs of the town of Laurens, which elected him mayor.

He was a leader in the church, too. The members of the church elected him deacon, and he proved himself worthy of their trust. His good sense of right and wrong and his commitment to Jesus Christ as Lord were evident to all who knew John Franks. He was an old-fashioned gentleman.

John Franks was a good, quiet man. Religion was not something he talked about, nor did any of the family. It was, rather, something that they lived. It permeated every aspect of their life together. Everything social in their life as a family was centered around the church. Sunday School, Sunbeams, circle meetings, worship, prayer meeting: All were a part of them and every one of them was a part of these. Martha had the greatest respect for her father. She was proud of him as a leader in the community and as her father. John was, like his mother, not one for wasting time with frivolous things. Each member of the family was expected to remember who he was and his own place within that circle.

Only once in all the years of their long life together did Martha ever hear her father say an unkind word to her mother. It had been an exasperating day at the store; nothing had gone right. As her father sat down at the table for his dinner, it was obvious to the family that something was out of kilter. They all sat wide-eyed as Mrs. Franks asked what he would like to drink. In a sharp tone of voice, he said, "Tea!" It was so out of character that Martha still remembered that "Tea!" after 80 years.

She also remembered the one "switching" from her father. Martha was a gadabout. She made the rounds of the neighbors' houses every day if she could get away. Across the street there lived a family with several children. Martha was drawn there like a moth to a flame. Against her mother's wishes she went; her mother called her home, spanked her, and back again she'd go. Most often she wound up in the kitchens and her too-frequent stops had already begun to show on her fattening body. She visited one neighbor so often that her mother one day sent her suitcase over before Martha's arrival. As Martha came in, despite all admonitions to stay home, the neighbor said to her, "Your mother sent your suitcase over. You won't have to go home now. You can just stay here." Martha burst into tears and ran all the way home vowing not to go wandering again. She kept her vow for all of three days.

On the day her father spanked her, her mother was not feeling well because of a terrible bout with bursitis which had persisted for days. She had taught Martha to be home by a certain time each day. It was summer and Martha and her little friends had enjoyed the day and hated to see it come to an end. They had spent hours playing hop-scotch and hide-and-go-seek and paper dolls until they had almost exhausted their repertoire of things to do. All day long the wagons, and buggies, and carriages had moved in a steady stream up and down those unpaved streets. Where there had been deep ruts after the last rain, there was now only the finest red dust left on the road. That dust ground by a thousand rolling wheels was as soft as silk and the most fun to play in. Late that afternoon, Martha and Margaret Wright sat barefoot wriggling their toes in that powder. It felt so soft and cool on their feet and they were enjoying themselves so much that Martha forgot the time. Her mother didn't forget it. As Martha got home, she knew she was in for it this time. Her mother glared at her as she came in late, coated as she was with that red dust which stuck like glue all the way to her knees. It was Sallie who always administered corporal punishment to the girls. This time she couldn't lift her arm because of the bursitis. When John came home from the store, he was told about Martha's behavior and asked to give the spanking. Martha remembered that he took a straw from a broom and switched her with it. John Franks was not accustomed to meting out punishment, and Martha was his baby.

Sallie Franks certainly wasted no time with straws with her baby daughter or anyone else. She was a happy woman with a good disposition. She had reason to be happy; she had a husband who provided well for his family. He was a deacon of the church, mayor of the town, and a respected member of the community. There were six healthy and bright children. Sallie Franks was a contented woman, and she equaled her husband in managing well what he made from his business. John and Sallie complemented each other as husband and wife, as partners in life. He cherished her, and she loved him.

They had brought up their children in such a way that by the time Martha was born, the others were old enough to take over many of the responsibilities of running a large house. Five bedrooms, a formal parlor, a dining room, a sitting room, a large kitchen — all made for plenty of work for the family and for servants.

The household chores were so alloted that things ran smoothly in Sallie Franks' house. She was an excellent cook and soon taught Rosalie and Alleene how to cook everything that was served from her table.

The boys took care of the outside chores: feeding the animals, milking the cows, and cutting wood. Having parceled out the responsibilities of the house, "Ma Sallie" could give her time to sewing. On her old foot-pedal sewing machine, she made most of the clothing which her family wore. The men's shirts and underclothing, the women's dresses, skirts, blouses, and bloomers — all were sewn at home.

Martha early on got the message of the importance of service. She watched one afternoon as her mother and her mother's sister Aunt "Tunie" cut out and stitched a bushel basket full of aprons. They were making the aprons for the Ladies' Aid Society. The aprons were sold and the money given to the Lottie Moon Christmas Offering.

While the older boys and girls took care of many of the simple chores inside the house and outside, Sallie pedaled, sewed, and sang. On summer days when the heat in the house rose to a stifling pitch, she moved out to one of the large porches which surrounded on three sides the big two-storied house. For hours she could be heard singing with obvious joy and contentment, songs of those who love the Lord. "Amazing Grace" and other old favorites rose into the air on those long, hot afternoons as Martha's mother joined her husband in providing for a big, happy family.

As she closed her sewing machine for the day, Mrs. Franks would begin her walk. Back and forth on the long, wrap-around porch she walked singing, "I Will Guide Thee with Mine Eye." As Martha trotted along behind her, she wondered what Mama meant by, "I Will Guide Thee with *My Knife*." One day the circus came to town, and she got her answer from the elephant trainer. As the parade passed down the street, there came a giant elephant. Riding on his neck was a man with a long "knife" in each hand. With those he touched the elephant, first on one side of the head, and then the other, "guiding him with his knife." Martha's mother sang reasonable songs.

The Frankses were in most respects typical of small-town, up-country South Carolina families in the first quarter of the twentieth century. Brothers and sisters teased and argued and helped each other. Clyde was sixteen when Martha was born. He was a born builder whose joy was to find and explore an old house. He dreamed of building and later entered the real-estate business as an avocation. As a young man, he built a playhouse behind the kitchen. He wanted a real, working, up-and-down window and finally tore an antique clock apart to get one. Martha's was the only playhouse in Laurens that had a movable window.

Clyde could be an awful tease. He delighted in taking Martha's long braids and tying them into a tight knot on top of her head. Not only did it hurt her head, but also her pride; and she would run crying to her mother or one of her sisters for comfort.

Although the other children were older than Martha, they delighted in seeing her enjoy so many things. In later years, they would all be proud of her and help her in every possible way in her work in China. Clyde might tease her, but he did not mind being seen with his little sister. One afternoon in the spring, a medicine show came to town. Oh, how Martha wanted to see that show! She begged Clyde to take her and the family agreed. After the playing, the singing, and the medicine man's pitch for his cure-all elixir, Clyde bought Martha a great big ice cream cone. As they neared the barber shop, Clyde suggested to Martha that she go in and get a haircut. An hour later, as they arrived home, they were greeted with cries of disbelief as Martha sported bobbed hair. Her beautiful, long braids were no more. In their place was the latest thing, bangs and a bob.

Martha's relationship with Rosalie was more serious. She was the first daughter in the family, and like her mother, a good cook and a good housekeeper. She was one of those good, solid women who felt no need to apologize for being female, nor for enjoying the running of a house. She kept a clean house. Because she was much older than Martha, she could order her to help with the tasks of cleaning. One day Rosalie sent Martha to dust the parlor. Martha returned from her chore much too soon to suit Rosalie. Without bothering to inspect, she instructed Martha to dust again. Martha burst into a fit of anger at such presumption, but it did no good, because Rosalie's order was supported by their mother.

Years later, as Martha came home on furlough from China, she lived with Rosalie. She always took care of Martha's clothes and got everything ready for another long stay in China. In 1986, as Rosalie entered her ninety-eighth year, Martha was caring for her as they occupied adjoining rooms in the Martha Franks Retirement Center. Martha said, "It is no burden. I am happy that I can help her now." When asked what

Martha had been like as a young lady, Rosalie, who was nearly deaf, upon finally understanding the question, laughed aloud, saying, "Martha was never a lady!"

Rosalie and Alleene might enjoy dishes, and cooking, and housekeeping, but not Martha. She never did learn to enjoy such menial tasks — those were for servants or ones who didn't know any better. Martha had rather hitch the horse to the buggy and go riding. As a little girl, she'd go to the fence with an ear of corn in one hand and the bridle behind her back. As the horse came for his prize, Martha quickly slipped the bridle on his head, and in short order she'd be out riding, picking up friends along the way.

Later, when the family had its first car, Martha begged to be allowed to drive. The boys refused to let her behind the wheel. She watched every move they made until she was sure she could drive as well as they. She got the operator's manual and read every word. One day, when the boys were all away, and Mrs. Franks had gone to her circle meeting, Martha saw her chance. She was to go for her mother in the buggy. Imagine Sallie Franks' surprise when ten-year-old Martha pulled up in the family Maxwell! She had never driven before, but Martha knew how to drive. Her father, who never learned to drive, soon made Martha his unofficial chauffeur as she drove him everywhere.

Just as Rosalie was the homemaker, Alleene was the teacher in the family. Even at home, as a young girl, she exhibited those qualities of what some have called a "born teacher." Alleene helped Martha, teaching her numbers and letters before she started school. Alleene delighted in teaching her younger sister new things and helped with her "recitations" as she entered school. In later years, it was Alleene who became Martha's closest friend and confidante in the family. They liked to read the same spiritual books. They discussed God's Word. After her retirement from the classroom, Alleene went to Taiwan with the intention of spending four months with Martha. The four months grew into four happy years as the two sisters worked with their beloved Chinese people in exile.

Brothers Henry and Charles were nearest in age to Martha. They were of kindred spirits, too. Their assignment was to take care of cows, horses, and buggies. The two of them were a familiar sight around Laurens as they spent much of their time together. Henry had the best disposition of any member of the family; he was generous and kind. He later followed his father, both in the farm supply business and as mayor of Laurens. Charles, who was nearest in age to Martha, graduated in textiles from what was then Clemson College. Soon after graduation, he went to work for one of the mills in the Greenville area. Within a few weeks, Charles was stricken with typhoid fever and died, a promising young man, of only twenty-one years of age.

In all, the Franks household was a happy one. It was respectable and respected. More than that, there was a respect within the family which parents and children had for each other. There was little show of affection and little talk of faith and religion. There was something else; there was security.

Many years were to pass before Martha felt close to any of the family. Her parents were older and occupied with supporting a family. Her brothers and sisters were too old to give much time to a baby. Martha was left to herself. She had to find her own things to do. It made her independent, resourceful, and determined.

One characteristic of her family that Martha would always hold dear was their commitment to education. From the end of the Civil War until the middle of the twentieth century, the South was a beleagured land. Before the War, there had been much emphasis upon education. The children of the gentry were sent to the best schools both at home and abroad. The widespread poverty resulting from the War virtually wiped out higher education for all but a privileged few. There were those families determined to educate their children. The Franks children were among those fortunate ones.

Martha began her formal education at the age of six. She was bright and learned fast, but was a somewhat indifferent student. Probably she was often bored with much that she experienced in the first years of public school. She had grown up with older people and knew many grown-up ways. Her grandmother, parents, brothers, and sisters had taught her much before she ever got to the schoolhouse. The process of osmosis gave her a knowledge that many without older ones in the home did not have. Old, middle-aged, and young often lived under the same roof. There they shared much of the reality of life with each other.

While Martha was not a particularly good student, she did adequate work and always managed to do acceptable work. She was one of whom it might well be said that she never allowed studies to get in the way of her education. She was a tomboy and a leader. Wherever she was, Martha made her presence known.

One of her early teachers told the story of how she could always tell when Martha had entered the room. Early in the mornings, or following recess or lunch, the teacher would be writing an assignment on the board. Every student would be quietly copying the assignment. The moment little late Martha entered the room, the students erupted in whisperings, giggles, and twitterings which came to be recognized as Martha-itis. Without so much as glancing around, the teacher would say, "Come on in Martha and take your seat." She made friends easily. Those friendships have lasted eighty years and more. She had the gift of laughter, and it was a contagious gift as she continued for decades to bring laughter to others. Matsu Crawford, one of her classmates from grammar school, told of how Martha would sneak down the aisle with a bag of cookies, sharing them with the other children. "We'd have been afraid of getting caught, but not Martha. While the teacher's back was turned, Martha would slither along the floor to the delight of everyone, passing out cookies from home."

On the way home from school, it was not at all unusual to see her swing up on the back of a wagon or carriage and ride for a block or two before hopping down to continue the walk with her friends. She was most athletic and a good swimmer. On more than one occasion, when one of the other children got into trouble while swimming, Martha, without hesitating, jumped in and pulled him to safety.

As a first grader, Martha became ill while at school. The doctor soon diagnosed the illness as scarlet fever got from drinking from the dipper at school. Martha and her mother were quarantined to an upstairs bedroom while her father stayed in the hotel uptown. Late every afternoon Mr. Franks came bringing small gifts which he tied on the string which Martha dropped from the window. After a day of hemming flour sacks for dish towels and covers for the biscuit pan, her father's face and gifts were more than welcome.

On those long days, shut away with her mother, Martha longed to play in that giant tin-lined tub in the well house. On long, hot summer days, the children filled the tub in the morning and five or six friends came to spend an afternoon frolicking in the water.

Other than looking forward to her father's daily visit, Martha's favorite pasttime was making a Bo holey. It was her favorite snack. To make a Bo holey, one bored a hole in a biscuit, not quite through, poured in syrup, squeezed and licked, refilled the hole, and enjoyed. Henry made the best Bo holies of all. But Henry could not come up to her room now. No one could come up to her room. It was just she and her mother.

When she was well, on Saturdays, Martha and some of her classmates could be found playing in that playhouse built by brother Clyde. They played with their paper dolls cut from magazines, shared little girl secrets, and dreamed of the day when they would grow up and dress up as they dressed those cardboard dolls in their beautifully frilled hats and dresses.

Martha always adored beautiful things and, as an adult, wherever she was she surrounded herself with the prettiest things she could find. There was one real disappointment she remembered after seventy-five years: She was never allowed to dress up in pretty things as a child. Her mother sewed for her good, practical clothes which were made to last. Because she was so roly-poly, her mother made blousy things for her to wear. There were no frills on her clothes; they were simple things just like her mother, who made them on the foot-pedal machine. As Martha looked around at her friends, she envied their pretty, frilly dresses. How she longed for the day when she too would be able to dress up in pretty hats and dresses!

She felt the resentment for years to come. She always liked pretty things.

More than one tree Gave wood To build this temple

In addition to public school education, there was the church. Almost every bit of social activity for the family was centered in First Baptist Church, Laurens. Sundays and Wednesdays found the entire family in Sunday School, worship, and prayer meetings. At other times they participated in the missions activities of the church. There were Sunbeams, Girls Auxiliary, Young Women's Auxiliary, Royal Ambassadors, and Women's Missionary Society.

It was through those missionary organizations that Martha and many other boys and girls first came to hear of the great need to share the story of Jesus with the rest of the world. It was in those organizations that they first heard fascinating stories of people with strange customs who lived in far-away lands and who worshipped other gods. They learned of the poverty, ignorance, disease, and oppression of countless millions of the world.

Some of the most dramatic stories were of China. The world's most populous nation (then and now) was sunk in poverty and ignorance. China had a long history of great wealth, and a culture and civilization which reached back hundreds of years before the Western world had emerged from the Dark Ages. But those privileges were the domain of a special few. For the vast majority, there was only a lifetime of struggle simply to survive. It was a struggle often interrupted by the cruelties of drought and flood, followed inevitably by famine and war and the deaths of hundreds of thousands and sometimes millions of men, women, and children. Most of them were born and died never knowing that there was a loving God who cared that they suffered.

There were stories of Lottie Moon, who had given her life to China. She had lived with them, loved them, and as much as possible, had become one of them. She had shared her own meager bowls of rice with them in famine, until, weakened from lack of nourishment, she died on board ship on Christmas Eve 1912, while returning to America. Martha would never have dared let anyone else know it, but she too was inspired by those stories of Lottie Moon and China. She heard the stories of how Miss Moon wrote letters telling of the plight of the Chinese until her hand would not work. She heard the stories of the inspiration for the Lottie Moon Christmas Offering for Foreign Missions.

Martha and others heard these stories and sometimes dreamed of going to China themselves as missionaries. Mrs. Clara Watts was one of those who first opened China's window to Martha. Mrs. Watts was a deeply spiritual person, who, as director of Young Women's Auxiliary, inspired the girls in her group with stories of China. She told of a lovely, cultured people who needed to know of God's love. As Martha listened to Clara Watts, she was moved to deep feelings of admiration for her and awe at the stories she heard. Her feelings were too personal to share with anyone. Her feelings, and the stories, were hidden deep within the inner recesses of her heart never to be erased. No one, not even Martha, would ever have guessed that within a little more than a dozen years of Lottie Moon's death, she would be in China and in another two, telling the stories of Jesus Christ in some of the same villages that Lottie Moon had traveled only fifteen years before.

Not only did Mrs. Watts influence Martha, there were others who were equally near and most visible as they worshipped at First Baptist Church. Martha was torn between the dream of being either a member of the church choir or a widow. Martha admired an especially striking lady who was a member of the church choir. She always came to church in the most elegant dresses and great big picture hats with long ostrich feathers drooping over her shoulders. Each Sunday Martha squirmed and impatiently waited to see what her heroine would be wearing. She would never die disappointed if she could only grow up to sing in the choir and wear such pretty things as Josephine Fuller. Even if she never realized her dream of singing in the choir, she could always be a widow. That might be even better. As she sat waiting for the choir, down the aisle, floating like a beautiful wraith on a soft and gentle breeze, came the lovely widow, Mrs. Joe Watts. All dressed in black from head to toe she came, her hat trailing a black veil reaching to her waist. There were only a white handkerchief, bordered in black lace and a little white ruching (ruffle) at her high, stiff-necked collar to break the spell. Martha never knew another woman to have a handkerchief bordered in black lace. Such elegance, such dignity! She would live a life of the greatest joy if only she could grow up to be a widow like that. Martha dreamed and ogled, but it was never to be. She never got to the choir and never made it even close to widowhood.

What would she be? What would she do? She had no idea. One thing she knew, she would not be one of those "religious" persons; she'd rather be caught dead than have someone accuse her of being "religious." Church was fine; it was expected, but there was no need to get carried away with it. Papa was a deacon, Mama served in Women's Missionary Society, and everyone worshipped: That was expected, but she would not have anyone think that she was religious, never!

He who carves
The Buddha
Never worships him

Martha continued to grow spiritually despite her protestations to the contrary. She was a leader among the other children and well-liked by most, but there was one area in which she did not lead. When they reached the "age of accountability" (knowing right from wrong as a choice), it was expected of the Baptist children that they would make public professions of faith and be baptized into the church. Here, as in so many other areas, Martha was determined to go her own way. The other children in her group did what was expected and what they felt moved to do, but Martha held back. Martha admired her pastor, but it was at a distance. Nanny Bennett, her Sunbeam leader, and Mattie Bobo, her Sunday School teacher, had much to teach Martha. She appreciated both of them but never felt close enough to any of them to share her real feelings.

Everyone in Martha's Sunday School class had been baptized except for her. Her teachers, pastor, and others began pressuring her, not to "know the Lord" as she remembers, but to "join the church." Something must be wrong with her. The others had done it, why not Martha? One day during the annual protracted meeting (revival) as the end neared, John Franks took his youngest daughter into the dining room. He gently asked her, "Do you know you are a sinner?"

Martha, horrified at the thought, quickly answered, "Certainly not!" She knew what a sinner was. Several months before a yegg man (itenirant burglar) had come to town where he had robbed the bank, was killed by a policeman, and had been buried in Potter's Field. That was what a sinner was. Martha was no sinner. She was embarrassed, hurt, but had no sense of personal sin nor of needing a Savior.

As the pressure mounted, Martha caved in. Down that long aisle she went feeling like a condemned yegg man going to his hanging, as all who knew her watched. As she walked, she saw the pastor whisper to each one, receiving a whisper in turn. What would he whisper, and what would she answer?

After an eternity, it was Martha's turn.

"Do you love Jesus?" asked Dr. Thayer.

Martha was certain the man was daft. Of course she loved Jesus. Before she had a chance to answer, someone in the congregation blurted out, "I move she be received." Martha was in, home free. She was a member of the church. But something was missing.

Though she had been baptized, she remained something of a tease and show-off even in church. The Sunbeams had prepared a program for presentation before the entire congregation on a Sunday evening. Martha had a few lines to recite but had missed her cue because she was busy talking to someone as usual. The program continued without her until everyone had finished. Before anyone had opportunity to see what was happening, Martha skipped to the center of the stage and proceeded to recite "Little Orphant Annie." While her family cringed (Sallie Franks sat wide-eyed in disbelief), the congregation had all it could do to keep from bursting into fits of laughter. They caught themselves just before applauding.

Martha was seldom timid about anything. She might be slow about going down the aisle to tell the world she was a sinner, but she had no qualms about helping to raise money for a worthy cause. Several times during the year, the missions organizations set about raising money to help support foreign missions. One year Martha won the prize for raising the most money in her group. Mrs. Bennett drove over in her buggy with Martha's prize. As she took the tin of marshmallows from her teacher's hand, she stood for a moment watching her drive away. As she thought of how many would be waiting and of how few marshmallows there were, she sat down by the hedge surrounding the house. Carefully opening the tin, she counted the pieces — What should she do? Then and there, making a momentous decision, she ate every marshmallow before going into the house.

It was not, however, eating all the marshmallows, nor reciting "Little Orphant Annie" in church that told the tale of who was inside that facade called Martha Linda Franks. Years later, her mother revealed that she had dedicated Martha to the Lord before she was born. As she matured, a sense of the reality of God became increasingly more pronounced in her life. It became more important to her that she have a personal relationship with God. In her immaturity, she could not begin to understand all that was meant by the surrender of her life to God, but there was ever-increasing awareness of his presence with her. It fits and starts and in halting ways, she reached out to God who had already marked her for His own.

It was the summer of her fourteenth year that Martha heard clearly the voice of Jesus speaking to her. Mrs. Fuller, the mother of Martha's sister-in-law, invited several girls to her home in the country. The Beaverdam Church was then engaged in a revival meeting. Every morning and evening the girls joined the community in services of praise at the large country church. Between times, they laughed, and sang, and talked.

Martha had been gifted with a musical ear, and while never having the discipline to study the piano, she played, as she liked to say, "for her own amazement." One day as she sat playing, she looked at a candlestick which seemed almost to speak to her. It was in the shape of a cross and there was the Christ on it looking at her. As she played and sang and looked at the image of Jesus on that candlestick cross, she realized for the first time that it was for her, for Martha Franks, that Jesus had died. That day, as they worshipped, she felt it again and heard the Lord speak to her. She received His love and salvation on that very day, and felt Him bind her to Himself "with cords of love."

During those early years, the seeds were planted which would grow into a tree of service to the people of China. China was a world away. At once proud, brilliant, poor, beautiful, lost, China was a mysterious and intriguing place where missionaries went to teach the "heathen" about God. Martha hardly imagined that she would have a place of service in that antique land. She never guessed that she was destined to be one link in God's chain of love to China. How could a young girl who had dreams of college, marriage, and a family know that her life in many respects would be totally unlike that of her family and friends? Who among her friends would ever have thought that laughing, boisterous, tomboy Martha would become a missionary?

The high school years found her only a maturing version of the fun-loving girl who so readily spread her gift of laughter. She liked nothing better than to dress up and show off her new clothes which were almost always handmade and too plain. She studied as she had to and planned for college as no more than a fuzzy probability. At the time she graduated from high school, there were only ten grades. Most graduates were only fifteen or sixteen years of age. Because they were so young and because of codes then governing behavior between boys and girls, Martha had never dated anyone. She had many friends, both male and female, and they partied together, but she never became seriously involved with any boy during the high school years.

Learning is weightless
Treasure you always
Carry easily

As her final year of high school came to a close, the state added an eleventh year. Martha had made no serious plans for college, and her parents decided that she would spend another year of school in Laurens. It would be good for her, helping her to mature.

Martha went to school that first day only to find it the most boring thing she had ever experienced. The fun was gone, having evaporated with her friends. All her crowd was away at college. She would never be able to survive another year at Laurens High School. After a few days, it became increasingly clear to Martha that she would certainly die if she didn't get out of high school. Returning from school, she burst through the door and broke into tears as if her heart were broken. Mama tried to console her and calm her enough to find out just what this horrendous problem could be. Finally succeeding in quieting Martha's sobs and drying her tears, she asked, "Martha, what's the matter?"

"I can't stand school," she said. "All my friends are gone. I don't ever want to go back again!"

"Well what do you want to do?" her mother asked.

"I want to go to college," was Martha's only answer.

Mrs. Franks, who had already sensed Martha's unhappiness, said to her, "Go talk to your father."

As she made her way downtown to her father's hardware store, dreams of college, of new clothes, of new friends, of good times, of being away from home — all were rushing through her head like cascading water that could not be stopped. She danced down the street with a new lease on life. She hoped no one would be in the store, so she could tell him right away. Fortunately, no one was there. Rushing through the door, Martha said, "Oh, Papa! I hate high school. I will die if I have to go back there again. All my friends are gone, and I want to go to college."

Quietly, reassuringly, her father asked, "Where would you like to go? You know that school is already in session."

With no hesitation Martha blurted out, "Coker!"

The Franks clan got in on the act. They called Coker and Martha was accepted into the freshman class. While her father and mother were making the necessary plans and her mother was packing all those items that would have to last until Christmas, Martha could think only of clothes. Oh! how good she would look! She wanted pretty new things bought from the store. She wanted to show everyone that she could dress with the best of them.

With Rosalie and Alleene to help, she went to town and bought the most striking navy blue suit she could find. There was a smart matching hat with three ostrich feathers and a pair of high-heeled slippers that would have made any girl proud. As she unwrapped her treasures for her mother's perusal, she heard the suit pronounced "practical," the hat raised eyebrows, and the slippers were anathema! Her mother declared that the shoes were "Outrageous!" Anyone could see that they threw one's body out of balance and were injurious to a woman's health. They would never do! Her lovely, longed-for, high-heeled shoes had to be returned.

Still, she had her feathered hat and a new suit. Others would follow. The day would come when she would buy all the clothes she wanted and just the kind of things she liked. With the plans all made and all her trunks packed, the long-awaited day of her departure dawned. Mid-morning, her train would leave Laurens for Columbia where she would switch for the trip to Hartsville and Coker College. She had plenty of time to go to school and show off her nice new clothes to those poor "things" being left behind. What a show-off she was! As she pranced around school talking a mile a minute about college and making jokes, she completely forgot the time. Returning home, she found that the train for Columbia had come and gone. She was left standing, looking so silly and childish in her new clothes. The family wondered if she would ever mature enough to be able to take care of herself. When they thought of Rosalie and Alleene and of the way they handled everything so responsibly, they could only look at poor silly little Martha and shake their heads.

That night there was a gathering of the clan. Martha had wanted to go to Coker because that was the place for the smart, well-appointed young woman. They all spoke of what was best for Martha. Her personal feelings were given scant attention. Brother Clyde let it be known that he opposed Coker from the word go. It would do her no good to go there. Rosalie and Alleene had gone to Limestone; why not Limestone for Martha? Better still, Em, a dear friend of all, had gone to Winthrop, and Em was the model of what a young lady ought to be. Clyde declared that Winthrop was what Martha needed. She would learn discipline there. She would grow up at Winthrop and learn to take responsibility. She should definitely go to Winthrop. Winthrop was the last place Martha wanted to go, but her wishes were ignored by everyone. She might as well not have even attended the meeting. They could all sit there and plan her life and never flinch at the knowledge that her feelings were not even considered.

Man concocts
A million schemes . . .
God knows but one

The day following that family meeting deciding upon a college for Martha found a somewhat sullen and pouting girl on the train with her father headed for Columbia. The former principal of Laurens High School had moved to Columbia, and he had to sign papers necessary for her entrance into Winthrop. After meeting with him and having him sign the forms, Martha and her father boarded another train for Rock Hill.

Upon disembarking in Rock Hill, they were driven to Winthrop and directed to the home of Dr. Kinard, Dean of the College, who was in his vegetable garden when they found him. Martha, who was there in body if not entirely in spirit, could only listen as the two Baptist deacons chatted about gardens, the church, and made decisions affecting her life. She was barely consulted at all. She was secretly hoping that she would not be admitted; after all, she had failed the entrance examination which she had taken earlier in the spring. Besides, there were no rooms available. As she listened, she added it all up again in her head: No satisfactory examination, no room available, no uniform — she might be able to beat the family at this game yet. She knew that there were several girls from Laurens who had got high marks on the entrance examinations, had been accepted, and were even then living in town waiting for rooms. There was little chance that she would be given one. Little did she know of the power of two Baptist deacons joining forces to work their will.

However much Martha tried to go in another direction, it was to be Winthrop for her. Dr. Kinard left the garden, washed his hands, put on his stiff white collar, and accompanied this dressed-up young lady and her father to North Dormitory. There they found the matron, Mrs. Walker, sitting on the porch with her staff. Dr. Kinard said simply and matter-of-factly, "Mrs. Walker, take care of Miss Franks." If the matron were taken aback, she made no such sign to the dean. There was one empty bed in North Dormitory and that only because the girl to whom it had already been assigned was then in the infirmary. Martha was given the sick girl's bed.

It was done. The impossible had been done. She never thought they would be able to do it, and yet here she was at Winthrop. It was where Martha least wanted to be. With words of encouragement that she would grow to like it and words of advice to study hard and behave herself as a Franks from Laurens ought to do, John Franks said goodbye to his youngest child and took the train back to Laurens. It had been a long day: Laurens to Columbia, Columbia to Rock Hill, Rock Hill to Laurens again. As he watched the landscape rushing by, he thought of the day and concluded that it had been worth the effort to have his youngest daughter settled into college. He had been able to spend only a few years in school himself, but every one of his children had attended college. Despite his weariness that night, John Franks had reason to be happy with his lot in life.

Her father gone, Martha was left alone for the first time in her life. She might huff and puff, boast and brag, but in the end she could always retreat home. She had never realized, and probably was not even aware of it then, but home was security for her. How she loathed Winthrop College, was determined to hate every minute of it until they allowed her to come home and find another school. The family had won rounds one and two, but she would win the deciding one. She might just as well have had no navy blue suit and tri-feathered hat. At Winthrop everyone wore the same insipid uniform of blue skirt and white blouse. Everywhere one looked there was that sameness, and nothing but girls.

For three weeks Martha cried and pouted and begged to be allowed to return home. Almost daily she called home telling her parents of the awful life she was leading at Winthrop. Her father was ready to agree to her leaving school when her mother got on the line. Taking matters firmly in hand, she said sharply to Martha, "Young lady, your father and I are making a sacrifice for you to be in school. You are not coming home. Now, you dry up and get to work!" There was nothing left to do but settle down and study. She knew any further resistance would be wasted effort. Sallie Franks had spoken law this time.

Martha had not even known how to fill out a schedule, nor what courses to take. As she looked at the big, monstrous-looking catalog, she felt lost. Elizabeth Young, a senior from Laurens, graciously came to the rescue. She led Martha sensibly to take basic courses so that whatever she decided as her major later on, she would have the right foundation. She had no place to stay when the young lady returned from the infirmary to claim her bed. Again, two kind and generous girls from home came to her rescue. Mary Ruth Copeland from Clinton and Mary Blackwell from Laurens invited Martha to move into their room. It was a little close for three. Except for those times when she got on the telephone with her parents, one might have thought she was beginning to like the place. The pouting and telephoning abruptly came to an end after three weeks. Martha was attractive, witty, and winsome; she made friends easily. Winthrop soon knew that Martha Franks had arrived.

There was another young lady in particular who soon knew Martha was at Winthrop. Her name was Olive Lawton. Olive had been on campus several days when Martha came sailing in on a cloud of pout. The two were as different as night and day. Olive was a world away from her parents in China. There was no crying, no pouting, no begging for Olive. She was much too mature for that. It was not that she did not feel the homesickness and uncertainty, it was the fact that she had experienced so much more than Martha. As the two sat one afternoon on the long veranda running the length of North Dormitory, each found that the other had been born on the same day, February 15, 1901. What a chance that the one born in the sleepy little town of Laurens, South Carolina, the other in far-away China on the same day in the same year should meet at Winthrop.

"Oh! I've always wanted a twin, and now I've got one," squealed Martha.

Olive only smiled her enigmatic smile of approval.

Twins she might call them, but two could hardly have been as unlike as they. Martha was impetuous, quick to speak her mind, haphazard about studies, quick to judge, generous, vivacious. Olive, on the other hand, was quiet, reserved, kind, equally generous in nature, studious, quick to laugh, and a genuine friend. As different as they were, there began between them a life-long friendship which continues after more than seventy years. Martha and Olive studied together at Winthrop. In their freshman year, both Martha and Olive were nominated for president of the class. After a score of votes, all of which were tied, Olive was finally elected.

At Winthrop, Martha came to associate with a number of people who were to have enormous impact on her life. Special among them was Olive Lawton, another link in God's chain to China: That link was inextricably joined with Martha's as the Lord paved the way before them.

Winthrop College in the 1920's was a beautiful place, with attractive new buildings, wide expanses of manicured lawns and spreading shade trees just beginning to mature. The atmosphere was one of discipline, both physical and intellectual. The discipline was evident to the eye in the well-kept grounds and in the deportment of the young ladies who wore the same blue skirts and white blouses. There was a rigid core-curriculum followed by everyone. Every girl had to know how to swim before she was awarded a degree. The aim was to train young women for the maturing twentieth century, and discipline was a necessary means to that end.

There was another element which many would find surprising, if not downright intolerable, in this more enlightened age. It was the unabashedly spiritual atmosphere. One can hardly imagine a Winthrop, state-supported school that it is, in which the president, David Bancroft Johnson, used to address the faculty and students in chapel with the words, "The sun never sets on Winthrop daughters in service to humanity."

Dr. John Lake, on a visit to Winthrop, told a group of teachers that Dr. Willingham said to him on one occasion, "I don't understand why we have so many missionaries from Winthrop College, South Carolina, a state school." Dr. Lake answered him, "I do; I know the president." Dr. Johnson was a Christian layman who emphasized the spiritual life both personally and professionally.

It was a fact that Winthrop graduates were serving round the world as Christian missionaries. That kind of service, and the training for it, were promoted by the leadership of the college. No one questioned such an approach; it was accepted as upright, responsible leadership.

Because of that leadership, there was a sense of mission, of unselfish service, which took many of those young women to new lands. In lonely, faraway places they lived out their working lives. In many ways they countered the image of a brassy, brazen country, sometimes drunk on its wealth and power. They revealed another face of America. It was a face of love and compassion, a kind and gentle face offering help to the poor, broken peoples of a world in need. In the process of living their lives in "service to humanity," they discovered the truth that though the customs be different, underneath all are alike. All share similar needs, physical, emotional and spiritual which make the world ultimately one. President Johnson and Winthrop were another link in God's chain which bound Martha closer to Himself.

When the tree waves
Wind is stirring

As she had done in high school, Martha continued to be the center of attention wherever she was. Singing, playing, acting, swimming, she made herself known to the entire college. Everyone soon knew Martha Franks, and she got to know everyone on campus. She was generous and kind to all who knew her. Some of her classmates spoke of those days with the "daredevil" again in the lead.

One night, in the midst of a terrible rain and windstorm, Martha had the idea of tying the sheets together to make a great flag to signal their distress to the world. Out the window they blew until finally the flag came loose from its mooring inside the room and sailed out across the lawn. As it was her idea, Martha had to be the one to fetch them back. She would not have dared let anyone else do it. As she came back into the room soaked to the skin, the resulting howls of laughter were heard all the way to the matron's room. As the matron opened their door, she found every girl fast asleep and Martha reciting Wordsworth's "Daffodils" even as she slept, perhaps, not too soundly.

Not only did her "antics" follow her to Winthrop, but so did her fund-raising. Another classmate from Laurens recalled seeing Martha set small saucers of chocolate pudding on her windowsill at mid-morning as the hungry girls passed on their way to and from classes. She paid a nickel for a package of pudding from which she made several servings, selling them for a nickel apiece. Martha and others raised several thousand dollars to pay for a portrait of President Johnson painted by E. Hudson Stuart, an Englishman.

Perhaps the most telling of her character is the story of

Martha's dear friend Matsu Wofford Crawford. One morning a message came, telling of the severe illness of Matsu's mother. Both Matsu and her sister returned from class to learn the sad news from Martha. Before they had got the news, Martha had their bags out and packed most of the things they would need. She had called the station and got tickets and made arrangements for a taxi to the depot. Martha set her own clock, got the Wofford girls up the next morning, and saw them off to the station. When they got to Laurens, the girls found that their mother had died while they were en route. Remembering their sadness, they never could forget Martha's kindness and generosity.

To light the lamp
Before God
First extinguish self

Martha was maturing. She was developing spiritually too. Winthrop girls were expected to worship in the local churches on Sundays. Martha went with many other Baptist girls to First Baptist Church of Rock Hill, pastored by Dr. J. Powell Tucker.

Southern Baptists were then engaged in the "75 Million Campaign." There was great excitement as Southern Baptists took on the herculean task of raising seventy-five million dollars from what were primarily rural churches. The money was intended for education of a pastoral and missionary staff who would serve at home and abroad, spreading the gospel.

One theme of the "75 Million Campaign" was "Calling Out the Called." One Sunday morning as Martha sat in the congregation, Dr. Tucker spoke of God's plan for their lives. "God has a plan for each of your lives," he said. "God will direct your life if you want him to." Many years later, Martha remembered that morning and that message. She had heard it so many times before. This time, God spoke to *her* about the directing of *her* life. As she sat listening to the preacher, she heard that the Lord of the universe wanted to guide the life of little Martha Franks from Laurens, South Carolina. She needed guidance. *Wouldn't it be stupid of her,* she thought, *to try it on her own? Why not let God do it for her?*

As Dr. Tucker issued the invitation to any who wanted God to direct their lives, Martha was the first to respond. She needed help; here was the answer. There were no flashing lights, no flutterings of angels' wings, no great emotional stirring; it was sensible, practical, and the right thing for her to do.

She had made a giant step in response to God's call. She sometimes laughed too loud, had difficulty getting down to her studies, and was often too impetuous by half, but she had made a public commitment of her life to God. She had always been a part of the church and had accepted Jesus as Savior; now she was out to make Him Lord as well. The full implication of that commitment no one could know, least of all Martha. It was a single step which would take her on a journey of a thousand thousand miles.

As an outgrowth of her commitment to the Lord, Martha began a practice which continues to this day. She set aside a time for Bible study and prayer. It was a personal thing between her and God. She had made the decision to answer God's call; now she would need to know what it was He wanted her to do. She needed the private time to talk with God and learn His will for her.

Before her second semester at Winthrop, Martha arranged her schedule so as to have the room to herself a part of every morning. While her roommates were in class, she read the Bible, talked to God, and He began to speak to her of China. Why China? From her earliest recollections there were stories of China. In Sunday School lessons, in Sunbeam programs, in sermons — Martha had heard of China. Now she began to hear a more compelling voice than any of those; it was the voice of Olive Lawton.

Olive, whose parents were missionaries, had been born in China. She knew the land and its people firsthand. Hers was a voice made more compelling by the obvious respect she had for the culture of the land which until Winthrop had been her home. It was clear that Olive loved China and its people. She spoke of the vastness of the land. She regaled Martha with descriptions of that land which covered much of the continent of Asia. She spoke lovingly of a gracious and erudite people. Olive spoke too of the physical needs of a people made poor by sheer numbers. She told of the spiritual needs of millions of men, women, and children who knew nothing of God's love for them. They needed to hear of the Lord's compassion; it was imperative that they hear. Olive was going back to teach her adopted people. She loved them as her own and would lead in the churches there. As she listened, Martha began to see herself as a part of that work also. God was speaking; Martha was listening.

As devoted as they were to the church, John and Sallie Franks were speechless when Martha told them of her thoughts of going to China. They had given their youngest child to the Lord before she was born; they never imagined He would take her to China. China was a hard land that had claimed the lives of many men and women before. Perhaps it was a passing whim. Martha was far too young to be making so momentous a decision. Not long ago she had missed the train to Coker. She had been fortunate to get into Winthrop and had cried and begged to come home. Now she was telling them that the Lord was leading her to China. What next! In the meantime, they would discourage, as much as possible, any talk of China. It was fine for people to go to China — they ought to go — but Martha would never be able to survive it, and they certainly would not survive her going. They would have to keep a closer reign on Martha. There were many other ways of serving the Lord and His people.

God works with parents, too. If He wanted Martha to go to China, he could lead her family to understand and accept that fact. He did. In time, they came to see God at work in Martha. They accepted the reality of her call to China and her commitment to it, and lived to rejoice in her work for the Lord.

As she prayed and planned, read and played and dreamed, she was often jolted back to the reality of academia. Martha really had to discipline herself to study. Studying was hard work for her. There were many other things she liked to do better and wanted to do. She had decided to train for kindergarten teaching. With a major declared, she began preparation for a life of teaching Chinese boys and girls.

When the time came for summer vacations, Martha headed for home and worked with her father or at one of the camps in the state. One summer's vacation found her working as a counselor at the South Carolina Baptist Sunbeam Camp. It was there that a friendship was born which proved to be like no other she was ever to know. Mrs. W. J. Hatcher was the state's Sunbeam Leader, and known to girls throughout the state as "Mother Hatcher." She became, as Martha called her, "My Chosen Mother." Carrie Hatcher met a need that her own mother had never been able to do. She became Martha's dearest friend and confidante. For years, she and her husband, who had no children of their own, made Martha theirs. They encouraged her with their letters and with gifts and entertained her when she came home on furlough.

The years came and went almost, it seemed, like birds on the wing. Martha had a good time at Winthrop establishing friendships which were to last a lifetime. Again, she managed to do acceptable if not superior work. Only twice, she recalled, did she receive double stars, which was the highest grade attainable. The one was for teaching, the other was for housekeeping. She gave credit for the latter to her roommate, Mary Blackwell, who was really the housekeeper; Martha never was.

In her junior year, Martha served as a marshall. As a senior, the college elected her president of the student body. Her friend Olive was elected president of Young Women's Christian Association.

Illustrative of the spiritual atmosphere then prevailing at Winthrop, eight women of the class of 1922 went on to serve as foreign missionaries. They were:

Mary Ruth Copeland — Presbyterian — India
Virginia Lewis — Presbyterian — South America
Alice Cobb — Methodist — South America
Sarah Glenn — Methodist — China
Anna Edwards — Baptist — China
Martha Franks — Baptist — China
Olive Lawton — Baptist — China
Alice Wells — Baptist — China

The American church's concern for China is obvious from a glance at the list of eight; five were for China.

Winthrop had proved to be a happy experience. Martha grew at Winthrop. Now she was ready to go on to other things.

New boots
Big steps

Upon graduation from Winthrop, Martha was employed as a teacher by the public schools of Schoolfield, Virginia. Her connection there was that same "Em" whose name had been used as proof of what Winthrop College could do for a young woman. Martha loved and respected Em, and had long ago come to see God's hand at the helm in her going to Winthrop.

Schoolfield, a suburb of Danville, Virginia, was a wonderful place for Martha to begin her work. Martha was most fortunate to have as her principal Miss Rosa Brimmer, who inspired her to do her best as a teacher. She loved every minute of it. She enjoyed the students, visited in their homes, and took the entire community into her heart. Em and other teachers

Student Government Council, Winthrop
Martha, President, center, first row

made up her social circle, helping her to enjoy a life outside the classroom. On Sundays she taught a Sunday School class. The abject poverty of many families in the area caused her to become deeply involved with the welfare department.

While she was much too involved in her work to spend time in dating, there were a few men who invited her to one of the school or church-sponsored parties. Besides her work, there were definite plans for seminary and nothing must stand in the way.

One long-time dream became a reality at Schoolfield: Martha began to buy clothes. They were not terribly expensive, but they were nice things: hats, dresses, shoes with heels. She could dress up as she liked, and she has never stopped dressing in pretty clothes. She bought her first car, paying $150.00 for it. With her new clothes and a car, Martha Franks had arrived.

The second year in Schoolfield found her teaching kindergarten for the welfare department of Dan River Cotton Mills at a monthly salary of $125.00. She had a beautiful, well-equipped kindergarten facility with an assistant and maid to help with 125 children under her care. There was a grand piano and any equipment she requested would be got for her in short order. Every Friday night the mill provided a big party for one of its departments. Those were exciting and happy social events. Martha had the pleasure of assisting the college-trained Director of Social and Athletic Activities. There was opportunity for advancement and her salary was considerably more than that of public school teachers. She went wild buying clothes. She spent all of her money on clothes and gifts, so that when Christmas came, she had to wire home COD to get money to come home. She had the world by its tail, but never once forgot that it was China for her.

During that wonderful year with Dan River Mills, Martha applied to the Women's Missionary Training School of Southern Seminary in Louisville, Kentucky. The seminary readily accepted her, providing a South Carolina Scholarship.

On the final day of her work in kindergarten in Schoolfield, she was torn between her love for the children and her call to missions in China. She loved the children; the work was good; it was needed. She could stay right here; advancement would come. She could be happy as a kindergarten teacher. The two years had brought new friends, new clothes, a car, a budding social life, and personal fulfillment in her work. As Martha thought of all those things, she would rush to the bathroom and weep into a towel so that the children could not hear her. Coming back into the classroom, she would work with the children until her emotions got the better of her again. All day long, the pattern was repeated until all the makeup was gone from so many washings. It was games and tears the whole day through. She loved teaching; it was her gift from God; He had other plans for those gifts.

Years later, on one of her furloughs, she returned to Schoolfield for a reunion with some of her co-workers. They gave a nice dinner for Martha, and she recalled the "Towel of Tears." While teaching there, she had thought to be head of the village welfare department would be the top of the totem pole. As she heard the conversation, she realized what a small circle was their world. All they talked about was that small village and their work. Driving back to her room, she was filled with gratitude to God for His blessing. She had been round the world and had studied a year in Peking. She had rubbed shoulders with spiritual giants: Ruth Paxton, Marie Monson, Jane Lide, Charlie Culpepper, and many others. She had been part of a great spiritual revival in China, experiencing for herself the life-changing truth of "Christ in You." Her horizons had been stretched to the limit. It seemed to her that in every way she had been lifted out of a small, narrow circle and set into God's great community of light and joy which included all the world.

Even her clothes were better than those who had more money than she. The Lord had provided for her a dear friend from Atlanta by the name of Billy Younts. Mrs. Younts was a member of the wealthy Camp family of Franklin, Virginia. Billy Younts always saw to it that Martha had a proper furlough wardrobe, providing for her simple but elegant dresses for speaking engagements all over the country. Through Mrs. Younts, God provided for Martha those beautiful things she loved, but could never have afforded for herself.

That night before lying down to sleep, Martha knelt by her bed to thank God for his goodness. She praised Him for choosing her to receive such wealth of experience. He had given her friends, experience of joy beyond telling; He had given her the world. She wept tears of praise to Him for all His goodness to her.

Mallet strikes chisel . . . Chisel splits wood 

Southern Seminary was the happiest experience Martha ever had in school. The studies were stimulating and soul-satisfying. Her teachers included John R. Sampey for Old Testament, A. T. Robertson for New Testament, E. Y. Mullins for Theology, and W. O. Carver for Missions. With those giants of the world of theology, Martha enjoyed studying for the first time in her life. She read, listened, learned, grew in her relationship to God and His world.

Infrequently, she dated one or another of the young preachers studying at seminary. Most of them left her with the same feeling expressed by Dr. Robertson who said that one of his callings in life was to take the wind out of the sails of inflated students of theology.

Only one young man really interested her, and unfortunately she got him on the rebound. He was suffering rejection by his girlfriend and confided in Martha. She was too busy thinking of China to get seriously involved with anyone who did not share that dream.

Her rebounding beau was later reconciled with his girlfriend whom he married. He went on to the presidency of a Baptist college in Mississippi. Many years later, his widow and Martha were on the same program as speakers before a large audience in Richmond, Virginia. At the conclusion of the program, the widow kissed Martha first on one cheek and then the other, saying, "That second was for my husband."

As much as she enjoyed the seminary, Martha felt an ever-increasing urgency to get to China. Why the hurry? She was a young lady; there was plenty of time. In fact, the door was closing fast. It was not unlike that great "Iron Curtain" of which Winston Churchill spoke years later in describing what had transpired in Europe. Martha was the last missionary appointed to North China during that period. Eleven long years passed before there was another, and then there were no more. Had she not gone that year, she probably would never have gone to China at all. It was North China because they needed a kindergarten teacher.

People fated to be happy
Need not haste

As one who had an urgent need to go, Martha applied to the Foreign Mission Board for appointment to China. Ever the optimist, she waited impatiently for the word to come that she had been accepted. The year was 1925. The Foreign Mission Board, deeply in debt, had ceased all appointments. Martha was crushed when the reply came: "We regret to inform you that because of a lack of funds we are unable to approve your appointment." An accompanying letter informed her that if a church, or group within a church, were willing to assume financial responsibility for a missionary, then the Board would make the appointment.

First Baptist Church Laurens was engaged in a building program and felt that it could not undertake the financing of Martha's work. Two doors had been shut; slammed it seemed to her.

And then a big, wide door opened through which rays of the warm sunshine of God's love caused Martha to rejoice. The Woman's Missionary Union of Grove Avenue Baptist Church of Richmond, Virginia approached the Board offering to support a single missionary. Through the leadership of Mrs. J. B. Yeamans, the women of the church firmly believed that God wanted them to give their efforts to help in the support of spreading the gospel in other lands. They agreed to raise $2400.00: $800.00 for salary, $800.00 for travel and $800.00 for supplies. Aubrey Saunders, chairman of Missions and

Education, was given the task of leading the effort. All women of the church, from little girls to old women, joined in. As the results were tallied, they rejoiced to have exceeded their own goal by $600.00. From the $3000.00 raised, Martha would be paid a salary of $67.00 per month. It was less than half what she had made in Schoolfield, but the amount was the furthest thing from her mind.

The trip to Richmond for her appointment was one of the happiest of Martha's life. Her mind was a jumble of thoughts of the service of appointment, of those wonderful people of Grove Avenue Church, and of China; it would be China at long last.

The Richmond experience exceeded by far anything that she could have imagined. Grove Avenue Baptist Church rolled out the red carpet for their missionary. She was given a royal welcome which was just the prelude for what would come over the course of forty years in which the church continued to pay her salary. Jesse and Ethel Wood and their daughter Ann took Martha into their home and into their hearts. During their time together one of the ladies joked, "It was like taking a pig in a poke when we got you." They loved their pig from the first, and she loved them.

In the early years, Sunbeams, Girls in Action, Royal Ambassadors, Young Women's Auxiliary, and the women worked hard to raise funds to keep Martha in China. Their work eventually inspired the entire church to join in her support.

One of the highlights of every furlough was a visit to Grove Avenue. On those visits Martha spoke to the congregation in worship services and to many groups of the church. Since her retirement, she has made two happy visits to them, thanking them again as she would say "for her bread and butter *and* jelly" for forty years.

One especially enduring friendship at Grove Avenue was that with Mary Cornett, head of the Junior Department of the church's Sunday School. It was in Miss Cornett's home that Martha stayed while on visits to the church during her furloughs. Miss Cornett became a vital means of moral support to Martha, sending a letter with interesting clippings of news from America every week. With the love and financial support of Grove Avenue Baptist Church, another link was joined with Martha's in God's chain.

A journey of a thousand miles Begins with a single step

After the royal reception in Richmond from the people of Grove Avenue Baptist Church and appointment by the Foreign Mission Board, Martha's return to Laurens was more than anti-climactic; it was difficult. Neither of her parents had been able to reconcile themselves to the thought of her going to China. They were not angry or hostile toward her; they were just unable to talk about it. Once, long before, as she and her mother sat shelling beans, Martha had asked, "Are you not happy for me to go to serve the Lord?" Her mother's words were full of pain as she answered, "Don't push me." Nothing more was said.

Making her return and the packing more painful was the fact that both her parents were confined to bed with a nurse to care for them. Martha was forced to pack her trunks on the side porch to avoid disturbing them and to shield from their sight what they knew was taking place. Emotions sometimes threatened to overwhelm her; should she wait until her parents were well? Was it selfish of her to go to the other side of the world rather than caring for them? As those and a thousand other questions crowded her head, Martha could not bring herself to cease her packing. God had called her to China, and she knew beyond any doubt that she must go.

One of the most difficult things she ever did was to leave her parents without a word of farewell. How she dreaded that parting. How they must have dreaded her going. The car arrived; all those trunks were loaded as quietly and as quickly as possible. Hardly daring to glance round lest she burst into tears, Martha took the road to Spartanburg.

If she were still feeling the weight of leaving her parents, it was soon lifted as she met that veteran of many China wars,

Sunday
November 29, 1925

Dear Tommies —

How do you like this loud stationery? I thought it was loud enough to speak for itself, which would save me from writing much — therefore I bought it.

You just don't know how glad I was to get that grand letter — <u>please</u> keep it up — I was always thrilled to get letters, but out here they are better than anything I know of — <u>anything</u>!

I'm getting fatter every day and sassier too — When I come home I expect I can get a job in the circus —

No, we surely don't have to bother about styles — its wonderful. You can almost always tell how long a person has been out here by the hat they wear — The old-timers examine our hats and clothes as if we newcomers had just stepped in from gay Paris — It makes us feel plumb stylish, whether we are or not.

Olive and I are having a wonderful time seeing the sights. She has been a mighty good tongue for me. I'm getting so now I can speak a little for myself and I'm mighty "biggety" and stuck up over it — I don't think I shall ever be able to read though — and I know I won't ever be able to write the stuff — But I'm going to talk!

I know that Ma Sallie is telling you all the news — I just wanted to say "thank you" <u>sure</u> enough for that letter and implore you to keep up the good work —

Love to both Tommies —

The Chink

P.S. There's something at my house for you — Maybe it will keep the rats away!!

Bertha Smith. Martha said she had never seen so many relatives in all her life as that hoard of Smiths who came to see Bertha off. Bertha said of Martha, "She was about the prettiest thing I had ever seen in all my life. All dressed up in the prettiest clothes: witty, bright, warm." Thus was born a friendship between the veteran and the novice that was to blossom and grow to a full-blown sweetness, ending after more than sixty years with Bertha's death at the age of ninety-nine (1988).

As they crossed the continent by train, Martha marveled at the beauty of her own country which she was seeing for the first time. Bertha took pleasure in Martha and found her good company. They studied and prayed together; they talked of China. Martha had a thousand questions; Bertha had two thousand answers. As unlike as they were, it is a wonder that they were able to stand each other's company. Bertha was a brigadier general, a real disciplinarian, disciplined; she believed in a place for everything and everything in its place. She was opinionated and frank, sometimes to the point of appearing rude. But she was well-versed in many areas and good company. Martha was a little flighty and somewhat lacking in discipline, but Bertha sensed in this impetuous young lady the makings of a real missionary. They liked each other. In time the two "generals" came to respect the strengths of each other so that they could live and work together with the greatest joy.

In late August, as they reached the West Coast, there was another case of nerves as Martha anticipated boarding ship to cross the wide expanse of the Pacific Ocean. When the trunks were duly hauled aboard with tons of other luggage, the two women stood on the deck of the *S. S. President Madison* along side several hundred people of many nationalities, all watching the shore of the United States fade in the distance. There was a big lump in her throat as she fought back tears and thoughts of her parents and friends and China.

Bertha, sensing those feelings which she had experienced a dozen years before, hurried the young lady off to the cabin where they unpacked their bags for the long trip ahead of them. After the fact of leaving land, there was little time for regrets or weeping. Martha was out to experience everything a single missionary girl could; there were deck tennis, shuffle-board, musicals, food galore, and the most interesting people she had ever encountered. She sat wide-eyed in her naievete, listening to tales of the Orient, especially from some of the wealthy, educated Chinese traveling with her.

To make her parting easier, there were telegrams from home and from former classmates at the seminary, particularly her roommate Rollie, who helped to salve the hurt. Martha in turn dashed off letters to family and friends which boiled with her excitement. She was discovering people, all kinds of people; she was discovering new foods (and already gaining weight); she was discovering new words and new expressions. There was little hint in her letters of the dignified lady who lay beneath that facade. She was straight from a small, secure circle of girls who could be as silly as they pleased (in private). She was being cast into a larger, more sophisticated company whose scope was the world.

As the first day of their voyage dawned, Martha crept with trepidation to the deck of the ship. Before stepping into the open, she closed her eyes, bracing herself for the fright-ening sight of giant waves which would certainly be lashing the ship. To her great astonishment, the sea was as calm as could be with hardly a ripple to break the beauty. She had determined, before sailing, that she would not be seasick. As the ocean did its part in helping to keep her stomach calm, Martha settled in for the time of her life. There were beautiful, moonlit nights, which set her thinking romantic thoughts having little to do with China. They were thoughts of which Bertha was never to know. They were revealed only to her dear friend Rollie.

Near the summer's end, they came to berth at Kobe, Japan. Again, the sights, sounds, and smells were almost more than Martha could absorb. Her senses were being bombarded from every direction, and she reveled in every new sensation. Much more of everything awaited her in China.

As the *S. S. President Madison* eased into the harbor at Shanghai, it was surrounded by a swirling mass of humanity unlike anything Martha could ever have imagined. Dozens of junks came alongside the ship, carrying hundreds of outstretched hands hoping for a coin from one of the "foreign devils" or one of the Chinese citizens rich enough to travel. As they disembarked, Dr. Williams, one of the missionaries, met them and quickly took care of the transportation of all their belongings. He had reserved several rickshas before their arrival, and the voyagers were soon settled in for the ride to the mission compound.

Martha looked round making certain that the familiar faces of her friends were nearby. In the mad rush, her runner saw a chance to take a shortcut and dashed down a narrow side street and away from the others in the group. When she realized that this strange man had taken her away from the others, she was suddenly frightened at the knowledge that she was in a foreign country, knew not a word to say, and had no idea where to go. What if? As the wheels rolled over the cobbled streets, every bump raised another doubt and question. She was on the verge of being overcome with fright when, with a sigh of relief, she saw the others in their rickshas as they all approached the mission. She had been in good hands after all.

After a short stop in Shanghai, it was on to Chefoo and Hwanghsien. As Martha alighted from her ricksha in Hwanghsien, she made her first *faux pas* in China as she ran up to one of the veteran missionaries, kissing her on the cheek. Poor Mrs. Hartwell was embarrassed beyond words at such show of affection before the Chinese. If it bothered her at all, the young lady recovered in short order as she drank in everything around her. She was like a giant sponge soaking up every element of China. Her letters reveal a genuine love affair beginning at first sight which grew with the passing of the years.

In Hwanghsien, she was introduced to the people with whom she would later be working. Some of them must have wondered whether the Board had made a big mistake this time. Martha seemed much too immature to be able to settle in to studies and the hard work with a distant and often unresponsive people. Not only the people, but also the land could be harsh for one unaccustomed to extremes of cold and a wind sometimes swirling a stifling dust for days. There was a multiplicity of diseases which could spread like wildfire among the millions of people living on the edge of life. The poverty and dirt in which the masses existed fueled epidemics like gasoline doused on a flame. When they struck, those outbreaks sometimes proved to be no respecters of persons high or low. Many a missionary had been buried in China before Martha's arrival.

No such thoughts dared intrude Martha's head. She'd never have entertained them if they had come. She loved the mission. Every new word from the missionaries, every tale of God's work were like music to her ears. She knew immediately that she was going to love China and the work God had sent her there to do.

Learning Is rowing upstream . . . Advance or lose all

Following that brief stop in Hwanghsien, the company made its way on to Peking, one of the most alluring cities in the world. Its narrow streets teemed with those people whom Martha had come to tell about Jesus. Shops abounded which sold every imaginable commodity including degraded human beings, male and female, both adult and child. There was the Forbidden City from which the last Empress Tz'u-hsi and her henchmen, the despised eunuchs, had hastened China down the road to ruin less than twenty years before. Martha said of Peking that it was "the most charming, exciting, interesting city in the whole world." She loved China, its people, and everything Chinese. Her respect for the people and their customs proved to be a boon in later years when she worked in the rural areas often encountering robbers and kidnappers in a country engulfed by anarchy.

She could see the tip of the iceberg and wanted to see the whole great chunk. She ached to examine every facet of that beautiful mass which proved to be like a many-faceted crystal revealing ever more fascinating colors with each turn of the hand. She would see everything possible; she would know everything she could learn about this great land and its people.

But for the present, there was the not-so-romantic necessity of unpacking and settling in for a year of language at the College of Chinese Studies. There were about one hundred students all boarding and studying together. They had come from several different nations and were studying the language in preparation for many varied occupations. There were, besides the missionaries, teachers, career government personnel, lawyers, businessmen, and others. They were an interesting group with varying degrees of likes and dislikes for China. For Martha, every day was a new opportunity for discovery; she wallowed in the new and was refreshed.

Entering the classroom for the first time was enough to jolt her out of her reverie. Classes began at 8:45 every morning, Monday through Friday, ending at 4:00 in the afternoon. The head teacher called "Dearest" was a master teacher. John Dewey, the American philosopher-educator, is reputed to have said of Dearest that he was the best teacher in the world. There was a different teacher every half hour, each one emphasizing what the last had taught. No English was spoken by the teachers. They used whatever method they could muster to enable their pupils to learn new words: *eye, ear, hair, hand, cloud, book, child;* there was no end with four to five new words each day. They were learning Mandarin, the official Chinese dialect. Mandarin has four tones and is monosyllabic. The word *sse* could mean *dead, persimmon* or *tomato, louse* or the numeral *four,* depending on the tone.

Martha had an advantage over many of the others in her group; God had given her an ear for music. She quickly came to distinguish the tones, learning new words every day. Bertha Smith, with her gift of hyperbole, said of Martha, "She could speak the language like a native. If you hadn't seen her as she spoke, you'd never have known she was an American." Martha laughed at those words. The fact remains that she was adept at the spoken Mandarin. "It's hard, but fun," she wrote to her family and friends.

If she needed incentives, she found them as she stepped outside the security of the walls of the college. There were

Martha, Peking, 1925

reminders everywhere — on every street, in the doorways, along every wall — of the poverty and despair into which China had sunk. There were wars and rumors of wars every day. Student demonstrations often left a score or more dead in the streets. There were dying beggars, lying helpless on the way. On one side, there was a naked beggar child, covered from head to toe with sores, his eyes swollen shut, wailing in pain to the attention of no one. As Martha passed the child, she almost jumped from her seat to grab the little boy and hug him to her breast. On another side one could see the stupor-faced addicts and prostitutes of both genders, as they moved from one dastardly deed to the next. As she observed those pitiful pieces of human flesh, entrapped as they were in the bondages of this world's evil, writhing in pain, she silently asked God to help her to learn their language. She desperately longed to be able to speak a word of comfort and hope to them. She wanted, needed, to tell them that there was a God who cared. She thought of how God had shown his love and compassion in sending his only Son, Jesus into this world. Everywhere Jesus had gone, he had shown God's love as he reached out to hurting people. The blind man, the epileptic child, the leper, the woman with a blood disorder, the demon-possessed man living in the tombs, the woman taken in the act of adultery: All had seen God's love in the flesh, as Jesus reached out to heal. Martha wanted to be one of His disciples, spreading that same love to those poor people of China.

Language school wasn't all study. There were the late afternoons, evenings and weekends which left a little time for exploring. It was not uncommon to see several of the students set off for the market places where Chinese art bedazzled the eye. Martha stared in wonder at the exquisite porcelains; embroideries; the water color paintings on silk; ivory, jade, cork and wood carvings of infinite variety. They gave her an insight into the Chinese character which spoke of a love of beauty and a patience in working with those ordinary elements from which such beauty emerged. Study, and daily discovery of the wonders of China led quickly to Christmas.

Martha had dreaded to see Christmas come that first year in China. Christmas at home brought all the family together for singing, cooking, eating, laughing. She would miss her family more than she dared say. She would miss making candies and fruitcakes. How would she survive it, half a world away?

It was the Lawtons who filled that one big empty spot in her season. Olive had been born in China, and it was to the old family home in Cheng Chow that they all met at Christmas time. The Lawtons were good, sensible people; there was little frivolity with them. Martha arrived with a breath of fresh air. Olive said she came with a large pack on her back looking like Santa Claus himself. She had gifts for everyone; there was a ham, a victrola, her saw for making music. Martha woke that old house in Cheng Chow.

En route, she had been greatly disturbed by the sight of so much widespread poverty. In Peking she had seen the beggars, but in the countryside, there were entire villages devastated by floods from the winter rains. She saw hundreds of villages made of nothing but tiny mud-walled single rooms with a little thatch on top. They looked to her like little covered wagons. Whole families huddled inside just to survive the bitter cold of winter.

Upon arrival in Cheng Chow, again she saw how wretchedly the masses of people lived. There was a fifty-foot deep moat surrounding the city which had been dry for generations. Many people had dug caves in the wall of the moat. In the caves whole families, made up of two or three generations, lived out their lives from birth to burial. As Martha stared, such scenes of poverty and pain grabbed at her heart. Over and over she thought of how she wanted to tell them of a Savior who cared that they were poor and that they hurt. She wanted to get to know them and learn to love them as His disciple.

She had opportunity to express her faith with them when Sunday morning before Christmas brought the community of Christians together for study and worship. Martha went to Katie Murray's Sunday School class for seven year olds. She was thrilled to be able to follow the Bible story and translate the motto text. At the close of the story, one bright-eyed boy stood to tell the story from start to finish, never missing a point. In the general assembly which followed, each class stood in turn giving the motto text which they had learned that day. In the worship service, Martha had another surprise. The preacher was Pastor Ding, whom she had known at Southern Seminary in Louisville, Kentucky. Christmas was proving to be better than she had imagined.

But Monday morning brought reminders of the fragile nature of life even at Christmas. Because of a recent outbreak of smallpox, Martha and Olive had brought vaccine from the city. Each girl and the workers at the orphanage had to be vaccinated. Mrs. Lawton made an instrument for scratching on the arm by pushing a needle through a cork. With Martha, Olive and Katie to do the scrubbing with alcohol and the scratching, Mrs. Lawton applied the vaccine. Martha found that she also enjoyed playing nurse.

Every day brought new sights, new faces, new experiences. One after another, old Chinese friends brought in baskets of vegetables or some other goody then available. The Lawtons placed money in each basket, the equivalent of goods delivered. It was not so different, Martha said, from gift-giving in America.

A highlight of Martha's stay with the Lawtons that Christmas came when a young Chinese couple by the name of Ding were married. Their wedding feast was the first Martha had experienced. There were twenty courses, the last of which had seven dishes. Thirteen main courses included duck, chicken, ham, sausage, and fish of different kinds. She thought she would never want another bite to eat during the whole of Christmas.

Another first for Martha came in seeing the commitment of Cheng Chow Christians sharing the gospel in the villages dotting the hills and valleys of that seeming endless expanse of China. The country evangelists were arriving for a month of study before returning to the villages where they preached the gospel. Some of them had walked thirty miles carrying bedding on their backs. Their faces showed plainly the joy in their hearts to be able to tell of God's love. Hearing them pray and sing and study, Martha was reminded again of God's goodness and wondered what place He intended for her. She must study, study, study this language.

On the third day of Christmas week, everyone was forced to stay within the compound all day because two war lords were threatening to fight. The women all busied themselves with preparing ingredients for fruitcakes and candies. They addressed cards, laughed and sang and plotted Christmas. The tranquility was broken with the news that Pochow had been sacked. Dr. Mary King and Clifford Barrett had lost all their possessions and were being held in the city for ransom. Other missionaries were negotiating their release. Amid the joy of celebrating the birth of the Prince of Peace, there were reminders everywhere of hatred and war.

More joy came just before Christmas when they all met to decorate the church. What an eclectic mix there was of greens, bows, Chinese lanterns and hangings of all descriptions. The program included traditional readings from the scripture, music by the orphanage band and two plays presented by the girls' school depicting the gospel story. The program took on added significance when Martha realized that there were parents present for the music and plays who were hearing the story of Jesus for the first time.

With Christmas Eve approaching, Martha and Olive could hardly contain themselves. The two twenty-four-year-olds were like teenagers. All day long they plotted, plundered and planned. In the attic they found decorations and a trunk full of dolls. It seemed an eternity before Olive's parents finally retired for the night. It was a wonder they ever got to sleep with the two young ladies whispering, giggling, and tiptoeing all over the place. They hung cedar in the hall and living room; there were red bells and other antique decorations. The victrola and a bathrobe were for Olive's father. There were lampshades, fruitcakes and candies for Olive's mother. After a trip to the cook's house where they placed in each child's stocking a small toy and candies, Martha and Olive settled in for a "long winter's nap."

The nap came to an abrupt end at five o'clock on Christmas morning. Girls from the school were standing under their window in the snow singing carols in Chinese at five o'clock in the morning! By six the day of celebrations began with a big breakfast. Seven-thirty was opening time! It was surprise time for Olive's parents. Olive and the other children had been away at school and there had not been anything like this in their home since the children were young. Martha's own gift was a beautiful fur rug to wear while riding in a ricksha. Later in the morning, the cook's family and all the neighbors came in to share in Christmas treats.

Happy, happy Christmas! Martha sat down that night to write letters. In one she said, "I thought Christmas meant all it could mean to me in America, but it means twice more out here, because I have seen what it would be like to live in a land where the blessed Christ child is not known."

Christmas break helped make it possible to go into another semester of language studies. There was a new incentive to learn this language.

Gold has its price
Learning is beyond price

Her first year in China was the most exciting time Martha had ever spent in her life. The people were fascinating to her. They came in all the varied shapes, sizes and personalities with which the mass of humanity is blessed. They were steeped in a culture and tradition which far outdistanced her own in both time and space. There were the foreign community, made up of officials of the governments of the world who had their fingers in every Chinese pie. There were tradesmen and fortunehunters who had been a part of the China scene for centuries. As in every ancient society, there were the scholars and Chinaphiles who poked and probed into every artery of China's body.

Martha enjoyed them all, but there was something which fascinated her more than any of the teas, luncheons, soirees, outings, games, and studies. Her one single most exciting event was to escape from the prison of those walls behind which Chinese authorities had generations ago shut all foreigners, and simply walk down the streets on her own. Sometimes

Aug. 18, 1926.

Dearest Rollie Girl:

Has it been hot in Virginia today? I feel just exactly like Epaminomdas' butter, or at least I did, it is getting cooler a little cooler now, and pretty soon I think we are going to have another glorious sunset. Come along and we will walk down the goat track to the river. We'll stop by some Chinese houses.

I got in from Chefoo Saturday. We had such a good time playing around in the ocean and seeing all the American ships out in the harbor right in front of our house and we had dinner one night on one of the biggest ships in the harbor, the Black Hawk. We had a real American brass band while we ate and a moving picture afterwards. There hasn't been any travel on the road since I came in Saturday and I thought at some of the slipperest places that maybe I might not get here but the Lord takes care of old maids, children and fools and I come under all three classes so I got here safely. The river has water in it for the first time in six years. They built a stone bridge over the dry bed five years ago and since there has been no rain since the people have all declared that the reason was because there were the rocks of the foundation on the dragon's head. The bridge washed away, so of course it really was on his head or tail and I'm afraid that we will never have another bridge. We were to have had a big wedding in the church Tuesday but the bride couldn't get across the river so the affair had to be postponed, isn't that tragic, just think of a little thing like water keeping you from the waiting bridegroom. Speaking of brides I was talking to my teacher yesterday about the tragedy of the bride not getting to the church and she told me of the superstitions regarding the weather that the wedding day brings forth. If the day is a rainy one there is sure to be sorrow, neither of the couple will live long. If the day is windy, the bride will have a very high temper and the husband will have to be careful, if the day is cloudy, she is hoo doo, stupid, but if it is snowing gently there will be much happiness, long life and many children, this is true too of a pretty day, not too hot, nor too windy etc. I hope that my teacher is going to tell me a lot of interesting things to help us pass the time a little. I like her fine if she just wouldn't eat garlic. I am studying three hours a day now and in two weeks I hope to work up to five hours a day. There isn't anything particularly thrilling or romantic about studying hard with one little woman for five hours a day.

We will be so glad when the river goes down and we can get mail across. I think I'll go down and do the side stroke across and get the mail and come along home. I could ride my bike to the riverside.

I stopped and ate supper. Just Charlotte, Ullin Jr. and I are here. Mr. Leavell has gone off to some kind of a meeting. We had a good supper, fried chicken, bran muffins, tomatoes, and peaches. We have awfully good things to eat. We have to be awfully careful of course.

Aug. 19.

I stopped again we forgot it was prayer meeting night so I had to get a wiggle on and go over to the Glass house for the meeting. We have such lovely prayer services just our little community, last night there were nine of us there. I came home and dreamed about you. I dreamed that you had gone to church history and I was packing my trunk and found that pink Japanese crepe dress of yours, except it was blue, but the dream had it pink. I thought it was so dirty and you would want to put it on when you came home so I washed it right quick and put some new Chinese filet lace on it and when you came home you were the tickled one!

I have finished my lessons for today. We studied the third chapter of John, it is so hard and it is so hot. Then I went by the hospital and Blanch Bradley took me in the operating room where they were grafting skin on a man's foot. I had never seen a grafting operation before, it was interesting but the poor man had just had a local anesthetic and I couldn't stand to see him suffer so I beat it on home. Right now I smell something so good cooking and I am starting to diet today, I'm just so fat I can't get in my clothes most hardly. Charlotte weighs 204 so she is dieting too and by next summer we are going to be the thin, slim sylph like ladies. Maybe.

Did you hear that V's little sister is going to get married? I was so surprised, she has been writing me this winter and hasn't said beans about getting married or even having a lover. I guess V her own self will be the next one. Then my little Rollie will up and marry that lawyer and I don't much care if she does.

I do hope you are going by Laurens, they were all so disappointed when you didn't come by in the spring. Alleene wrote me that they could have shed crocodile tears. Please go.

The mail may get out today and if it does I must get some several letters off so I'll hang up on this line. You know that I love you a lot! I had such good pleasure thinking about you last night in my dreams. Aren't dreams nice when you haven't eaten too much pie for supper? My love to all the family.

Melindy

when she was all but exhausted from her studies, or perhaps when she began to think too much of home, or when she ached to begin the work that she had come to China to do, she walked to the gate and stared out into that other world. At every opportunity, she escaped her own ghetto, her prison, tuning her eyes, her ears, her every sense on this strange magical place called China.

There were the long daily sessions in language studies. They were at once a source of joy and pain. She knew that she was learning to speak their tongue, but after six hours, one felt drained. She wanted to learn, was determined to learn. Without the language she would be of little use to the work. It seemed sometimes to be so slow in coming, but she knew there would be no assignment for her until she had a proper working knowledge of the language.

Following a day of language studies, there were often expeditions into the city. On one such occasion, darkness overtook Martha and Olive as they returned to the school. Suddenly Martha was frightened to see a large group of white-robed figures carrying lighted torches. In an open space, at the turn of the road, she saw them stop, making a bonfire, as they tossed their torches into a heap. On the lighted torches they piled life-sized paper horses, carts, flowers, money and servants to assist the dead man in the next world. Riding on she sat in silent disbelief. She was glad to be in China and determined to learn to tell of God's love which receives the souls of those who accept his love with no strings attached.

The two young ladies soon had opportunity for sharing their faith with the Chinese. On Thursday evenings, she and Olive taught a class of thirty young men, aged seventeen to twenty-five years. Following the formal English lessons, there was a question and answer period. The young men, many of whom worked in shops frequented by the foreign community wanted to know everything American. "What is a parlor? What is in one? How big are napkins? What is on a napkin? Why an initial?" The boys were a refreshing outlet to the two young students.

The two shocked their fellow students at the language school when they announced they were moving from the school dormitory to a YWCA hostel for Chinese girls. Because of the uncertainty created by the never-ending wars, there were only five girls living in the hostel designed to house many more. What better way to learn the language, culture and manners of the people than by living with them? The food would be Chinese, but its preparation was supervised by an American. They had a sitting room with southern exposure and a wall of windows. There was a large general living area with a grand piano, and the two shared a large bedroom. To top it all, the cost for room and board would be $40.00 as opposed to $70.00 per month at the school.

Thus the two young ladies managed to escape the closeness of the school to make another place for themselves. Following her usual pattern, Martha surrounded herself with beauty and life. The room soon sprouted potted geraniums, begonias and a bowl of goldfish. She found a lovely brass bowl at the market and brought out the blue desk set which a friend had given her before she left America. Martha had done what few would have dared; she was living with the Chinese themselves. Perhaps it was not in quite the way most of them lived, but she was closer to them than most foreigners. She liked what she saw up close even better than what she had only been able to observe before at a distance.

Moving to the YWCA was typical Martha. As a child and later in college, as a teacher and in seminary, Martha had always cut her own path. In China she would remain true to pattern.

To know the road ahead
Ask those coming back

The novelty and excitement of being in China had worn a little thin by the end of the session in the early summer of 1926. Martha loved China and all things Chinese still, but language studies had become a burden. She was glad for the summer to follow at Chefoo. The missionaries had a beautiful, large stone house on the seacoast overlooking the harbor.

Language studies continued, but there were walks on the beach, entertainments, and a trip to the Great Wall. It had been eleven months since Martha left home in Laurens. They were eleven eventful months filled with more excitement and adventure, more experiences than most people have in a lifetime. Martha thanked God upon every remembrance, but on those long, hot days when no mail arrived, she felt the distance. Every day as she came down the stairs or came in from a walk, she went immediately to the table where the mail was placed, hoping for words from home. Any letter from home was like a drink of water to one in a thirsty land. She described the anticipation and receipt of an unexpected letter during that summer at Chefoo: "Coming into the house, I found a letter when I had not expected any mail. Dropping down on the stairs, I hastily drank in every word. Then I walked out the door and along the beach a way before dropping down in the sand where I read the words over and over again until I'd memorized every line. As I read your letters, I forgot how hard John (gospel) is to read in Chinese, how hot it is, and how I wish all the folks would come along home."

In an attempt to escape the hot and humidity, they traveled to the hills for the weekend. Riding through the countryside, they saw evidence of the awful conflict between so many

Culpeppers leaving for America in a Shenza (mule litter)

fighting forces in China. The Chinese Communist Party had been organized in 1921. But it was often the forces of the Nationalist Government, in its attempts to bring some semblance of law and order out of the raging chaos, that resulted in more and more fighting. Soldiers as often as not, received no pay and had become roving bands of brigands themselves. They took from the people whatever they wanted and sometimes burned the remainder; they were especially hated and feared for their habit of carrying off the women and girls of the villages. As the Nationalists' reputation for cruelty increased, the people's hatred for them grew. When the final showdown with the communists came, the people sided with the communists over the Nationalists. Communist leaders cunningly laid a trap for China, in part by disciplining their soldiers to be polite, give way, and take nothing from the people. The day would come when they would take everything; by then it would be too late to save China.

Despite the scattered skirmishes and rumors of wars raging in the country, the trip to the hills that late summer was a most refreshing one. The views were almost breathtaking. They spent the night in an ancient temple courtyard, sleeping under a sweetgum tree.

The next day found them all riding donkeys over the mountains to visit another temple to see the renowned "Black Dragon Pool." Gazing into the shimmering waters of the pool, they heard the legend of the great dragon who lived under it. Long ages before, during a time of drought, the Emperor had traveled to the pool telling the dragon that if he didn't soon release the rain, he would not come there to play any more. Before the Emperor got back to Peking, there was such a deluge that the Emperor was forced to return to the pool to placate the dragon. Everywhere one turned, there were equally beautiful sights and interesting tales of the long ago.

The summer was a happy one, but Martha knew that with the coming of autumn, she would have to continue and even redouble her efforts at the language. This year there would be an added incentive as she would begin timidly to enter the world of the people in school, church, hospitals, and orphanages. She wrote home, "I do not know what my place or work will be, but I know that in His plan there is a place and I am trying to be patient about seeing it. I feel a tremendous appeal in City Evangelistic — probably through our church in the city — I do not feel that I am 'cut out' especially, for school work. Our station has certainly suffered from loss of workers. The Stout family is here now en route to America. How we do need someone for our seminary!"

Summer's end approached too rapidly, finding Martha both longing for and dreading its coming. She traveled by open car along rough, unpaved roads to Hwanghsien. The other missionaries were more than happy to have a new worker. The scripture "The harvest is plenteous and the workers are few" was truer than an outsider could possibly imagine. There was a dinner in her honor and words expressing great expectations of her work. Before going to the Pruitts for dinner, Martha had to pin a handkerchief to the neck of her dress so as not to appear indecent in public. No decent woman could show her neck nor arms above the elbow. On the other hand, one could show all the leg one liked. There were so many things to learn; so many things to remember!

Martha had already learned that speaking was not all there was to know in order to communicate with the Chinese. The written language is made up of more than 40,000 characters, which, to the untrained eye, appear at first to be hardly distinguishable one from the other. In order to be considered fit for graduation from language studies, one must learn to write a mere 800. A musical ear is no help at all when it comes to learning the written characters. Martha grabbed the "Gordian Knot" when she began to learn those characters, but there was no cutting of the knot; she had to labor over it. Sometimes it seemed like slave labor almost, but there was no way round it; it had to be done. She wrote over and over to family and friends, "I will learn this language."

Martha had spent a year in the cosmopolitan city of Peking, and she now was plunked down in the provencial town of Hwanghsien. The amusements and diversions of Peking were suddenly replaced by the real, work-a-day world. Martha found hardworking men and women who were committed to the Lord and to their work. They were kind to her and helped wherever they could, but she had to do much on her own; they were all busy every day with their own tasks.

Hwanghsien is situated on a fertile plain between the ocean which lies five miles to the north and the mountains lying fifteen miles to the south. The surrounding fields produce in great quantity wheat, millet, cabbages, sweet potatoes, turnips, and many other fresh vegetables and fruits. The year 1927 found that area of North China in relative peace which, as it happened, proved to be the proverbial calm before the storm. It was a good time for a beginning as a missionary in China.

The people of Hwanghsien were a source of joy to Martha from the first encounter. She remembered the men as being large and handsome. The women were skilled in the culinary arts and with the needle, especially embroideries. The children were rosy-cheeked and happy and were almost always receptive to joyous, laughing Martha. There was another quality which impressed her: It was their patient endurance. The Chinese themselves referred to it as "the ability to get over the days."

She found that Chinese Christians exhibited in their lives a spirituality that she had found all too rare among the Christians she had known back home in America. Unlike herself and most of the people she had known at home, Chinese Christians paid a price for their faith. They were often ridiculed, ostracized, and sometimes physically abused for their faith.

Here she was a spiritual "pygmy," as she saw herself, surrounded by spiritual giants. Martha came to see in Charlie Culpepper, W. B. Glass, Jane and Florence Lide, Alice Huey, Anna Hartwell, and others, an awareness of God, and a relationship with the living Christ, all of which she knew too little. Likewise she recognized a deep commitment to the Christ and His church in many of the Chinese Christians. Tzang Pao Chin, Wang Sue, Wang Li Mei, Dr. Chu, Wang Ge Sung, Wang Kwang Sung, Tzang Tien Pao, and Fan Ming Ging all made a lasting impression upon this young lady who wanted desperately to serve the Lord among them.

As Martha observed the joy they took in their work, she was hardly able to contain herself. She was eager to try her hand at being a messenger to them of God's love. She was slowly but surely learning to speak their tongue; she had come round the world to tell them; she longed to join in the work.

She had made a good beginning in Peking, but before she could begin her own work, Martha had to have a working knowledge of their language *and* a knowledge of their manners and customs. One missionary, in ignorance, could wreck what many had worked years to accomplish. There were certain questions considered impolite, if not downright insulting to the Chinese. Women in that area of China never wore short sleeves and no low necks. Certain colors were not to be worn. Only brides wore pink or red. Missionary women had to know and respect those traditions if they were to gain the respect of the Chinese in return. A teacher must never allow himself to become overly familiar with students. In the classroom in China, all students stood and bowed when the teacher entered the room.

One must never tell a joke in which an animal represented a person; that was considered in the worst taste. In ignorance, Martha once asked her Chinese teacher whether he thought it would rain. The man answered her not a word, to her complete amazement. It was several hours later that Dr. Hartwell, principal of the school, told her that the man had come to him in the greatest anger. Indignantly, the man said, "Miss Franks reviled me! She asked whether I thought it might rain!" To her great chagrin, Martha learned that one never asks that question of a Chinese. Only turtles know whether it will rain. In Chinese thinking, the question is connected with the turtle's reproductive system. If a Chinese wants to revile or insult another person, he draws a turtle on the gate. There was so much to learn, so much to know. It was difficult getting everything straight in her head.

The Lord provided help. There were those kind and loving new-found friends in the mission who helped to ease the way. By God's grace, Lois and Eloise Glass were there. The Glass girls had just graduated from the China Inland Mission High School and were waiting for their parents to complete another year of service before furlough at which time they would begin their college studies in the United States. Lois and Eloise were

Martha and her teacher

nearest in age to Martha of all those in the mission and provided a much-needed companionship in tennis and other recreational pursuits.

Friday nights brought delightful, formal suppers in the Hartwell home, meals well-served by a trained Chinese staff. Mrs. Hartwell had brought her china, silver, and crystal with her when she left Charleston, South Carolina, and had no intention of allowing the distance and environment to change her style of entertaining. After supper, as the men engaged in business talk, Mrs. Hartwell read to the women from some excellent volume which proved to be a source of joy and strength to them. Martha always remembered those Friday evenings as delightful diversions.

Her teachers in Peking had been of the first class. In Hwanghsien, she found a teacher who had never taught a foreigner before. To further complicate matters, the dialect was very different from the Mandarin she had studied the year before. For five hours each day she sat across a small table from this plodding Christian woman. They used the Bible as a text. Martha came to like the woman except for the fact that she always ate garlic. Sometimes she felt that she could not face another hour of those garlic fumes. Hour after hour, day after day, she studied the characters. It seemed that they twisted and changed shapes from one day to the next so as to deliberately confuse her. Some days, she had to fight back the tears of frustration. Mondays were the worst of all; so much seemed to evaporate in just two days.

Every two months Jane Lide examined Martha's progress in learning Chinese characters. Despite the monotony, she continued to show respectable progress in memorizing that line of never-ending characters. Some days they seemed to sneer at her like a bunch of twisted-limb demons; Martha was learning to glare back at them, calling them by name. She was learning to communicate with the Chinese. As halting as were her words, she was eager to make a beginning.

Whenever the studies threatened to overwhelm her, Martha's teacher, sensing her frustration, took her for a walk in the mission's gardens or into the city on market days. Martha described in a letter, the beauty of the hollyhocks, snapdragons, rose-covered arbors and trees laden with huge apricots, peaches and cherries. She spoke of the priceless pieces in the market to be had for a pittance, if she had only had the pittance. There were porcelains, brasses, semi-precious stones, silk paintings, silver and gold pieces and needlework. Such beauty was always enough to rejuvenate her sagging spirit, at least temporarily.

On such excursions, Martha's teacher taught her much of the folklore, mores, and manners of China. Her old friend, Bertha Smith, remarked that Martha came to identify so well with the Chinese because she "learned every nuance of Chinese culture and etiquette." She listened to every tale about China and absorbed as much of the life as she could.

She delighted in being a part of a Chinese wedding. Before the ceremony, there came a big rain, washing away a bridge which had stood for five years over a dry river bed. The people declared that the reason for no rain was the fact that the bridge

The young wedding
couple, Tsining

had been built on the dragon's tail. The dragon had finally roused himself, flooding the country and washing the bridge away. The destruction of the bridge spelled disaster for the poor bride-to-be stranded on the other side. Her teacher explained that it portened an unhappy marriage. If there were rain on the day of the wedding, there would be sorrow; neither would live long; if wind, the bride would be high-tempered, and the husband would have to be careful; clouds meant that the wife would be "hoo doo" (stupid); if a gentle snow fell, or the sun shone, there would be great happiness, long life and many children.

At any rate this wedding had to be postponed. When the day arrived for the rescheduled wedding, the entire mission community helped with arrangements for the marriage of the two young Christians. Martha helped the other women gather flowers of pink and red from all the mission's beds. Red was the color for happiness and thus for weddings and was used as liberally as possible. At 9:00 a.m. the bride arrived in a red chair; at 9:30 the groom arrived in a green one; the two were feasted separately in the pastor's house. At 10:30 the wedding party arrived at the church. The bride was dressed in a pink skirt with silver dangles on the hem, a pink blouse, and a pink organdy veil with a huge pompom on top. The groom was dressed in the traditional wedding garment of a Chinese gentleman. The bride was escorted down one side aisle by two school girls who supported her as she walked. The groom proceeded down the aisle on the other side of the church. The two almost met, standing three feet apart. As the couple arrived at the altar, the congregation stood, singing "Praise God from Whom All Blessings Flow." Martha commented to a friend afterward, "If I ever get a man that far, I admit I'd feel like singing those words, too."

Four men sat on the rostrum to do the ceremony. There were the pastor, the master of ceremonies, a relative, and a middle-man. After the middle-man spoke, the pastor had read from the Bible and spoken of the meaning of Christian marriage, each of the other men spoke. The couple then bowed to each other, to the congregation, pastor, and parents, and were considered married. The bride and her attendants left by one door; the groom and his by another for a wedding feast. The bride was not allowed to dine with her husband in company with others. Martha did not appreciate the men's feast nor did she generally like the treatment of women in China.

Of these and other events, she continued to write long personal letters in which she poured out her new-found wisdom, her frustrations, and her dreams of the work to come. One day, upon receiving a copy of the South Carolina *Baptist Courier*, she was shocked to find on the Woman's Missionary Union page a copy of one of her letters to Mrs. Hatcher. There was little dignity in it; she was just being herself. In her next letter to Mrs. Hatcher, she implored her to correct punctuation and edit future letters before allowing them to appear in print. Martha's sister Alleene and their father both scolded her for the use of so much slang in her letters to others.

While it is still Good weather . . . Clean the drainpipes

Upon her arrival in Hwanghsien, Martha was invited to live with the Leavells. The Leavells were a young couple, not much older than she, and were especially kind to her; she enjoyed being in their home. At that time the women did not go into local shops to order cloth; merchants were invited to bring samples of their cloth for the women's perusal in their homes. Martha needed new dresses of a different cut ("fit for an old maid," she said). When the merchant arrived to show his wares, Martha was shocked to learn that the man thought her to be Dr. Leavell's concubine. She decided then and there to find new lodgings.

That one move was perhaps one of the most momentous decisions of her life. She simply walked up to Alice Huey's door asking to move in with her. In a letter to Martha's sister Alleene written from Alabama, December, 1947, Miss Huey, in response to a request from Alleene, wrote of that day,

Martha Franks proved to be a great judge of character. Alice Huey did indeed have something which Martha lacked and needed. In future years she would have to get that something lacking if she were ever to fulfill the mission in China to which God had called her. As one examines the happenings of those years, it is easy to conclude that Martha might never have survived in China, but for that fateful decision to move in with Alice Huey.

Life with Alice Huey was an experience that helped Martha endure the burdens of being separated from home and family and the seeming endlessness of Chinese characters. The girls' dormitory at the mission school housed seventy-five girls who were themselves a source of comfort and joy to Martha. The two women had a comfortable apartment in the dormitory. Both of them were busy during the day with studies and many other duties, but when the day's work was finished, they sat down to talk about God, home, and the people of China. They read the Bible, discussed its meaning, and prayed together. Martha had found a mentor in Alice Huey.

September 29, 1926, proved to be a red-letter day for Martha and a turning point in her relations at home. On that day she received the very first letter her mother had written her. She could hardly believe her eyes when she saw the handwriting on the envelope from America. It was certainly Sallie Franks'. Ripping the letter open, she burst into tears before she had read a word. At the words themselves, she variously laughed, cried, and squealed until old Huey was forced to go to her aid. Jane Lide was on furlough to the United States and had traveled to Laurens for a visit with the Frankses. Jane had told them of Martha's joy and progress; she reassured them concerning her health; she convinced them of the feelings of the other missionaries that Martha would become a good missionary in time.

Both John and Sallie Franks had been sick and were hurt at their youngest daughter's leaving. They knew how immature she was and really wondered whether she could possibly sustain the effort. God was now beginning to help them to see that He was a part of the plan, that it was indeed His plan for Martha to be in China. They could not continue to disagree with God. Martha received letters from home telling of her mother's improving health. A year before, as she walked out the door on that late summer's day, she felt certain that she would never see her mother's face again; now she had hope.

Despite her lack of facility in language, the administration invited Martha to take the job of gym teacher for the girls. As they watched her play and laugh and dance, the students decided that she must certainly be a rather large monkey from the circus. The poor girls whose feet had been bound long before had never learned to play. This young missionary was out to teach them. Soon they too were learning how to run, and laugh, and dance.

Language studies continued in good times and bad. Martha had attempted to learn each chapter perfectly before continuing to the next. The older missionaries had good advice for her, born out of their own experience. "Don't worry about learning every new term. If one proves to be difficult, you should continue on to the next passage. You will find the terms again, and they will eventually become clear to you." Martha said of her studies in a letter home, "This language has to be rubbed in, it can't be absorbed in a day. Someone said that the devil created this language to keep the gospel from being proclaimed and I believe it. The old boy certainly did a good day's work."

Letters from home helped relieve the tedium. In her own letters Martha poured out the story of need in China — health care; education; poor, abandoned children; abused wives; and, sad to say, most of them were lost. They had never before heard of God's love for them. They did not know of the coming of His Son Jesus who had died on the cross to save them from their sins. Martha told the stories repeatedly; some responsed. The gifts were not large; they didn't have to be to help. One concerned friend sent a check for fifteen dollars; it would make thirty dollars in Chinese money. Thirty dollars would support a Chinese evangelist or a Bible woman for three months. It would pay the cost of an average surgery in the mission hospital. Every dollar was gladly received and acknowledged; every dollar was spent only after prayerful intercession with God.

Martha soon discovered that attempts at witnessing to the Chinese were not always welcomed by any means. Alice Huey tried repeatedly to talk to an old letter carrier who came every day to pick up and deliver mail to the mission. The snaggle-toothed man, who seldom moved faster than a turtle and who did nothing except deliver the mail to them, always responded

The old postman — headed for heaven for delivering missionary mail

71

that he was too busy to stop and listen. Huey asked, "What about when you die; will you have time then? Do you expect to go to heaven?"

"Oh! Yes ma'm, I expect to go to heaven all right, certainly!" he answered assuredly.

"But why would you expect to go?" Huey continued.

The old man broke into an ear-to-ear grin, "Why, I've carried you preachers' mail all these years. You know *I'll* get in!"

Martha often told such stories in her letters; she also told of needs. One reason for sharing so much of the need in China was the fact of a shortage of personnel. Not only were there not enough teachers, doctors, nurses, and evangelists, but some of those on the field were growing too old for the rigor required. Travel was extremely hazardous to one's health. Mrs. Pruitt had recently come in from Chefoo with a broken arm. The Chinese driver had turned the car over at 9:00 in the morning, and they had arrived home late that night to have the bone set. Not long before, Anna Hartwell had been in a similar accident, while traveling to Harbin, in which she had an ankle broken. Not only were the unpaved roads treacherous, but the drivers were often untrained and careless.

With the shortages of personnel and two workhorses hindered by broken bones, Mr. Hartwell had an attack of gallstones. There was no surgeon in town, and it looked as if the man would surely die. The entire mission knelt to pray for God's mercy. Mr. Leavell was returning home from a trip to one of the villages when he chanced upon a Chinese Christian by the name of Mr. Woo pacing the road and praying aloud. Mr. Woo was begging the Lord to spare Mr. Hartwell and take him instead. He said in his prayer that China needed Mr. Hartwell far more than it needed him. God heard all their prayers, sparing Mr. Hartwell's life and Mr. Woo's. The attack subsided, and he was able to travel to Chefoo for surgery which enabled him to continue his work.

Mission policy, strictly adhered to, stated that no missionary could begin work before the completion of two years of language study. Cautiously, almost gingerly, as Martha became more proficient in the language, the other missionaries began to encourage her to venture out just a little. She would not be allowed to work at the expense of her studies. Martha began teaching English in the girls' school one hour each day. She had no plans to become a teacher, at least on that level, but she enjoyed every minute with the students, and they responded to her.

The beloved old pastor Chen came to school to hold evangelistic services. He was a most convincing preacher. Kind, gentle, and loving, he preached of the need for conversion. Martha accompanied the girls, along with one other foreigner, to the meetings. She had never before experienced anything like it. It seemed to her like a little *Pentecost*. She began to see the moving of God's Spirit in response to the prayers of the young Christian girls. She heard them pray for poor, war-ravaged China. They prayed that God would save the millions who were lost. Martha felt the presence of God as she had never done before. The book by S. D. Gordon entitled *The Power-Full Christian* was the one chosen by Alice Huey for their reading at that time. It was a book on prayer. That book and Huey's guidance proved to be another great source of strength to Martha during those trying days.

Even as the missionaries continued their work, war swept the country. There were intermittent skirmishes and student demonstrations, sometimes resulting in many deaths as the struggling giant attempted to rouse herself and throw off the bonds which held her down in the pit of ignorance, poverty, and despair. Bandits roamed the countryside, stealing, raping, and murdering. There was news that Pastor Lin had been shot and killed in Laichow.

As if all the rest were not enough, news arrived from Richmond, just before Christmas, that there would be a thirty-five percent cut in appropriations for the next year. The entire community was dejected. They worked so hard; they were careful with every penny. What they really needed was a hundred percent increase. How could they continue the work they were then doing? It looked as if they might be forced to close the girls' school. They would be forced to cut back in every area.

Christmas was not going to be the happy time she had experienced last year with the Lawtons. In a letter to Mrs.

North China Baptist Mission about 1930. Most of the older missionaries worked with Lottie Moon

Pictured on row one are J. T. Williams, C. L. Culpepper, Mary D. Willeford, Mrs. Glass, W. B. Glass, Mrs. Pruitt, C. W. Pruitt, C. E. Maddry, Mrs. Maddry, Mrs. Newton, Anna Hartwell, Mrs. Evans, P. S. Evans, M.D., M. T. Rankin, J. W. Darves

Row two: Mr. Gillespie*, Pearl Todd, Bonnie Ray, Lois Glass, Bertha Smith, J. W. Moore, Mrs. Moore, Alice Huey, Mrs. Ayers, Lila Watson, Doris Knight, W. C. Newton, Blanche Bradley, Jane Lide, Dever Lawton, Robert Jacob

Row three: Ts'ang T'ien Pao, Wang Chi Sheng, Frank Connelly, S. E. Ayers, M.D., A. Yocum, M.D., Wilson Fielder*, Victor Koon*, Charles Leonard, Mrs. Leonard, Martha Franks, Mrs. Adams, W. W. Adams, Florence Jones

* = Visitor to the mission meeting.

Hatcher, Martha wrote, "I'm going to tell you the truth — I have tried so hard to be happy and joyful especially for the children's sake — when all the time deep down in the depths of this selfish heart of mine was an ache. I just wanted my own ones so badly. Seems like at Christmas time there is just a 'homing instinct' that comes out! Everybody has been so good to me my first Christmas here, but there wasn't anybody I could go to to admit my aching void."

Easy to run down hill . . . Much puffing to run up

As the year 1927 neared its end, the others in the mission felt Martha was ready to try her hand at the work. The big question was where to begin. She wanted to begin, but how? What could she do? Martha prayed for God's guidance. Dr. Glass asked her what she would like to do, to which she responded that she was praying concerning the matter. He had suggested a Sunday School to be held on Sunday afternoons in the church in town. It would be up to the Chinese pastor to make the decision. While she awaited an answer from the Lord the Chinese pastor met her one morning saying, "Miss Franks, would you like to start a Sunday afternoon Sunday School for the street children? No one will be there then and you would have plenty of space and time." There was the answer. The pastor had been unaware of the discussion between Martha and Dr. Glass, and yet he had seen the need for a Sunday School also. Martha felt certain that God was guiding in the matter. She was about to begin. The Chinese have an expression, "A journey of a thousand miles begins with one step." Martha was soon going to take the first exciting step on a long, long journey of a thousand, thousand steps.

The Hwanghsien church was a large, urban, institutional church which met many needs of Christians and non-Christians in the area. The first floor of the building housed a medical clinic and a reading room. There was more than enough space for a Sunday School. The pastor and deacons all agreed, and plans for the children's Sunday School were soon underway.

Martha could not undertake the job without help, and help was nearby in the large boarding high school operated by the mission. There were a large number of lovely, intelligent, mature Christian girls who were eager to help. With a little instruction from Martha, and the barest minimum of materials, the girls made good teachers.

They were an attractive sight as they marched into the city on Sunday afternoons. A chaperone led the way, followed by the young girls walking two by two, who were in turn followed by Martha and another chaperone. They marched from the mission, through the city gate, down narrow streets to the Hwanghsien church.

Inside the church, a large number of children gathered to hear the stories told by Martha and her school girls. The children were well-behaved and receptive to Martha and her obvious joy in sharing her faith. All week long, between her continuing daily studies of those wicked characters, Martha planned every word of the devotional which she would give the children. Martha played the tiny Japanese organ and sang with them. When the children were assembled, she spoke to them in

Sunday School Class, Tsining

her halting Chinese of God's love for each one. She told them about Jesus who came to show God's love in the flesh. The children liked Martha and were much too polite to laugh at any mistake she might make. After the general assembly, the children were divided into several age groups which were led by the school girls. Martha assisted where needed and played well the part of general, all-purpose leader — the beginnings of a real missionary.

Every Sunday after lunch, the little gospel troop could be seen marching to their station. On a Sunday, seemingly as like the rest as could be, Martha had finished her devotional and was waiting for a call from one of the girls, when she observed two country-women-come-to-town stopping at the gate to the church. They had never before seen a church, and in addition to the strange architecture, they had never seen a two-storied building. The two women, with their tiny bound feet, supported each other as they walked and talked non-stop about the strangeness of foreign ways.

Martha, seizing the opportunity, invited the women into the church. The women graciously accepted her invitation, examining everything in sight. After they had seen the clinic, reading room, and Sunday School classes, Martha persuaded them to climb the stairs to the second floor. What a novelty that was. Among the common people of that area of China, it was considered an invasion of privacy to have a second floor — one might look down into another's house or into one's courtyard.

The two women saw nothing scandalous that afternoon. They heard the young American woman's endless chatter as she explained every item in the sanctuary, even playing tunes on the organ for them. When the time came for them to be on their way, there was more than a little bemused activity as the women faced the fact of having to descend the stairs. With their bound feet, coming down would be like walking downstairs on stilts. They looked, twittered, hesitated, and finally sat down, bumping one step at the time until they were again safely on the first floor.

With sighs of relief, the two began to thank Martha for her hospitality. The thought had come to Martha at first sight of them that these two women might never again have opportunity to hear of the love of God. This was her chance to tell them of Jesus, and they needed to hear. Surely they would be happy to hear such glorious news. Martha told them as best she could with the words she had already learned. The women listened patiently to every word she had to say. When she had finished, their only response to the message of God's love was "Is that so?" As she accompanied the two women to the gate, rather than a grateful response to her invitation to faith in Jesus Christ, they issued their own polite invitation, "If ever you visit our village, you must come for tea."

Sadly, hardly believing that they were going, Martha watched the two hobbled women move off into the street where they soon disappeared from her sight. She would probably never see them again and they likely would never again hear of God's love. Martha felt the world caving round her. When she had returned to the mission, she slowly closed the door to her room and locked it behind her so that she was alone before God. Falling on her face, she asked, "Lord, have I made a mistake? You told me to come and I'm here. I know those women are lost. I know you want to save them. You said you would be with me. I did the best I could. They understood,

Evangelists and Bible Women

but nothing happened. Is this the way it's going to be? If so, I want to go home. Lord, where is the truth? It has to be in the channel — me!"

Firewood alone will not Start a fire

That first timid step into her work would prove to be both a joy and pain. It would not be Martha's Waterloo; rather in a sense it would be her Hegira or flight. She was not escaping any physical persecution except the doubt in her own mind. Her first attempt to communicate the gospel to the Chinese raised questions that she had never before considered; they had never arisen before. They were questions, the answers to which, would make Martha Linda Franks as a missionary or send her slinking home in defeat.

That old demon, doubt, had planted his seeds. Before any fruit could be harvested in the garden she was tending, those wild vines threatening to send their runners everywhere choking the life out of her work would have to be uprooted and dealt with — every one.

What makes a missionary? Is it training? College? Background? Seminary? Ability to speak the language? Identifying with the people? Each of these certainly plays a part in the molding of a person into a fit vessel for the Lord's use, but there must certainly be other considerations.

As Martha recalled sixty-five years later, she went to China thinking that she was doing the Lord a favor. After all, she was from a "good" family, well-trained, talented, well-linked. She was making a sacrifice to go to that land on the other side of the world taking the gospel to those "heathen" people. She knew she could do a good job in China. She had been President of the Student Body at Winthrop, a successful kindergarten teacher in Virginia for two years; she was equal to and above the average of her peers at WMU Training School. God was certainly getting a good one in Martha Linda Franks! He must have been proud of her.

Despite all her upbringing and training, the next six months were filled with agony for Martha as she sought the answer to her dilemma. She wept, she prayed, she begged to know. She had to know if she were to continue. She was nearing the end of her language studies only to find a far greater difficulty than words confronting her. This was a crisis of the spirit, and no amount of words and symbols could possibly answer the ache she felt in her heart. Every day, in every experience, she faced her dilemma. What could she do? How would her missionary dream end? Would she go home a failure as so many had done before? Would this undertaking prove to be too much for her? Would she be forever broken by her experience in China?

As these and a thousand other thoughts tumbled day and night in her head, she began to look round her for answers. Observing the seemingly never-ending suffering of the poor millions of China, Martha began to see that the answer must lie in her lack of suffering. She had never suffered, had in fact in many ways led a charmed life.

Chinese women knew about suffering only too well. As children they suffered the pain and agony of having their poor feet bound just at the time in their physical development that they needed most their freedom to grow. They have a sad maxim among them, "For every bound foot, there is a barrel of tears."

Following the pain of footbinding, there came for many women the terrors of being bound to a mother-in-law: A woman's family engaged a middleman to find for her, not a husband, but a mother-in-law. A family bought the girl as one might buy a donkey and brought her to be servant, first to her mother-in-law, and second to her husband. A mother-in-law who showed kindness to her daughter-in-law was a rare exception in China. Most of them, having been treated cruelly as daughters-in-law, in turn vented their own anger and frustration upon those who came to dwell under their roofs. The young wife became the property of her husband and his mother. She could not go home again. She could not work outside the home. There was no recourse but to knuckle under, making the best she could of what was often a bad situation.

Martha, observing the stoic acceptance of suffering by those Chinese women, concluded that the answer to her dilemma lay in her lack of suffering. Perhaps if she could suffer, then she might be able to identify with them and thus reach them with the gospel. She prayed for God to send suffering and braced herself for the blow. It never came. The only suffering she experienced was continual harassment by those two demonic gadflies, distress and discouragement. Martha had the plague in double-dose form.

Little did she know that God was not through with Martha Linda Franks. Indeed, He was just about to begin with her. Long ago in her own home and in Sunbeams at First Baptist Church, Laurens, South Carolina, He had planted the seeds. Through her family and those Godly servants of His church, God had been laying a foundation upon which He was going to build a magnificent structure of faithful service. He would not allow anything to overwhelm this one who had come such a long way to do His saving work. The day did come when Martha affirmed with the apostle Paul,

> "In the same way the Spirit comes to the aid of our weakness. We do not even know how we ought to pray, but through our inarticulate groans the Spirit himself is pleading for us, and God who searches our inmost being knows what the Spirit means, because he pleads for God's people in God's own way; and in everything we know, he cooperates for good with those who love God and are called according to His purpose. For God knew His own before ever they were, and also ordained that they should be shaped to the likeness of His Son . . . and it is these so fore-ordained, whom he also called . . . ." (Romans 8:26-30, New English Bible). Paul concluded his discussion with this assertion of his faith in God, "For I am convinced that there is nothing in death or life, in the realm of spirits or superhuman powers, in the world as it is or as it shall be, in the forces of the universe, in heights or depths — nothing in all creation — that can separate us from the love of God in Christ Jesus our Lord" (Romans 8:38-39, New English Bible).

Those gadflies, as annoying as they were, would never be able to separate Martha from the Lord who had called her to China to help with the building of His church. They might slow her down for a bit, cause her to swat and slap blindly at what she could surely feel but not see, but in the process she would learn to trust the Lord as she had never imagined she would need to do. She would learn to let God lead the way. He had chosen Martha for His own, and He would lead her each step of the way.

Jade and men . . .
Both are shaped
By bitter tools

The commencement of God's help with Martha's distress came in the person of Jane Lide, who was herself a native South Carolinian. Jane, who had graduated from college in the year of Martha's birth, was a wise and experienced veteran of many a spiritual battle in China.

In February 1927, Jane and Florence Lide returned from furlough in America. As was the custom, returning missionaries led the "Foreign Service" (for missionaries) on the Sunday afternoon of their return. As the Hwanghsien mission met that Sunday afternoon in the home of Ullin and Charlotte Leavell, it was Jane who led the service. Martha remembered how lovely Jane looked in her new American clothes — brown skirt and blouse, brown shoes, brown kid gloves — all topped off by a brown velour hat. How Martha envied her beautiful new ensemble. Jane told them all the latest news from America and they hung on every word. Modestly, almost before they quite grasped the shift in her presentation, she began to speak of an extraordinary experience in the United States which had changed her life. They had already noted the change; now they were about to learn the reason.

As a hush fell over the assembled missionaries, they heard Jane speak of their trip home and of subsequent events. When the sisters left China, Florence had been ill. Weeks on the ship had simply aggravated her condition. Upon disembarking in California, it was obvious that she was too ill to make the long trip to South Carolina by rail. The sisters, who had little money, found lodging in a hostel run by a group of Pentecostals. What they saw and heard living among that group was new to them. It would change their lives.

Almost two hundred years before, John Wesley had a similar life-changing experience crossing the Atlantic. On the ship from England to Savannah, Georgia, there was a terrific storm which greatly frightened Wesley. In fear for his life, John Wesley witnessed the calm assurance of a group of Moravians who, even at the storm's most furious temper, showed no fear. Wesley's life was forever changed by that encounter with people of another religious persuasion. Later, he went to Moravia to observe their community. Even though he disagreed with them on other issues, he never forgot their faith in God's care.

Likewise, the Lide sisters found aspects of the faith of the Pentecostals which they could not understand and others which they could not accept. They had little but time on their hands, and in that time Jane began a search of the Bible for an understanding of the truth concerning the person of the Holy Spirit. She told of how as the Holy Spirit began to teach her, she learned the meaning of being "filled" with the Holy Spirit.

In her talk that Sunday afternoon, she did not use the expression "Filled with the Holy Spirit." Instead, she used terms common to Baptists: "Christ in you the hope of glory" and "When Christ who is our life shall appear." She spoke of the change that had come to her as she accepted a truth learned in her encounter with a group of Pentecostals in California. Jane Lide left China for furlough reading philosophy: she returned from the United States passing out little pink tracts. Before her fellow workers, she gave her testimony simply, sincerely, earnestly. There was no shouting, no speaking in strange tongues; she spoke of the Holy Spirit in her life.

Jane's message went straight to Martha's heart. As the service ended, Martha stood before the other missionaries confessing that she had nothing of what Jane had spoken. Jane's new-found truth was a mystery to her. She told them that she was in extreme spiritual need and asked for their prayers. Eloise Glass stood to echo Martha's words, also requesting prayer. The mission left quietly, soberly to think again and again on Jane's words. Something definitely had happened to Jane Lide. No one knew quite what to make of it.

At the time of Jane's speaking, Martha was house-sitting for the Pruitts who were away for a few days. As they left the meeting, Alice Huey wisely said to Martha, "I think I'll come and spend the night with you in the Pruitt house." The two talked until 1:00 in the morning. Martha argued. Alice listened and tried repeatedly to help the younger woman to listen.

"But Huey, I want the Lord to use me."

"Martha, that is none of your business. What God does with you is not the issue. The issue is your total surrender to Him to do as He will with you. Get off the throne and put the Lord Jesus there."

At one o'clock, they felt they could not add more fuel to the fire because it was so terribly expensive. The night had grown bitterly cold when the two crawled between the heavy covers with Martha still arguing, still struggling to keep the reins of her life in her own hands.

Alice described the events of that evening thus,

"We had good times. Gradually, I saw in Martha a little dissatisfaction. Someone criticized her singing of Negro spirituals — thought she was too frivolous — etc. I didn't object to any of it. She didn't tell much of her heart yearnings. One night Jane Lide on her return from home brought echoes of wrestings (sic) of blessing to her own life. She had asked Martha and me to sing, 'Once it was the blessing, now it is the Lord.' As we practiced the music, Martha was critical of the music. Later she confessed it was the sentiment of the words. She was heart hungry. She wanted a closer, deeper touch with the Lord. I don't recall much that Jane said that night. We went to a nearby home (and) slept in the home of a friend who was away. As we lay there in the dark, Martha's hand in mine, I began to pray. I asked God to reveal Himself to Martha in a way she had not realized before — to satisfy her longings, etc. I hadn't prayed long till she squeezed my hand hard. No word was ever passed, but she was different. She walked like one in a dream for days and days. Fundamentally, she was the same girl, yet different. She saw the Lord high and lifted up (Isaiah 6:1).

"After that came the call to more exalted positions. Humanly speaking, there are other women over there who might be considered as well able to do her work but somehow God chose her. Her personality enriched by that transforming vision made her a fit vessel for the Master's use. I'm so glad I had a little part in helping to mold such a life. Psalm 34:5 ("They looked unto Him, and were lightened: and their faces were not ashamed") is literally true of Martha Franks.

God bless everyone of your name.

Lovingly,
Alice Huey
Bessimer, Alabama
December 7, 1947.

Despite the spiritual change, the endless parade of Chinese characters was still there; she was still, at the age of twenty-six, several thousands of miles away from home, *and* she was still surrounded by a sea of hundreds of millions of Chinese who knew nothing of the Savior whose love she had come to share with them. But there was a difference now. She did not have to see each step; it was not even necessary that she see the way. It was enough for her to believe with John Henry Cardinal Newman in his song, "Lead, Kindly Light amid the encircling gloom, Lead thou me on. The night is dark and I am far from home; Lead thou me on! Keep thou my feet; I do not ask to see the distant scene; one step enough for me." She was learning to trust God's timing and learning to let him lead the way.

All her life, especially in seminary, she had thought of the Holy Spirit as the "One called alongside to help." She felt she could keep the reins in her own hands, sit on the throne of her heart, be in charge. The Holy Spirit would be there to help her carry out *her* plans. She was learning a lesson, painfully so, that she didn't have what it takes to bring one person to Christ. By God's grace she came to understand that the Holy Spirit would not come to help, rather she must give place to Him, put Him in charge of her life. By faith she must allow the Spirit of the Risen Christ to be Lord of her life. *He* would take charge; *He* would make the plans. That was the essence of God's love for His children, that He operates through those who put their trust in Him. Incredible as it seemed, the Creator of the

Universe, Omnipotent, All-Wise God loves His children so much that He wants them to share in the joy of His saving work. Martha came to see that for everyone with faith enough to give the reins to God, making Him Lord of one's life, that one becomes a part of God's great work of salvation.

Martha's Sunday School and Sunbeams in the church in Hwanghsien began to be enfused with a joy that she had not known before. One Sunday a five-year-old who was usually there ahead of the others came late holding a six-year-old friend by the hand. The older boy, who had never been inside a church before, was reluctant to enter the gate. Martha found her little pupil tugging at his friend, urging him to come inside. "Why don't you come on in?" she asked.

"He's afraid," answered the friend.

"But why?" asked Martha.

"He's scared of Jesus," the little boy said. "I told him he didn't have to be afraid of Jesus. He's up in that old woman's little room."

It took a while, but she finally coaxed the two boys inside and spent the afternoon telling them of God's love for them. Before they left, they could respond to "Who is Jesus?" with "He's my friend." Martha was learning that He was her friend, too, and that He wanted to help give her joy in her work.

As Alice Huey said, Martha did not indeed tell much of her "heart yearnings" even to those closest to her. There was, however, one person who knew everything that she was able to reveal. Carrie Hatcher was the one person to whom she was able to pour out her joys, her fears, her longings, her hurts and pains. Reluctant to tell her family of the turmoil in China for fear they would worry unnecessarily for her safety, she continually wrote to Mrs. Hatcher of every problem in the country.

It had seemed earlier in the year that there might be some conclusion to the ceaseless fighting between the Nationalists and Communists or "Reds" as they were called. From the papers they read of the imminent defeat of the Communists. The next edition brought news of new outbreaks of war in one city after another. There were horror stories of atrocities committed by both sides. Sometimes there were stories of scores of students being shot down in the streets. The Nationalists had executed seventeen Communist students in Peking, including one young girl. To further burden the young peasants, by late spring a famine of such severity swept Shantung province that the people were reported to be eating dirt and a thin soup made of leaves from the trees. They were dying from hunger and poisoning from the leaves. The mission sent all the money it could spare to relieve their suffering.

By April of 1927, it was obvious that rather than lessening, the war was intensifying. At the advice of the American Consulate, the missions were closing school early, leaving the work with Chinese Christians. The Hwanghsien mission was closed by April, and the missionaries and their families moved to Chefoo.

In Chefoo their chief concern was not for their own safety; it was rather for those Chinese Christians left behind. Their peril was for greater than that of the Americans who had gunboats waiting to evacuate them at any time. The poor Chinese had no means of escape. They were at the mercy of their fellows who had proven already how merciless they could be. There was little of their work to do; so it was that they came to spend their days in Bible study and prayer. "We are here," they said; "We cannot work. Why not pray?" Daily, as rumors spread first of conclusion to the war, only to be followed by equally convincing words of an all-out conflagration, the band of Christians from several stations waited and prayed.

As they waited in the relative calm of Chefoo, it hardly seemed possible that such devastation was being wrought on the land that they had come to love so much. There was talk that they might never be allowed to return again. Martha sat sometimes on a hill overlooking the ocean, wondering how it would all end. Even as she waited, she continued her studies. In the evenings after the sun had set, several of them walked to the beach. Sitting on the sand in the twilight, they sang of their joy and faith. Martha's teacher, Miss Wan, sat by her side, drawing in the sand or in her hand as Martha continued to learn her 800 characters.

Late in April, they helped Mary Crawford and Lucy Wright off to America. The Leavells left in May, followed by the Glasses in June. In 1924 there had been thirty missionaries in Hwanghsien; by summer's end there would be four. In a letter to Carrie Hatcher, Martha asked, *"What does it mean? Is the Almighty trying to get us out of His way?"* The American Consul advised going to Japan. The Executive Committee of the Central China Mission sent a request to the Foreign Mission Board in Richmond for a leave of two years for any who desired it. They asked for traveling expenses and three months salary. It would save the Board a great deal of money in the event they were not able to return to their stations. The only thing they could do was wait and pray. Oh! how they prayed, not for themselves, but for poor, war-torn China. It seemed that China was daily being plunged deeper into the pit of hell itself. Famine, plague, war, disease, each battered her first from one side and then the other. Would China survive? Would any of them survive it?

There was another spiritual problem for Martha; it was the matter of her baptism. She had been baptized as a young girl. She became increasingly convinced that it was not believer's baptism. Knowing that the act of baptism was not necessary for her salvation, she felt ever more keenly the need for following the command to be baptized *after* confessing Jesus as Lord. The other, older missionaries advised caution and patience, knowing that the decision would be hers. When the time came, Martha stood in the little Chinese Church to confess that it was two years after her baptism that she had come to real faith in Jesus as Savior. While her confession raised some eyebrows among the missionaries, the Chinese Christians expressed their sympathetic support. The young Chinese pastor had never baptized anyone before and was more than reluctant to rebaptize a missionary. But he did it graciously. On the occasion of Martha's baptism, several young students, a number of men, and a seventy-year-old woman were all baptized into the church on that same day. They had studied for a year to be allowed the privilege of baptism; Martha had been studying all her life. She felt a new sense of peace with God.

Priests return
To the temple
Merchants to the shop

It became increasingly obvious that no one would soon be returning to Hwanghsien, nor to any of the other interior stations. Martha then made a decision which confounded her compatriots; she announced that she was going home. It was at her own expense and with no salary. They begged her not to go. She had grown so, was continuing to grow in her faith and in relationship with the Lord. They were afraid that she would never return once she got home again. They had no idea of the depth of her commitment, nor of the plans God had for her. She was no quitter — never had been — but she was well aware of the fact that many would think her so. As she hastened to America, all she could think of was home. She longed to see her parents, her brothers and sisters, her dear "Chosen Mother" Hatcher. "Please don't think me a quitter," she begged. She just wanted to get home.

The ship was far too slow for Martha's liking. She wired from the West Coast before she had left the ship. The country was as beautiful from the train as it had been two years before. But she hardly saw it. South Carolina was her destination. It was home and family she longed to see.

As the train pulled into the station, there was the whole family waving, weeping, staring in disbelief. In two years she had gained forty pounds. After a big hug and several kisses, her father said, "Take this child and buy her some clothes; she looks like a missionary!" Walking into the house, she found the cook waiting for her. In wide-eyed disbelief, Ella walked all around her. Shaking her head, she said, "We got to cut this girl's rations and 'juice' (reduce) her down."

Martha spent four joyous months with her family. Her mother had been hurt at her going; she had worried over her youngest child every day since her leaving more than two years ago. The two spent many long hours cooking, sewing, driving the buggy calling on everyone in Laurens, and worshipping together. All the while, they talked and loved, getting to know each other as they had never done before: They talked of China, of home, of God's work, of the church, of Martha's place in God's plan. They enjoyed each other.

There were only a few speaking engagements. There were several precious days with "Mother" and "Daddy" Hatcher in which Martha poured out to Carrie far more of her self than she was ever able to do with anyone else.

While she was home, Nannie Bennet, her beloved old Sunbeam leader, invited Martha, her mother, and sisters Rosalie and Alleene to lunch. As they listened to tales of China, Mrs. Bennet remarked, "Of all the children who ever passed through my hands, you were the least likely to go to China as a missionary." The words were spoken in love and admiration.

At the end of four gloriously happy months, Martha said goodbye to her family, setting out by train for the West Coast again. Before losing sight of home and her parents, she turned to wave a final farewell to her mother. It was the last time she ever saw her face. In future years, she thanked God repeatedly for the four months they had spent together.

In January 1929, Martha returned to a China in greater turmoil than that which she had left six months before. Even before her arrival, the women of Hwanghsien church had written their hopes that she would soon join them in the work in that city. Martha's and Doris Knight's return was marred by the sad sight of dear old Mrs. Hartwell awaiting passage to America. Mr. Hartwell had died of meningitis, ending a long career of faithful service reaching back to the time of Lottie Moon.

After a long trip on a small Chinese boat filled to the limit with peasants carrying every imaginable thing, Martha finally arrived in Chefoo. The American Consul refused permission for the trip to Hwanghsien because of the continuous fighting. What would she do now? The Lord provided good company in her dear friend Bertha Smith. The two women, thrown together for several months, began to study in greater depth the Holy Spirit. They rested, prayed, studied, talked, laughed, and learned together.

That respite in Chefoo was not wasted. In addition to her readings with Bertha, there was a steady stream of men and women who came to share their own convictions concerning the meaning of faith in Jesus as Lord. Miss Tippet spoke on "The Cross — Pivot of the Ages;" Chinese preachers came to share the gospel with the boys in the mission. They heard of the work of Marie Monson, and of scores of people living a renewed faith in Jesus as Lord.

Month after month, the Consul refused Martha passage to Hwanghsien. She no longer resented his refusal, but came to see it as the will of God. She would not stupidly court martyrdom by traveling when she could continue language studies where she was.

"I heard" is good . . . "I saw" is better

It was then that she made another momentous decision, which, while it may have confounded some of her fellow workers, was nonetheless acceptable to them. They had already seen enough of Martha to know that she would do what she felt was right. She was invited to move into the home of a young Chinese couple newly married. Mr. and Mrs. Lan were a well-educated pair from a family of means. Mr. Lan was the son of a teacher, and Mrs. Lan the daughter of a Baptist minister. The two had a small home in the native style, with lovely silks and brocaded pieces all round. They were most happy to have such a bright, eager American under their roof. Martha learned more language, manners, and customs than at any other time. She especially enjoyed learning Chinese cooking.

There were numerous opportunities for work in Chefoo — country evangelism, city evangelism, and others, but Martha had come to teach kindergarten and she was not ready to give it up. Putting out her fleece (Judges 6), she asked God for twenty-five children the first day if it were to be kindergarten for her.

When the day arrived for kindergarten to begin, Martha rose early, breakfasted, prayed, and carefully placed twenty-five chairs in a circle. She had the pump organ ready to accompany their singing, and a helper standing by to assist.

Soon after the door opened, in walked *twenty-four* bright-faced little boys and girls. Where was the other? Martha reasoned that the twenty-fifth chair must be needed for her. But she was not quite satisfied as she had asked for twenty-five children.

As Martha, the children, and assistant sang, there was a knock at the door. Martha turned the knob to see an old Chinese gentleman in a long garment, wearing a little black skull cap topped by a red tassle. Holding his hand was the cutest little four-year-old boy. Confidently the old gentleman said, "Teacher, I have brought you a scholar."

Later, the same old grandfather, in appreciation for Martha's teaching, offered to act as middle-man in finding a husband for her. She thanked him profusely and refused.

Old Mr. Li and his grandson the "scholar"

There was plenty of work for everyone in Chefoo. Martha took two classes at the Boys School, teaching Old Testament, and Acts and the Epistles. The boys responded to Martha's interest in each of them. She loved them and continued to pray for those tempted to turn to Communism as the answer to China's troubles. Often, on the streets, one could see banners screaming, "Down with Christians," "Down with God," "Let's Behead God." To many Chinese, Christian was equated with America and everything American.

Continual fighting plunged China ever deeper into the quagmire of anarchy. There was the daily reminder of the precariousness of their position in the American warships anchored in Chefoo harbor. China's own leaders, the governors, and the hated warlords bled the people poorer and poorer until it seemed impossible to take anything else. The local governor, who had more than fifty wives to support, had already collected taxes from the people years in advance. Now, he demanded four months rent from everyone who owned a house. Everyone had to pay, native and foreigner alike. Some people were made so poor as to sell their children. A message came from a local woman, offering to sell her little girl for fifteen dollars. Beggars lay on the street dead and dying. Martha awoke one morning to find the pitiful body of an abandoned baby lying in the field adjoining her house. The child had one head but two faces. The mother would not be blamed for abandoning such a baby to the elements.

Poor suffering children obviously saw in Martha someone approachable. They came up to her on the streets to take her hand or bury their faces in the folds of her coat. They followed her back to the school for a late afternoon of ball playing. They came to sit by her in worship. She would have been glad to have a hundred of her own. She worked with Sunbeams, recalling her own time as a Sunbeam long years ago in Laurens.

Late in the year, a new American Consul gave permission for Martha to make the trip to Hwanghsien. She felt that she was coming home at last. Hwanghsien was where she most wanted to be, with her own people. Although she had spent only one year with them, she had come to think of Hwanghsien and the missionaries and Chinese Christians there as her own people. In Hwanghsien a fragrant flower would grow, the seeds of which had been planted in the fertile soil of refugeeing missionaries in Chefoo in 1927.

Enough shovels of earth
A mountain . . .
Enough pails of water
A river

Many words have been written concerning that experience referred to variously as the Shantung Revival or the Great Awakening in China. It is doubtful whether any except those who were a part of it could begin to comprehend its impact. It was a spiritual awakening of the first order. The revival manifested itself in a personal sense of guilt for past sins, a confession and righting of wrongs, and in a renewed commitment, through prayer and Bible study to Jesus as Savior and Lord of one's life.

Sunbeam Band, Hwanghsien, 1930's

Tsining, S'ung
May 20, 1932

Dear Friends:

*It seems impossible that I have been back six weeks . . .
quite long enough to forget those seasick days of travel! The
many golden memories of furlough are safely stored away in
memories' treasure chest and are taken out almost daily to
delight in. I do thank you every one ever so much for all you did
to make my furlough such a blessed one.*

*I have come back to Shantung in the midst of a gracious
revival. How wonderful it is to see how the Lord has worked
here in the past year. It has been one of the leanest years finan-
cially, but the richest spiritually that many of us have ever
seen. There has been a mighty outpouring of the Holy Spirit in
most of our North China stations. Pingtu and Hwanghsien
seem to be the centers of the flood but Tsining has come in for a
share too and we believe that our drops are going to be increased
into showers. A letter received here a few days ago from a
Chinese brother in Pingtu tells of one of his country trips —
twenty, thirty, forty, sixty being saved in the different villages
and many being filled with the Spirit. I went to Hwanghsien
for a few days and felt it was good to be there. Such prayer
meetings! Such love for the unsaved! Such fellowship in the
Lord! When I left China there were only six or eight students in
the Seminary in Hwanghsien — now there are forty young
people there preparing themselves for the reaping in those
whitened harvest fields. It was my job to be in several of their
prayer meetings and I was never more conscious of God's
presence.*

*I am safely and comfortably settled down in my own little
home and am having a delightful time at "playing house." My
three rooms and store room are furnished throughout in period
furniture. Some of it is the "Queen Lila" period — relics of the
sojourn of dear Lila Watson in Tsining. Other periods*

95

represented are "The Field," "The Littlejohn," etc. A Watson dresser with the mirror taken off makes an excellent buffet, a cot with some bright pillows makes a wonderful davenport and day bed. I forgot the dining-living room has five windows and only prepared curtains for three but an extra curtain donated cut in two with a little lace on the end to make it just the right length takes care of the two extra windows and leaves plenty of sunshine space. The rats have eaten rows of holes down the entire length of the new ceiling paper but we will know to put some arsenic in the next paste. The unpainted floors will be varnished and "rugged" gradually. The walls are nice and fresh and with a few homeside pictures, a quantity of flowers from the Connelly garden and a few extra dashes here and there my little home is very cozy and fairly attractive. I am near enough to my neighbors the Connellys to use such necessities as their piano and bathtub. An old copper chafing dish with six copper plates brightly polished by my faithful Chinese boy lends an air of real elegance to my house. And a blue vase purchased on the street for less than twenty cents with a Japanese parchment shade makes a very beautiful lamp for my desk. My only need is a co-worker — when will she come??????

I returned Monday from my first country trip. Mr. Conelly took Pastor Wang, Sue's brother and me out to the "North country" and we were there several days. We had good crowds, but there was not much evidence of a deep work of conviction. How I did miss Sue on this trip. I am beginning to realize that she is not here — somehow I've been expecting her to come in any minute. Everywhere the people speak so beautifully of her and her fruits are to be found in every corner of our field where she has been. The people in these country villages are poor past description. In this village where we stayed the people had nothing to eat but the leaves of trees and a little soup. I went to see a woman whose face was so swollen from eating leaves that her eyes were entirely closed. Her one and only chicken had disappeared that day and her distracted daughter-in-law was searching for it everywhere — it never came back.

The loss to her was as great as a fine cow would be to you or me. She was very ugly to the daughter-in-law about it and told her if she didn't find it she could just go and die. Another neighbor's daughter-in-law attempted to end her wretched life while we were there by jumping in the well. The water was shallow, so her life was spared. I can think of nothing worse outside of Hell than the life of some heathen women.

After a few days in this village, we went to Yuan Twang a village in the "east country." It was to this village that Sue and I made our first convert and it holds a very dear place in my heart. It was a joy to see the few women there who have tasted grace — how I do love them! We had good meetings there and saw some real conviction for sin and the beginning of a real awakening in that place. I have been especially interested in a Mrs. Lee, there in that place. Mrs. Lee recognized one of the kidnappers as a neighbor's son and they were able to get the girl back in a day or two but she killed herself soon after she came home. Mrs. Lee realizes that she has sinned against God these many years and I believe she is very near the Kingdom. She is a very intelligent, capable woman and I do covet her for the Lord. The last morning we were there she came with a large kerchief full of hot, hard-boiled eggs for me and one for Mr. Connely. Please pray for her and the seven children left. They are not as poor as most of the people are.

Mr. and Mrs. Connely and Pastor Wang have gone to the West country for a week or ten days. For the first time I am left alone on the compound — two boys, Stockwell, and Billy are here and the Chinese workers but I feel very small being the only white face on the compound — except the children.

The old postman has just come with American mail! Thrills!!

I believe with all my heart that the highway to victory is prayer — Oh will you not pray with us that we may reap an abundant harvest of precious souls on this Tsining field? Our heart's desire for these people is that they may be saved. Hold on in prayer with us to that end, will you?

May the God of peace fill you with His blessed Spirit and use you abundantly in the homeland.

Yours in Him,

Martha Linda Franks

Address: Miss Martha Franks, Tsining, S'ung, China

Postage on letters to China: 5 cents for first ounce or fraction thereof; three cents for each additional ounce or fraction thereof.

The Shantung Revival came as a result of sustained, believing prayer. The genius behind it was a little Lutheran missionary from Norway by the name of Marie Monson. Martha said of her, "I have rubbed shoulders with a good many spiritual giants and many of them have made tremendous impact on my life. The one through whom I saw the Living Lord flow most clearly, deeply, quietly was Marie Monson . . . . To be in her presence you felt you were in the presence of the Lord — completely at ease, no putting up a front, coming to grips with your relationship to the Savior, rock bottom realization of anything phony, and the deepest desire to be totally abandoned to the will of the Lord and His work."

Martha first met Miss Monson in Chefoo in 1927 when the American Consul had ordered all Americans to the coastal cities where they could be quickly evacuated in case of emergencies. China was then in great turmoil. Sun Yat Sen and his Nationalist Government under Chang Kai Shek were moving from South to North in an attempt to sweep the entrenched warlords from the countryside. The people were already irreparably splintered; and in addition to the warlords, communists, supported by Russia, were infiltrating the entire country. They wormed their way into every institution in China; even school children stood to recite communist slogans to their teachers.

The decades of the nineteen twenties and thirties were difficult for everyone, physically as well as spiritually. For a young missionary, still in the process of learning what it meant to serve the Lord in a strange land, it must have been especially so. Her great good friend, Bertha Smith, years after their retirement, said of Martha, "No one ever went to the mission field more spiritually unprepared than Martha Franks. But she learned, and she did wonderful work."

That spiritually-unprepared missionary had the good fortune to meet one who was well-prepared by 1927. In that encounter, God forged another link with Martha's in His chain of service to the church in China. Marie Monson was residing with the Wellers on the China Inland Mission Compound. Martha met with Marie personally, coming away from the experience encouraged, inspired, and happy beyond words.

Here was what she was missing. That meeting in the presence of an older, more experienced servant of the Lord spurred the younger one to a recommitment of herself to God's work. Martha, and several other missionaries who experienced the Shantung Revival, firmly believed that it was through this one woman that the impetus came for the Great Awakening in China.

As a young missionary serving in Hunan, Marie Monson had felt the lack of spirituality in the people in the churches with whom she worked. The people were faithful in attendance, they had thrown out their idols, they sent their children to mission schools, many of them endured ridicule and persecution for their faith, but something was missing. The spontaneity, the joy, which she believed a personal relationship with the risen Christ should have brought them were sorely lacking. There was little urgency to share the gospel. There was an obvious shallowness in their testimony and an absence of reality in their Christian experience. She observed that the people were selfish, apathetic, as dry as bones in their faith, and showed little desire to share their faith with others.

Speaking to an older missionary of her concern, she was told, "You can't expect to see the kinds of Christians and the kinds of churches you saw in Norway until the third or fourth generations of Christians out here." The younger missionary didn't dare say aloud what she thought; silently she was saying, "My Bible doesn't say that."

One cold Chinese New Year's Season, Marie Monson set about seeking an answer from God concerning her distress at the situation as she saw it. She had heard of a great revival in Korea which had begun with a revival of prayer among missionaries. She said to herself, "Oh! to be able to go to Korea and bring back some glowing coals to our own field!" But Korea was a long way and she hadn't the money. She prayed for funds to enable her to go to Korea so that she might see and experience that revival for herself. As she prayed, God spoke to her, saying, "What you want through that journey, you may be given here, where you are, in answer to prayer." From that moment, Marie gave her solemn promise to God's challenge. Her response was, "Then I will pray until I receive."

Millenia before, the prophet Jeremiah had spoken similar encouraging words to the captives in Babylon. His people had been swept away as captives into the strange land of Babylon. They felt abandoned by God and felt there was no way to approach Him in that land of their enemy so far removed from home. The prophet Jeremiah then wrote them a letter in which he told them that God had a message for them, "Then ye shall call upon me, and ye shall go and pray unto me, and I will harken unto you. And ye shall seek me, and find me, when ye shall search for me with all your heart." (Jeremiah 29:12-13) And again, "Call ye upon me, and I will answer thee, and show thee great and mighty things which thou knowest not" (Jeremiah 33:3). The same lesson which Jeremiah taught those poor captives so many hundreds of years before, Marie Monson was now to learn in China. God could be reached through prayer no matter where one was.

In her own words from her book *The Awakening*, "Having pledged myself, I set out to cross the floor of my room to my place of prayer, in order to pray this prayer for revival for the first time. I had not taken more than two or three steps before I was halted. What then followed can only be described as follows: It was as though a boa constrictor had wound its coils round my body and was squeezing the life out of me. I was terrified! Finally, while gasping for breath, I managed to utter the one word 'Jesus! Jesus! Jesus!' Each time I groaned out the precious Name, it grew easier to breathe, and in the end, the 'serpent' left me. I stood there dazed. The first conscious thought was: 'Then prayer means as much as that, and that my promise must be kept means as much as that.' That experience helped me to endure through the almost twenty years before the first small beginnings of revival were visible. Truly, God works unhurriedly."

Before the first signs of revival were evident in Shantung, Miss Monson was visiting in the area. While there, the Norwegian missionary spoke to Dr. Culpepper, "A great awakening is coming in this area, and it is going to begin with you missionaries in Shantung." Dr. Culpepper, who was somewhat taken aback, asked, "Why do you say that, Miss Monson?" Her reply was, "Because centuries ago, God made a covenant with His people, 'If my people, who are called by my name, shall humble themselves, and pray, and seek my face, and turn from their wicked ways; then will I hear from heaven, and will forgive their sin, and will heal their land' (II Chronicles 7:14). You missionaries in Shantung have met the terms of the covenant, and God is going to meet his part of it."

And indeed the prelude to revival came when the missionaries were forced to flee the interior for port cities. Housing was in extremely short supply. There were four Baptist missionary residences in Chefoo which were occupied by those working in the area. Martha and a large group of other refugees arrived from Hwanghsien by shentze (mule litter) to find that housing was not to be had at any price. What could not be bought, could, however, be given. The missionaries in Chefoo graciously opened their hearts and doors to the refugees. Martha's new residence was now home for eighteen unmarried women. They jokingly referred to themselves as UB's or "Unclaimed Blessings."

What do eighteen single women in one house do? There is a saying among the Chinese referring to two wives in one house, "Two women under one roof won't work." The women, each of whom was wedded to her work, now found that work snatched away. They were frustrated and unhappy as refugees. Eighteen old maids, each of whom was accustomed to acting the part of brigadier general, now found seventeen others of like disposition. For several days each tried as best she could to adjust to the enforced restrictions and to each other. It was not one bit easy being confined in such close quarters with so many even though they were all Christians.

Finally someone said, "Well, we are here. We don't like it; we didn't choose it; but we are here, we are together, so why don't we pray?" All agreed but without overmuch enthusiasm. There was, however, a sense of the need for prayer. They felt an almost desperate need to pray for God's guidance in their work, for the suffering people, for the government, for Chinese Christians left behind, and for their own inadequacy to cope with the present situation.

The following morning, the eighteen women and other missionaries met together for prayer. Martha recalled that it was a nice, proper kind of prayer meeting. Someone read from the Bible, made a few perfunctory remarks, and they began to pray in the same ordinary manner.

To their amazement, a most extraordinary thing occurred! The first miracle of the Awakening was prayer. God impressed upon each of them a spirit of prayer. It swept over the assembled group like the Holy Spirit at Pentecost! It seemed to them that there were burning flames in their hearts. "The result," Martha said, "was united, fervent, sustained, extraordinary prayer." To their surprise, they found themselves on their knees praying all morning long. No one was bored; no one was tired. Instead, there was genuine expression of concern for the people they had left behind in the interior. They prayed for revival in the churches and chapels and for their beloved Chinese co-workers. Some declared that it was the best missionary work they had ever done. Revival was born out of their desperation. As they had worked in their various fields of service, they had sometimes been so busy doing, that they forgot to ask what God wanted. Out in their stations nothing in the way of revival had happened. Now that they had been forced together against their will, they saw the hand of God moving them to see the need. Out of their personal sense of need, revival was born.

For several months, the missionaries remained in Chefoo until the national situation stabilized sufficiently for their return. During the entire time of their enforced stay, they had continued to pray for revival for themselves and for their people. After being allowed to return to their stations, resuming normal activities, they continued to pray. The spirit of prayer would not go away, indeed it intensified. They could not all get together each day, but they established the habit of meeting together in groups of two or three. Florence Lide, Lucy Wright, and Martha became a prayer group. Each day at 5:00 in the afternoon, they met for almost an hour to pray. On Sundays they went inside the city for worship with the Christian community in Hwanghsien. Market day came every fifth day. When it fell on Sunday, the streets were crowded with donkeys, bicycles, and people. On those Sundays, the three of them remained at the church where they fasted and prayed between morning worship and visiting in the afternoon. Their praying was united, sustained, persistent prayer. For one full year they continued to pray before they saw any definite results, one year of praying, believing that God would answer their prayers.

One afternoon when they had finished praying, Martha said to the others, "I feel that Li Ta Sao (wife of the cook) may be ready to pray with us. I will go down to the back where she lives and ask her." Li Ta Sao was a very intelligent woman but had had no opportunity for formal education. While her husband (the cook) was a Christian, she had refused for years to accept the Lord. She attended family prayers daily, heard the Bible read, went often to worship on Sundays, but had never professed belief. As Martha opened the door to go for her, she found the woman standing just outside the door. It was most unusual for the Chinese woman even to be in the missionaries' house and never at the top of the stairs. Neither woman spoke. After a moment Li Ta Sao burst into the room, fell on her knees, and poured out a torrent of sins. What no power on earth could have extracted from her, she now willingly gave by way of confession and repentance.

God's Holy Spirit was beginning to do His work. When she had finished, Florence Lide read to her several verses from the Scriptures. As Florence read, she substituted Li Ta Sao's name on the second reading. Li Ta Sao then repeated each verse phrase by phrase as Miss Lide instructed her.

> "If Li Ta Sao confesses her sin Jesus is faithful and just to forgive Li Ta Sao's sins and cleanse Li Ta Sao from all unrighteousness." (James 1:9).
> "Come now let us reason together saith the Lord. Though Li Ta Sao's sins be red as crimson, they shall be as white as snow" (Isaiah 1:17).

After three or four verses, she was assured from God's word of her salvation. The light of heaven broke upon her heart and through her face. The three praying women realized that they had witnessed a birth. It was a spiritual birth brought about by other than human means — it was of God — and they had acted as midwives. This was just what Jesus had meant when he said, "You must be born again."

Li Ta Sao's experience was the first of many; it was a single drop followed by several drops in quick succession, which became a trickle and in only a short while a steady flow and finally a mighty rushing stream.

Marie Monson was scheduled to visit the mission in Hwanghsien in the spring of 1929. Her arrival was greatly anticipated by everyone. There was an air of expectancy in all the churches. The ground had been well prepared by their continuing prayers.

On April 19, Miss Monson took a small steamer from Tiensin for an overnight trip to Lungkow. Martha and Jane Lide traveled to Lungkow to meet her. They went to the ship's office to ask for an expected time of arrival only to receive a vague, non-committal answer. They found lodging for the night with a Chinese Christian woman who practiced medicine in Lungkow. On the following day, they returned to the office several times only to be told that there was no news. The third day confirmed what they had suspected early on, that the ship had been captured by pirates!

On July 29 of that same year, in an address at the Peitaiho Conference, Miss Monson told the story of twenty-three days among the pirates.

    Psalm 119:89. "Forever O Lord thy word is settled in Heaven."

    Matthew 24:35. "Heaven and earth shall pass away, but my words shall not pass away.

    Numbers 23:19. "God is not a man that he should lie; neither the son of man that he should repent. Hath he said and will he not do it, or hath he spoken and will he not make it good?"

    Psalm 138:2. "I will worship toward thy holy temple and give thanks unto thy name for thy loving kindness and for thy truth: for thou hast magnified thy word above all thy name."

    If it had not been for this Book, the Book of promises and for the God who gave us this book of promises, I would have been, during those twenty-three days, the most miserable person that possibly could be. This *Book* and the promises in it made the time a very different one to me.

I came from Shansi and was going to Miss Lide's station, Hwanghsien. I had told her that I did not have Hwanghsien as a burden on me, but that the Lord allowed me to go, that was all. I had planned to have a few days of rest in Peping and had come to the conclusion that I would leave Tientsin for Shantung on the first steamer after the 20th of April this year. But every day when praying, these words came to me: "If there is a ship on the 19th, you may as well go on the 19th." This came to me again and again and at last I had to write Tientsin and tell them that if there was a ship on the 19th, I would be ready to go on that ship, and I got a wire back, "Come." When I came to Tientsin, I was told that there was a ship, but I would probably not be able to go on it; but late in the afternoon a telephone call came saying that the second officer was willing to give me his cabin, if I paid double the price of the ticket. That afternoon in Tientsin, the whole afternoon, I heard the words: "Go and buy a few pounds of apples." I could not make it out. It was a fifteen-hour journey across. I did not need a few pounds of apples, but at last the thought came, maybe there is someone else who will need them, and so I went on the street and bought three pounds of apples, and I want to tell it here lest I forget it later. The pirates, every one of them, asked me if I had oranges, and said, "If you have we want them." "Have you got any pears?" "If you have we want them." But not one of them asked me if I had apples!

We left Tientsin on the 19th about noon. Going down the river, I was outside handing out tracts and speaking to the people. We had then, but I didn't know it, twenty robbers on the ship. I had been handing out tracts and recognized them later. I remember I turned around again and again and looked at three of them. If I had been down in Honan, I would have known that they were robbers. I looked at them and looked at them; but I was in Tientsin, not in Honan. So I did not believe they were robbers, though they looked it. The ship was going all right and the next morning we were near the Shantung coast. Just before daylight, I heard pistol shots all over the ship and I knew immediately what we were in for. I immediately remembered those three men. As I heard shots all over the ship, the words came to me: "This is the trial of your faith." I remember the thrill of joy that went through me at the thought of it. I was immediately reminded of the word that I had been using much in years gone by in Isaiah 41:10, and I will read it to you as I had been reading it down on the Honan plains, "Fear not, Marie, for I am with thee, be not dismayed, Marie, for I am thy God. I will strengthen thee, Marie, yea I will uphold thee Marie, with the hand of righteousness." "Fear not, Marie." Long ago, down in Honan, the Lord had told me not to fear and I had answered, "I will obey, I will obey."

Suddenly the doors were opened and the passengers were commanded to go outside on deck. The sea was high. I heard the passengers going outside. They were commanded to leave everything behind. My door had been opened, too, and two or three times one or the other of these robbers came and asked me to go outside. But I did not move. I knew that I was on that ship that left Tientsin on the 19th because the Lord wanted me there, and I knew that I had that cabin in answer to prayer, so I did not leave it. There was another word that came to me, I almost kept singing it for days. It is a line in a Danish hymn: "My doorposts have been marked by the blood of the Lamb." I kept saying it, it must have been hundreds of times. And I did believe it was so. After a while, a young robber came into my cabin and locked at my watch, I had forgotten that I had things that I ought probably to take care of. I had been repeating the promises. He said, "Take that watch and hide it somewhere, or else you will lose it." I took it off and put it behind what I used for a pillow. I had no bedding. I was going to rough it for the night, just fifteen hours across, and save taking my bedding along. The boards seemed hard the first nights without bedding, but it seemed quite soft before I left the ship. I put the watch away. I did not realize that this same man meant to come back after it when he had better time. He did so. Another came, quite a young man. He said, "Have you a watch?" "Yes I have." "Have they taken it?" "No, I have it here." "Well, I want you to give it to me as a present." "No," I said. "I cannot give you that watch as a present, I never in my life have given away such presents to people that I do not know. If you want it as a present I cannot give it to you." He said, "Don't you understand? If you give that to me as a present, I will be your friend." "Thank you," I said, "I don't want that kind of a friend, I never had such friends before." "Well," he said, "Don't you understand, if I become your friend, I will ask all the others to protect you?" "Well," I said, "I do not think I need their protection. I have better protection. The living God up there had promised to protect me." He jumped up and pointed his pistol at me saying, "I will shoot you." "Oh no you cannot shoot me. You cannot shoot me whenever you like." I quoted the promise and told him what it meant. My God says that "No weapon that has been formed against thee shall prosper." I repeated that to him four or five times. I heard the young man repeating those words almost every day on that ship for those twenty three days. They just stuck.

Another man came and turned him out of the cabin. That was the first man who told me to put away my watch. He said, "Let me see your watch." "All right," I said "If you want to see it here it is." "Foreigners have good watches, and this is a good one too." "Yes," I said, "It is." "I will give you twenty dollars for it." "No," I said, "I would not sell it even if you offered two hundred dollars for it. Your money is not clean money, and I have never used anything but clean money all my life. So even if you offered me two hundred dollars I could not use one of your dollars." He said, "I will give you another in place of this. It is not as good as yours, but I will give you another one." "No thank you." I said, "If you gave me another one, that would be one you had taken from other people, and I could not use that watch." "Well" he said, "There is no help for it," and off he went with my watch. At the door he turned round and said, "You gave me this watch as a present, didn't you?" I said, "No you are quite mistaken: you are robbing me of it." I wanted him to be quite clear. He went away with it.

The passengers were looted for money, spectacles, rings, watches, even the clothing they had on, bedding, everything. Half an hour after the man had gone with my watch, another man came. He sat down, and told me not to fear, not to be afraid. "No," I said, "Do I look it?" "No," he said, "You do not look it." "No, I am not afraid," and thank God, I was perfectly delivered from fear all the time. He said some of the robbers at least had belonged to Chang's army in Shantung, but they could not make a proper living there, so they were making a living this way. "You need not fear," he said, "We have to protect this ship. We are on this ship just to protect it." "Yes?" I laughed. "I see that, I quite understand it. Do you call this making a living? I don't. I call it being robbers, and I call it violating your own consciences." I had a good long talk with that man. He proved to be my friend all the time, and he was really the one who saw to it that the other women passengers were not actually ill-treated. There was one promise that I had been claiming since I understood what we were in for. I will read it. Malachi 3:17,18: "And I will spare thee as a man spareth his own son that serveth him. Then ye shall return, and discern between the righteous and the wicked, between him that serveth God and him that serveth him not." From the beginning, I asked the Lord that there might be a real difference between me, a child of God, and the others. I asked the Lord, on this promise, that there might be such a difference, that the heathen people on that ship — two hundred passengers — might see that I had a living God, that my God was God, that my God was to be praised. I did not care about my things. I had before taken joyfully the spoiling of my goods, and I could take that again; I believe I could. But it seemed to me that those heathen people on that ship should have a chance to see and realize that there was a living God and that there was a difference between His children and those who did not belong to

Him. This man proved to be my friend. After we had talked together for, I believe, more than half an hour, he said to me, "Have they taken anything away from you?" "Yes," I said, "They have taken my watch." "Who took it?" I told him. "I will bring it back to you," and off he went. I didn't believe he would, but he did! As he handed it over to me, he bent down, and said, "Look here, don't you leave this cabin one moment. If you leave it, you won't have it any longer and your things will be gone too." "All right," I said. He said, "If they want to take your things away, just tell them the General says they are not to do it." "All right." They came one after the other; one came and one went all the time, and they asked me for the watch again. The first thing they asked for was the watch. "Well, it has been taken and it has been given back to me, so you cannot take it again," I said what I had been told. "The General says you are not to take my things, you are not to rob me." Some of them very cleverly asked me, "Who is the General?" I said, "I think you know him." The second day a junk came with guns and ammunition. To start with, we had twenty robbers on the ship; later on, we had from fifty to sixty. We had a lively time with fifty to sixty of them on the ship. After they got the guns and ammunition they looted every single junk they came across and they came across many. We were Vikings. I could see all from my door. I had a door just slightly open to get fresh air, and I could see those junk men when grain and everything they had on the junks had been looted, how forlorn they looked. I still seem to see some of those faces when they stood there with their empty junks.

When the ammunition came, it was brought into the cabin next to mine on the left hand side and I heard a voice saying, "Lock the foreigner's door." They evidently didn't want me to see how much ammunition they had. "Shut the door and lock it." It was shut and they tried to lock it, but the key broke as they tried to turn it. Two hours after that, my door having been opened again, I saw two of these robbers standing outside, looking into my cabin, two of those vile-looking men. I have seen quite a few robbers down in Honan, but I have never seen more vile looking men than those two. One pushed the other one into my cabin and shut the door and tried to lock it, but the key had been broken. There was the man in that little cabin; I felt the devil himself was there. His face and hands were all covered with hideous sores, open sores. He sat down on my suit case, almost breathing in my face. I repeated the promise that had been very precious to me many times down in our robber province, "The angel of the Lord encampeth round about them that fear Him and delivereth them." And there was another promise that I went over that moment, "The Lord is like a wall of fire round about His people." Round about me. Once when I had to travel through a robber district, the night before, the Lord allowed me to see it. I suddenly awoke and it seemed to me the roof was lifted off the house and I saw a wall of fire higher than the house, round about me, and I heard a voice saying, "The Lord is like a wall of fire round about His people." I could see the arrows coming from the outside, arrows without number, and I could see the flames consuming them and not a single one passed the wall of fire around me. I had known these words for years and years, but I had not known what they meant before that time. So I claimed the promise that He would be like a wall of fire round about me then, and that vile man sitting there was up against the wall before he could touch me. I started the conversation. "Is your mother still living?" "Yes," he said. "How old is she?" He told me. "Well, she is about my age." I asked him about his father and the rest of the family, and we had a good long talk together. I had asked him to open the door and he obeyed me. It could not be locked. I found out that he knew a missionary and he said about him, "Truly he is a good man, there is no better man in this world." He knew some real Christians too. I believe we talked together for an hour, and when he went out he had tears in his eyes, and he went out very quietly indeed. I never saw him again near my door.

For five days and nights they looted, looted, looted, every junk they came across, and sent the loot ashore. As to the food, the passengers got it; of course they had not been expecting to eat anything on that ship except what they had brought along, but now they had to eat, the loot, of course. I felt I could not do that. I seemed to see the faces of those junk men before me all the time after they had been looted. I had those few pounds of apples and I had four boxes of chocolate. I never before in my life carried about with me four boxes of chocolate. From the last part of February, I began to get those packages of chocolate, and every time I got one, I heard the words, "Keep it for an emergency, keep them for an emergency." I had a few biscuits, dry biscuits, fourteen or fifteen of them. Many, many times I had been wanting to leave them behind and not carry them along, but I always heard, "Keep them for an emergency." I remember when in Peking I wanted to give the chocolate away. I did not want to carry it along. "Keep it for an emergency," came again and again. I began to be quite troubled about myself. I said more than once to myself, "I am getting old and stingy." For nine days I had those apples, that chocolate, and those biscuits. They lasted me nine days, and during those nine days, I couldn't get any one of the crew near me. I could not get them near enough to speak to them to tell them I wanted anything, or ask them any questions. They feared the robbers and did not dare to speak to me. After nine days I had nothing, but I did believe that the Lord had a way. I did believe that. I did not fear. I did not believe He wanted me to eat of the loot, and the tenth day in the morning before daylight, I heard someone scratching at my door. I opened the door and there was the second officer. He came into my cabin and he said, "Have you got anything to eat?" "No," I said, "I have not." "Well," he said, "I have a box of eggs in this cabin, which I bought in Tientsin from my own money, clean money, you needn't fear. I have a box of Chinese cakes too. You can have it all." I was occupying his cabin, and from that day he came every day before daylight, scratched at the door, took out three or four eggs, sometimes three, now and again four, and boiling them he brought them back to me. From the tenth day till the end of the twenty three days, I had for breakfast one egg, for the noon meal, one egg, sometimes two; and for the evening meal one egg. In the middle of the forenoon, one of those sweet cakes and in the afternoon again one of those sweet cakes. I did pray that the Lord would make that egg into a real meal and that He would make it good for vegetables and fruit and all that I needed; and He did. I had no trouble whatever on account of the food and when I had eaten one egg I seemed so satisfied I don't think I could have eaten more if I had had it. The Lord showed me too that it was enough. When I could get food, for the first four days I didn't need much. I remember the first day when I got a bowl of rice it tasted just lovely; but I could only finish a little of it. I didn't need more. The pirates came again and again, every day, every meal, "What do you want?" "Don't you want food?" "Can't we give you any food?" "Just say what you want and we will find it for you." "No," I said, "You know I can't eat what you looted; and if I said I wanted this or that, you would just go out and loot people. I cannot do that." "Well you will die." "Well," I said, "I can die, but I cannot eat loot; but you needn't fear, I shall not die. My Father in Heaven is able to keep me alive." Once, one of these robbers came, and standing there with tears in his eyes, said, "Pastor." — They always called me Pastor. I have been Pastor for twenty three days. — "Pastor," he said, "Do you know, whenever I eat my food, I can hardly get it down for thinking of you without any food. Pastor, if I could get anything I would run and get it; but you know we cannot buy anything here. I would just get some of your own clean money and I would go ashore and get it for you." By the way, they asked me how much money I had. I told them I had fifteen dollars, "But you cannot take these fifteen dollars away from me, I need them for traveling money, you understand, don't you?" "Yes," they said. Strange enough before I left Tientsin, I had in my hands sixty silver dollars, but the very morning I left — I went on board right after breakfast — as I prayed in the morning it was said to me, "Don't take all that silver money along." So I just left $40.00 behind in Tientsin.

In five or six days, the sanitary condition on the ship came to be a real danger, the smell and the filth! I realized, — you will excuse my saying so, but you will understand it — I realized that I was the only sensible person on the boat, so if anyone was to look after it, I would have to do it. I prayed about it, and came to the conclusion that the Lord who makes the winds His servants, could make robbers be my servants too. By that time I had discovered that they smoked opium every night about six or seven o'clock and at that time I just went outside my cabin door to get some fresh air. They were, most of them at least, smoking opium. The second night I was standing there, the chief came. At least the one who wanted me to look upon him as chief. He was a very nice man and educated. I had a good long talk with him about many things, and in the end I said to him, "Look here, where is the captain?" "He is in his cabin." "Oh, you don't allow him to come out I suppose?" "No, indeed we don't." "Well," I said, "If you don't allow him to come out, you understand that the crew won't do what they ought to; but if we are to be on this ship, you and I and the passengers, and be without the captain's help, you must look after it that this deck is cleaned, swept, and washed every morning." He looked at me and said, "Whatever you say shall be done." And then and there he called one of his men, and told him what the "Pastor" had said, ordered him to go down and tell the crew, and it was done. The next night I had an opportunity to speak about the passengers. They needed fresh air, and he must allow them to remain on deck for awhile and get fresh air, "As the Pastor says it shall be done." And it was done. It was quite hot after a few days, and one night I told the chief that generally they had on such ships awnings, and I told him to ask the men to find the awnings and put them up outside the cabins and over them too. He did it and in the same way drinking water had to be attended to. They all did as they were told. They had their meals usually outside my cabin door. They looted all the fishing junks they found. They had lobsters and shrimps and many good things, and every day as they were sitting there, having their meals, I handed out tracts and they read them. One of them read aloud and the others explained them. Sometimes they asked me if it wasn't so. I happened to have a good many of those with the black and red hearts, and gave them each one of them. They read them. Many and many a time I saw tears in the eyes of those men. They said we cannot but be bad, and the one they wanted me to look upon as chief and to deal with came every night as I was standing outside the cabin door to get fresh air. We talked for hours together. Even the last night before they left the ship — I didn't know it was the last night — we talked together for two hours, on what I wanted to talk about. I told him what was coming, the Lord's return and the Lord taking His own people unto Himself, and the tribulation that was to come on the earth. I must confess it, the day I saw those robbers leave the ship I sighed. I sighed because my work amongst them had come to an end. By that time I had been made perfectly willing to go with them, to be carried off with them, although I could not see how they could carry me off as long as I had this Book and all the promises in it. They often said to me, "Don't you understand that you are worth much money?" "Indeed I do," I said, "You have probably met many foreigners before. You may have met many who are not worth as much as I am because I belong to the Kingdom of Heaven, and I am a child of God. Indeed I am worth much money." "We want much for you too." "I am sorry you do," I said, "You won't get a dollar for me, not one dollar, you'll see. I am a child of God and He has promised to deliver me out of your hands but He won't give you money for me." I had been reminded of Isaiah 45:3 and was filled with peace all the time, just full of peace, and not once was I impatient to get free. I had been one of the most impatient persons that ever existed, but I knew I had been delivered from my former impatience and it was lovely indeed to discover that I had been freed in such a way that under such circumstances I was perfectly delivered from impatience to get free. They said it again and again those robbers, "Cannot you be impatient?" They tried to get me in many ways to be impatient. "No," I said, "I have been delivered from that. Do I look impatient?" "No, that is the worst of it, whatever we do you don't look impatient." And they remarked as they were eating, "Can you understand the peace she has got? You can see it on her face. Look at the passengers; they look more yellow and worn and impatient every day." I knew it was so and I thanked God that they could see the difference. They said again and again, "Are you not impatient to get on shore and be free from this?" "No, thank God," I said, "I am not." The Lord has sent me to China to preach the Gospel and at present He wants me to preach it to you, and as long as I am here I am satisfied. It does not matter to me to whom I am preaching."

We had been on the ship I believe nineteen days, when two men came on board. I do not know to this day who those two men were; probably sent from the ship's company. I could hear, as the chief's cabin was next to mine, every word they said. The robbers demanded $200,000 for the ship and these two men asked, "Cannot the foreigner pay half of it?" I heard the chief answer, "Well you have to be quick; I will tell you the truth about the foreigner; she has not been eating anything now all this time and she is on her dying bed." I thought these men could not be allowed to go on shore and tell the people I was on my dying bed, so I just went outside my cabin door and walked up and down on the deck. The chief was sitting with his back toward me, but those two men saw me. I nodded to them and smiled, so they were given the impression that I was not dying yet. The last five days, the one question was to carry me off from the ship and take me with them. By that time, the gunboats were outside. I didn't hear them mention gunboats, but as I heard them every day saying they must get off the ship, I reckoned that the gunboats were outside. They had been in search of us a for night before they found us. At three different times, we had forty or fifty junks that the pirates commandeered at the ship's side, and the junk that I was going to be put on had been pointed out. I knew which junk I was going to be in. Bedding had been taken down into the junks, and also the food they wanted. They were just on the point of leaving, taking me with them, when a sudden storm arose, and the junks had to go near the shore for cover. So they didn't leave the ship that time. Every day for hours and hours they talked it over, how they should take me away with them, and where to take me. They mentioned places but I did not know them. I had a few wonderful promises that I held on to like Psalm 31:20, "Thou shalt hide them in the secret of thy presence from the pride of man. Thou shalt keep them secretly in a pavilion from the strife of tongues." That was one promise, and then another one in Isaiah, 49:24,25, "Shall the prey be taken from the mighty or the lawful captive be delivered? But thus saith the Lord, even the captives of the mighty shall be taken away, and the prey of the terrible shall be delivered: for I will contend with him that contendeth with thee." As they were discussing carrying me off again, and again, and seemed on the point of doing it, — I wonder if you will believe me, but this is so, whether you believe me or not — I was just sitting there laughing at all their plans. I remembered that the Lord in the heavens, He laughed, and I just laughed with Him. The second time they were going to carry me off something happened. One of the messengers came back with a message, and they talked it over. The time for opium smoking came and we didn't get off that time. The third time I heard the order given to one of the men, "Go and tell the foreigner now to get into the junk, we have to get off today." That was the day before the deliverance. That man came and opened my door, and he stood facing me and I stood facing him. He looked at me and I looked at him. It seemed to me that we were staring at each other for five minutes at least; but it could not have been that long. At last he shut the door with a bang, and I heard him say outside,

"No, I cannot say that to her; I cannot tell her that she has to be carried off, it will be wronging her the second time." And just then one of the spies came back again and they consulted, and again the time for smoking opium came and we didn't get off. On the twenty-third day, it was Sunday, three o'clock in the afternoon, we suddenly heard the shot of a cannon. Some of the robbers, — we had about fifty of them on the ship — immediately left the ship. Ten were left behind. The captain was ordered out of his cabin and we had a race for two hours, and what a race it was! The pirates saw that they couldn't make it, the gunboat would overtake us. During those last two hours, and especially the last hour, I heard nothing but the words, "We must have the foreigner with us; we must have a foreign face with us; we cannot go without that foreign face; they won't shoot us if we have that foreign face with us." At last they had to go into the junks and left the ship and I heard one voice saying, "What is the use of carrying the foreigner with us? She has not been eating anything for twenty-three days; she won't be able to run; she won't be able to walk: You see the circumstances we are in; leave her behind." And I was left behind; of course I was. "Even the captives of the mighty shall be taken away and the prey of the terrible shall be delivered." They never had once, as far as I could hear, spoken of taking the passengers away with them, but they carried off twenty of them. But they were released that same day.

When on the boat, the only difficulty I had — I got enough water to drink, though I had no washing water for twenty three days, except a few drops of the drinking water — I say the only difficulty I had on this ship was about how my old parents would take the news. They are over eighty years old and my mother not strong, and the thought came again and again; but the Lord said to me, "Be anxious for nothing, Marie." He had said it long ago to my heart, and I had answered Him, "I will not be anxious, I will obey, I will not be anxious." But the devil tried his hardest to get me to be anxious for my old parents; but every day I told the Lord, "Lord take care of them. I will try not to be anxious. I will try to obey, not to be anxious for them." The Lord took care of them. One day papers at home said that a young missionary, a Miss Monsen had been taken by pirates in China. My sister read it in one of the papers and knew immediately that that young missionary must be her sister. She went home and told mother that a young missionary, a Miss Monsen had been taken by pirates in China, and my old mother answered, "I am sorry for that young missionary. It would have been better if it had been our Marie, she has been so long in China and she knows the people." When they got the word that after all it was not a young Miss Monsen, but this one, my mother said, "Well, I am glad that it was not that young missionary." They had the news of that on Monday, but on Thursday a wire came to Norway saying that I had been set free. The word came to Norway seven days before my deliverance. So the Lord undertook for them. Now, I want to mention one thing more; what prayer did those days. I did realize it when on the ship; but as I heard things afterwards. I have been putting two and two together. The first four or five days, people didn't know we were missing so no one prayed for the missing ones, of course. Those five days I felt like one swimming against the current, but I felt that strength was given to me and that I would be able to make it. After people got to know we were missing and started praying for me, there was a marked difference. I felt like one floating on the waters, just floating, resting on the promises. And those seven days that they were having praise meetings at home, the hardest part of the time really because there was this terrible struggle between the powers of darkness and the powers of light, during those days I was so filled with joy that I felt like bursting with joy more than once. I was very glad that I had some writing paper, and that I had pen and ink, and that I had a coat I could hang up, and I could sit behind it, and write to some of my friends, and send some of the joy; that had to go out, send it to them in letters. After the pirates had left, those passengers swarmed around me, and I had two busy days before the loot could be cleared out of the ship and we could leave. They were fighting for tracts that I had, and they asked questions, and said, "We have seen that your God is God, and we want to believe Him too." The robbers had told the passengers all about me, and all they heard and all they saw. "We have seen that your God is good and we want to believe Him too." I had two very busy days amongst them.

Friends, I thank God for the Book of promises and I do thank Him that He is faithful to His promises and that I was allowed to see His faithfulness to His promises.

By the time of Marie Monson's release (after twenty-three days), the time scheduled for her visits in Hwanghsien had passed. It was to be another full year before she had opportunity to visit them again. This meant, in effect, that they had another year to pray. They prayed! Daily they prayed. By the time Miss Monson finally got to Hwanghsien, the field of grain was ripe for harvest. With the news that this diminutive woman who had held her own against a band of pirates for twenty-three days was about to appear among them, the people came in droves. The atmosphere was electric with anticipation. Wherever she spoke, every seat was occupied, the aisles were full, and people hung in the windows so as to see and hear.

As Marie Monson rose to speak, there came an awesome stillness in the church which remained the entire time she stood before the people. Everyone felt that the presence of the Holy Spirit filled the sanctuary. The little woman spoke quietly, sincerely, simply. Martha remarked afterward to a co-worker, "She didn't say a thing I couldn't have said." She realized that it was not the words; it was the power of the Holy Spirit in her words.

Her main topic was "The New Birth." The first message was, "What the New Birth Is Not." Quietly, simply, but firmly, she explained that the new birth is not going to church; it is not being baptized; it is not being moved to emotion; it is not doing good deeds.

At the end of each meeting, she stationed herself at the door. As each one came, she asked in a loving way, "Have you been born again?" If the person responded with a "Yes," she asked, "What proof have you?" If the answer were vague, she rejoined simply but earnestly, "I do not rest my heart about you." With such a word from that saintly little woman, the person thus addressed would leave with the feeling of having been pierced through the heart with a sword. Some were offended and angered at what they saw as Miss Monson's unorthodox methods.

In each succeeding meeting, Miss Monson spoke for about an hour on one particular sin. Speaking of only one specific sin, she illustrated from the Bible the results of such sin. She followed Biblicall illustrations with stories of persons she had known who had been guilty of the same sins. She told of one after another who had come to realize their sin. She spoke of their being "pricked in their heart." She spoke of conviction, contrition, repentance, confession, and restitution and forgiveness.

The sense of sin and guilt were so real as the Spirit of God moved among them that whole audiences were made aware of their need. The first person to be so moved was a Chinese woman who rose to her feet and began to confess to the congregation. Miss Monson asked the woman to be seated and to come to her privately following the meeting. There was to be no public confession. Nor was there any speaking in tongues. The movement had nothing to do with glossolalia.

The woman who had stood that day was a beloved Godly Bible Woman who had been in charge of the kitchen during an Inquirers' Class. The classes were arranged for those persons who had made professions of faith in the several chapels or preaching points in the surrounding villages. They were brought to the mission for a week to ten days of study and instruction before the church members examined them for baptism. At the end of the class, the Bible Woman had about two pounds of millet left from the supply for the class. Millet, cooked into a gruel, was the morning meal for many Chinese families. She had taken the leftover grain, cooking it for her own family. Her intention was to pay for the millet later, but she had neglected to do so. The piercing question, "Have you been born again?" often resulted in similar reactions. It was so direct, so personal, that it required a definite "yes" or "no."

There were so many who came to the meetings that Marie asked the missionaries to help by putting the question to each other in their inner circle, teachers to pupils, nurses to students and other workers, chief cooks to dietary staff, and so on until each had been confronted. Lucy Wright said that when she began to ask her nurses that all-important question, it stuck in her throat and came back to her pointing like a finger, asking, "Lucy, have *you* been born again?" She said to herself, "I must have been — I'm here as a missionary. I surely must have been born again." Then she admitted to herself, "I just don't know."

Early on while the meetings were in progress, Lucy went into her bedroom, got down on her knees, and prayed, "Lord, I don't know if I've really been born again or not, but if not, I want to be right now. And I will not leave this room until I know beyond a shadow of a doubt." At that point, the Holy Spirit began to convict her of her sins. Like cars on a freight train, they passed before her in quick succession. She had experienced a disagreement with her brother over a small matter. She got up from her knees and wrote him a letter of confession and apology. Once, she had cheated on an examination at Shorter College. She had a good mind and had no need to cheat; she had done it to see whether she could escape detection. Again, she got up from her knees, took her diploma from the wall, removed it from its frame, wrote a letter of confession to the president of the college and prepared the letter and diploma for mailing. Now she remembered that time when she was a child. Her mother sent her to a neighbor's house on an errand. There she found a quarter lying on the table. Lucy stole the quarter and lied to her mother about it. Again and Again, the Holy Spirit had reminded her of that theft and that lie. This time she got up from her knees and wrote a letter of confession to the neighbor. She enclosed a dollar because of the Old Testament's teaching to restore fourfold. Much of that long night was spent in praying and writing. As the sun rose the following morning, Lucy had a stack of letters of confession ready for mailing.

After all the "cars on the freight train" had passed, each sin confessed, and everything made right in so far as possible from that distance, she claimed God's promise, "Lord, you said if I would confess my sins, you are faithful and just to forgive and to cleanse me from all unrighteousness. I believe you, Lord. I receive your forgiveness." In that moment, her heart was filled with a peace and joy she had never known before. It was a new Lucy Wright who walked to the hospital and her nursing that morning.

Martha was then living across the hall from Lucy. She had no idea what was afoot in Lucy's room. Martha had to leave early for prayers at the seminary. When she returned for breakfast, Lucy had already gone to the hospital. There was a brief note pinned to Martha's pillow; it said, "I am saved and I know it!"

Before that night in which she came to know that she was born again, Lucy had been a superior person. Her father, uncle, and brother were all medical doctors. She herself had always been taught and firmly believed that the superior person was one who lived a life of service to others. Ingrained in the very fiber of her being was the desire for service — especially to the sick and suffering. Many who were brought to her for care were unspeakably dirty. None was too much for Lucy Wright. She simply rolled up her sleeves and set about cleaning them up. She was an excellent nurse. Martha said to her, "Lucy, if I needed surgery, I'd much rather you do it than some doctors I know."

During the time of the Great Awakening, Martha and Lucy undertook the care of three new-born babies. As a child, Martha had sometimes prayed that some unwanted child would one day be left at her door. She would love and care for it as though it were her own. One morning her wish came true when she discovered a little girl lying just outside her gate. The poor infant had a cleft palate and had been rejected by her family. Martha and Lucy eagerly undertook the care of the baby whom they named Mong En (Received Grace). Shortly thereafter, they learned of a child left with an old grandmother when her mother had died giving birth to her. They found the old woman who had no cow and no money to purchase milk. The grandmother had attempted to feed the baby bean soup through a nipple attached to the end of a hollow reed. The grandmother was happy to have them take the little girl until she was weaned. Martha named her Mong Ai (Received Love). They had no crib, but the hospital lent them a youth bed in which both Mong En and Mong Ai slept. The two girls were flourishing when a third was added to their family. A little boy was born in the hospital with a bent finger on each hand. His mother said to Lucy, "My mother-in-law would beat me if I took this baby home." Lucy took Mong Fu (Received Happiness) home, adding him to the pair in the youth bed.

The two unmarried women were surely objects of amusement to the Chinese servants who watched them as they washed and fed the babies assembly-line style. A Chinese woman cared for the babies during their working hours, but Martha and Lucy could hardly wait to get home to care for "their children." They learned much about children and great lessons in human nature as they watched them grow.

Mong En had corrective surgery for the cleft palate and grew to be an attractive and bright little girl. She was later adopted by a loving family. Mong Ai later happily returned to live with her grandmother. Mong Fu brought smiles to all who saw him and was later adopted by a childless couple. Mong En, Mong Ai, Mong Fu, received a great deal of love from the two missionaries and brought great joy in return.

Martha often visited the nurses' dormitory with Lucy. It was on one of these visits that Martha gained possession of a mirror that had once belonged to Lottie Moon. Indeed, it was Miss Moon's personal dressing mirror. One day as she walked into the dormitory, Martha spied a beautiful walnut dressing mirror with a marble shelf sitting on top of a small chest. It was a handsome piece and by its style, not Chinese. Martha asked the housekeeper the source of the mirror and was more than surprised to hear that it had belonged to Lottie Moon who had worked in the same area of China. Martha asked, "If I get another for the nurses, may I have this one?" Upon being told that she could have the mirror, Martha went into town, got a full-length mirror for the nurses, and took Lottie Moon's mirror home with her. So it is that Miss Lottie Moon's dressing mirror adorns a chest in one of the visiting parlors at the Martha Franks Retirement Center in Laurens, South Carolina today.

As the meetings in Hwanghsien continued, some became uncomfortable with Marie Monson's talk of sin, confession, restitution, and of being born again. A senior missionary went to Miss Monson to speak of his concern. Martha was sitting in the room when he said to Marie, respectfully but firmly, "We are Baptists and we believe in grace." Marie answered, "Yes, I also believe in grace, but it has been my experience that unless a person has an awareness of sin, he feels no need for the Savior. When the Holy Spirit has done His work of convicting for specific sins, and there is real contrition, then one just lifts up the Savior and people run to Him."

One by one, even the missionaries (or perhaps better) especially the missionaries were moved to think of their own positions. A senior missionary confessed that he had harbored anger toward a man who, years before, had made a pass at his wife. With the passing of the years, his anger had turned to hatred until he said to God, "If we both go to heaven, put me on the opposite side from him." He later confessed his sin and was able to rejoice in the freedom he knew in forgiveness.

Another missionary, while a student at Baylor College, had been in charge of the cafeteria. On a Sunday, a stranger and his family came in for lunch. They were first in line to pay and the student had no change to give the man for his ten-dollar bill. The man said, "That's all right; I'll pick it up later." The man never returned and the student kept the money, thinking that the man would come for it one day. Not long after, he received a message that his sister was critically ill. As he had no money of his own for train fare, he spent the stranger's money to go home. Although he had not thought of that incident in years, listening to Marie Monson, he was now convicted of his sin. He felt an urgent need to make it right. He argued with the Holy Spirit that he was too old and well-respected to bring up such an old sin. After all his arguments failed, he wrote the president of Baylor, enclosing a check. He was convinced that he would certainly be disgraced and that no one would ever have any confidence in him again. Many months passed before a letter arrived from the president of Baylor College. He said, "Dear Charlie (Culpepper), I think more of you than ever. I wish Baylor had more graduates like you."

A Chinese Christian brought to the church a bag in which he had seven hundred Chinese silver dollars. It was a large sum of money, but the man said, "Over the years, I have robbed God of his tithe and I want to get everything right in my life."

Even the children caught the spirit of doing and saying the truth. Five-year-old Mary Culpepper was riding on a bicycle with her father as he returned from prayer meeting. "Daddy, if children die when they are very young, do they go to heaven?" she asked. Her father patiently explained to her the meaning of sin. After he had finished, she said, "Then I wish I had died when I was very young, for I have so many sins." After she went to bed, her mother heard Mary crying. "Why are you crying?" Ola Culpepper asked. "Because I have so many sins," she sobbed. Lovingly, her mother offered comfort as she helped her confess sins and accept God's forgiveness. Put back to bed, she was soon heard crying again. "Mama, I've thought of another one." The pattern was repeated until she seemed to have exhausted her list. Her mother read to her of God's promises and she slept soundly the rest of the night. The next morning Mary came to tell Martha of her experience of salvation. She said, "I didn't have to confess the worst one because Mama caught me at it."

A painter who had worked for the mission for years came to confess his sins after hearing Miss Monson speak. He had never professed faith in Jesus but felt his need now. After only a short time with the painter, Marie, to everyone's surprise, sent him away. Her explanation was, "Don't pick unripe fruit." A few days later, the man returned, and she, discerning that he was "ripe," helped the man to understand the consequences of his sin. He confessed and accepted God's forgiveness and made restitution.

Martha's own experience was similar to that of many of the others. Upon her graduation from Winthrop College, she took with her one of the college hymnals. She reasoned that she needed it for the Lord's work in China far worse than the college would ever miss it. She remembered Satan saying to her, "You deserve it." During that time of revival, years later, she too was reminded of her sin. She sat down one night, packed the hymnal for mailing, and included a letter of confession and apology. Upon her arrival in South Carolina on her next furlough, there to greet her was a letter from Winthrop. Martha was afraid to open the letter for fear they were recalling her degree and stripping her of her rank. Instead, it was an invitation to the college for graduation where she received the Mary Mildred Sullivan Award for her service. It is Winthrop's highest honor; they gave it to Martha.

Seminary, Hwanghsien, following "Great Awakening"

Shantung Revival brought more, far more than confession of personal sins and restitution. It brought a sense of freedom in the Lord's forgiveness. Personal relationships fractured or broken long before were healed. There was a renewed sense of the need for patience with others. There was abounding joy among Christians and an urgency in sharing the gospel. A love for God and His people was reawakened in their hearts. The greatest result was in the addition of young men and women to the church. Each morning at 5:00 newly-awakened Christians met to pray. They took their maps and went each day by two's and three's to the surrounding villages to tell the good news. By the time the revival began, the enrollment of the seminary had dwindled to four people. After the Holy Spirit took control of their lives, the people were moved to serve the Lord. They rushed to the seminary for training, finally reaching a total of 150 men and women. The Great Awakening was a revival which did not end with the coming of the Japanese, nor with the defeat of the Nationalist Government and the resulting takeover by the Communists. Not even the exodus of the missionaries could halt it. Although it seemed to have died, it had in reality gone underground during those years of persecution (1950-1980). It was alive and well in the hearts and homes of the Chinese people. It continues to this very day.

Easy to enroll
A thousand soldiers . . .
But ah, one general!

Every year the annual mission meeting for North China convened in one of the port cities. The annual meeting was always a time of great joy and excitement. Everyone came with news of the latest developments and reports on progress in their own stations. After the beginnings of the Great Awakening, there were many wonderful stories of men and women coming to faith in the Lord. There was time for sharing hopes and frustrations. Their work brought both great joy and sometimes the most heart-rending pain. Each helped the other with plans and made decisions concerning directions for the year to come. Budgets were drawn up and monies allotted as available.

The meetings were occasions for worship, spiritual refreshment and a renewed seeking of God's will. Each missionary had opportunity to lead in worship and to make plans for assistance in his/her particular area. It was at the annual meeting in the summer of 1930 that Martha met the Reverend and Mrs. Frank Connely and heard them beg for help in their work in Tsining. Martha had no interest in going to Tsining, nor anywhere else for that matter. She was quite satisfied with the work in Hwanghsien.

Whatever Martha's personal feeling, the need in Tsining would not go away. In one of the worship times, a missionary spoke of the questionable character who knelt at Jesus' feet. He told of how she broke her precious box of ointment with which she soothed the tired and dusty feet of our Lord. Martha could almost see Jesus smiling at Mary in recognition of the fact that she was giving her very best to Him. At that moment she knew that she must give her best to the Lord; no second best would

Mary and Frank Connely

ever do. As Mary had given to the Lord her most precious possession, so Martha would give herself to help in God's work in Tsining.

Each missionary was encouraged to work as he or she felt led, and as long as it seemed reasonable, the others usually concurred. Everyone agreed that it was right for Martha to go to work with the Connelys in Tsining. She had come to the annual meeting as a worker in Hwanghsien, and happily so; she left the same meeting with her face set in the direction of Tsining.

There were no illusions as to the difficulties awaiting her. Tsining was the farthest outstation of the North China Mission; the country was poorer, less well-educated. But the need! What need there was. Everywhere one turned there were people by the thousands, many of whom had never seen a foreigner and had certainly never heard the gospel. There would be joy in telling them of God's saving love! Martha and the others in her group would be given the privilege of being the first to tell those poor suffering people in the villages that God loved each of them! They would witness as some of them heard, believed, and gave their lives to Jesus Christ!

Martha had begun in cosmopolitan Peking; she had moved down to the provincial city of Hwanghsien; now it was to be a much more isolated place called Tsining.

Life with the Connelys was different from what she had experienced in Hwanghsien. The Connelys lived in a big two-storied brick house in the American style which Mary Connely had furnished (out of her own pocket) with comfortable furniture to remind one of home. There was a bathtub. To take a real bath in a tub was quite a luxury. Frank Connely had one of the few cars in Tsining.

Mr. Connely had grown up the son of a plumber. His sensible upbringing in Missouri had been good training for his work in China. He had earned his way through college working as handyman to a wealthy family. He put his experience to good use in China. Whenever a piece broke, Frank Connely fixed it. When one wore out, he often made a reasonable facsimile of the original. One way or another, he kept most things working most of the time. He was a sensible, practical, and good man.

Mary Connely was a kind, generous, and well-organized lady who kept a good house, set a beautiful table, and served excellent meals. The two children, Billy and Julia, were a joy to Martha, as was Stockwell Sears (nephew of Mary) who lived with them. The children attended the American School in Peking, but were home for holidays and summer vacation. Mary supported Frank in his work, played the organ for worship services, and worked with the women of the church.

In front of the Connely's big brick house sat a small house in the Chinese style. It had a row of rooms with a kitchen, two bedrooms, and a nice sitting room. Martha was soon settled into that little house where she could entertain some of her own friends without being a bother to anyone else. Dining arrangements were especially helpful for both families. Mrs. Connely and Martha took turns preparing and serving noon meals. Martha dined at the Connely's table two meals and they shared one meal with her. Mr. Connely's specialty was strawberries and shortcake. Martha said he grew the biggest and sweetest she ever ate.

Frank Connely's days were spent working with Chinese evangelists in his area. He was responsible for getting necessary supplies to each of the workers. There were tracts, Bibles, study materials and the many other necessities required to keep everyone going. He looked after the residences, the church; supervised the school; helped the pastor and Bible women in their work; and paid all the salaries.

In Tsining, Martha had opportunity to put into practice one of the latest attempts to teach reading to illiterate Chinese women. If they could only teach these women enough so that they could read the gospels for themselves — that would be cause for rejoicing. The great problem confronting non-scholars was the multiplicity of Chinese characters. Unlike our own alphabet with its twenty-six characters, Chinese script has thousands and thousands of them. To learn those characters was a horrendous undertaking, even for scholars.

Martha had experienced the precarious undertaking of

memorizing so many when she wrote a note to one of the teachers at school. She sent a note by one of the students to an older Chinese teacher. She intended to address the women in a traditional Chinese greeting, "Dearly Beloved Old Lady." The characters for "old lady" and "puppy" are very like each other and, sure enough, Martha had addressed the teacher as "Dearly Beloved Puppy." Only later, when the pastor told the story on her as a joke, did Martha learn of her mistake. One little jot made the difference.

With her new opportunity to teach in Tsining, Martha wanted to use the phonetic script. Mr. Connely was skeptical but told her to do what she thought best and subsequently assisted her in every possible way. Phonetic charts were brought and the signs and sounds repeated until the women and children learned them. There were primers, New Testaments, and hymnals printed in the phonetic script, but love and veneration of the ancient characters doomed any widespread success. In the villages, as the women and children gathered in a circle, Martha took a stick and drew the symbols on the ground. The pupils, following her lead, would draw the same symbol. Again and again and again a single symbol was drawn

Street children, Tsining

in the dirt, sounded, erased, and drawn again. One symbol and sound followed another until a complete sentence was done. They learned short Bible verses and texts such as Mrs. Crawford's simple catechism, which had been widely used by Lottie Moon. The pupils were eager to learn. The children who were especially adept at memorizing the symbols were a great help in teaching them to adults. There was satisfaction in watching the simple, unschooled village people learning to write the phonetic symbols and reading the gospels for themselves. Martha was right about the phonetic method. In many of the more isolated villages, there had never been even one person who could read the Bible; now that was changing.

Doctors who ride chairs
Never ride them
To hovels

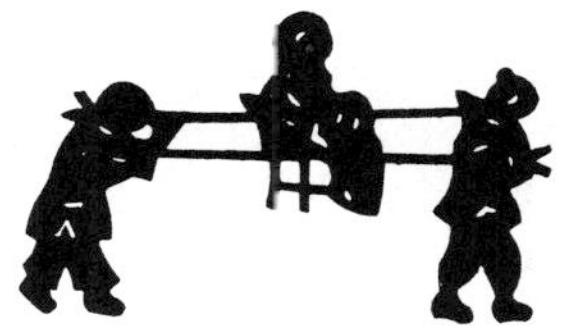

Reading, worship, study, prayer — all were important, but it was village evangelism that Martha had come to do. Everywhere one looked there were tiny little villages, numbering literally in the thousands. They were of the meanest sort, as poor as poor can be. Little mud houses with a bit of thatch for a roof, they huddled together as much against marauders as against the vagaries of nature, dotting the hills and valleys like so many ant houses. In them, sunk in ignorance and often despairing for their very lives, dwelt countless numbers of God's Chinese children. The sad fact was that they did not know of His love; had no idea that a loving heavenly Father cared for their misery and wanted to offer them hope.

Work in the villages of Tsining was all Martha had ever hoped it would be. She came to love those poor, beleaguered people. Multiple stories circulated of bitter reception given foreigners. During Martha's sojourn in the villages, there was no blatant, anti-foreign movement. Everywhere she and her co-workers went, they were received graciously and treated with great kindness.

The city of Tsining was the center of the village work, but it was out in the rural areas that the actual work was done. One was born, learned, married, reared a family and died in the context of the village, many of them never traveling more than a few miles away in a lifetime. Those villages, as isolated as they were, provided all that most people knew or needed in the way of necessities for the simple life they led. Except for a change in allegiance demanded by the warlord most recently to win a particular battle, life in the villages continued much as it had for generations beyond counting. The men (and women at planting and harvest time) worked the fields during the day and retreated to the villages every night.

One entered the village through a large wooden gate, which was closed at night or when bandits were on the prowl. From the gate a street led to a central square where business was transacted and marketing done. Narrow side lanes led to the simple homes of village dwellers who lived privately behind the walls of their own houses.

One entered a house in the village through the kitchen. The floor was packed earth. On either side was a large iron wok for cooking. Heat from the woks was directed into a kong or bed in the adjoining room. A kong resembled a chimney lying flat and was the source of heat for the room. On cold days the family sat on the kong, doing their needlework and mending; at night, they unrolled their pallets to sleep there.

The kong was a real life-saver in the bone-chilling cold of North China. It could prove to be too much of a good thing when its capacity was underestimated. On a cold winter's day Martha, Eloise and Lois Glass, and Alice Huey got caught in a snowstorm short of their destination. They were forced to spend the night in a simple Chinese inn. The women, dressed in fur-lined coats and padded garments in the native style, were all shivering as the innkeeper led them to the room where they were to spend the night. A dirty little boy was instructed to build a fire heating the kong where they would sleep. The boy built the tiniest of fires while each of the ladies urged him on. "More fuel," they said, "More fuel." Despite his protestations that it would be too much, the "foreign devils" forced the little boy to add more fuel to the fire. They were proud of their insistence as they rolled out their bedding for a good night's sleep. Everyone carried his own bedding when traveling in order to ward off the bedbugs called "China's millions." In such severe weather, they slept in their heavy clothing. It was not long before the women got up, one after the other peeling off first a coat, and then another piece or two. Eloise declared that she was "frying like a fritter." They had to keep turning from side to side so as not to be burned. Sleeping on the stove can prove to be most uncomfortable for one who has not mastered the art of firing it up.

Every Chinese house had its kong and was surrounded by its own wall. The family treasured its privacy, and that privacy was sacred. The simple house opened into a courtyard. The house, entered from the street, was attached to others like it. In these houses, all of which likewise faced the same inner courtyard, there lived sons and their families.

Most people had few personal possessions, and furnishings were sparse. Besides the kong, which was a necessity in that harsh climate, sometimes a small cabinet held the few extra clothes if they had enough money to afford them. The most precious clothing one owned was one's burial clothing. They were beautifully embroidered and lovingly preserved for the time when one would be laid with his ancestors. Sometimes, (for those who could afford the luxury) a coffin was another piece of furniture found in the room of the head of the family or of the mother-in-law. A coffin in the room was a source of comfort to an older person. Bertha had heard of a son who made a long journey. Upon his return, he brought his aged father the gift of a coffin. The man's mother was so angry that he had not brought one for her that she went into a fit of rage. She cursed and swore louder and louder, reviling her son for his ingratitude for several hours. Finally her rage overcame her and she fell with a stroke which shortly killed her. She got her coffin. To illustrate how little respect a single woman was given, no coffin was provided for her. She was often buried apart from the rest of the family, by the road. Because of the passing of strangers, no one wanted to be buried by a road.

Life within the family compound was firmly fixed. The father or eldest man was its head. He made decisions which were to be followed by everyone. His sons were expected to do what he told them to do. He allotted work in the fields and directed the planting and harvesting. There was great respect for age, and one of the cardinal virtues was proper respect for parents and ancestors. Just as the man ruled the family (in most cases), so the woman or mother-in-law ruled her daughters-in-law. She reigned like a queen, expecting to be attended hand and foot. While there could be good relationships between the two, many mothers-in-law were absolute tyrants. Women simply treated their daughters-in-law in the same fashion they had experienced. Many daughters-in-law shed rivers of tears within the confines of their own little rooms. Tension between the women made many Chinese marriages miserable. The only recourse a poor wife had was to wait for the day when she herself would get to be a mother-in-law. She was bought and belonged to her in-laws and could only go home for stated visits. The daughter-in-law's position changed only when she had born a son. Afterward, she was known as someone's mother, and referred to as the mother of so-and-so rather than by her own name.

Martha remembered once having seen a man bringing his wife on a wheelbarrow, which was not an uncommon practice. With tiny bound feet, it was difficult for a woman to walk without assistance. As Martha and a group of Chinese women watched, the man carefully helped his wife from the wheelbarrow and gently, solicitously escorted her into the adjoining house. At the sight, all the Chinese women burst into tears. Astounded at their reaction, Martha was told that they had never before seen a man treat his wife with such kindness.

Children were polite and well-behaved. If one were spanked on the hand for some offense in the classroom, the pupil bowed, thanking the teacher. Martha never knew the secret of their discipline. It was obvious that it worked. Children were loved and indulged but expected to obey.

As the people jealously guarded their privacy it could be a formidable undertaking to enter into the life of a Chinese family. Martha had set out to do just that. Her determination was much more than a brash American's desire to succeed. She had a story to tell which most of them had never heard. It was a story of life and death which they needed to hear. Her burning desire was to tell them of the love of God which Jesus had come to show all peoples. Hardships of travel and primitive village living paled in comparison to her joy in sharing the gospel story. Village evangelism was like going on a camping trip for Martha. It was an exciting adventure.

Village work required careful planning. The week before arrival of the evangelism team, someone went to the village, putting up posters announcing the coming of the "Jesus

Alda and Miss Ku rode sixty miles on this wheelbarrow to attend WMU Convention

people." Fan ta Ke, who was transporter and cook, took bedding, a portable kerosene cook stove, cooking utensils, and other necessaries. He loaded everything he could carry on a wheelbarrow. The Chinese wheelbarrow had a large wooden wheel standing as much as three feet in height. On either side of the wheel was a shelf large enough to carry a person or a great bundle of supplies and equipment. The wheelbarrow had to be carefully loaded so that it was balanced for traveling long distances. A novice could spill everything through lack of experience. After posters were placed announcing their coming, Fan ta Ke would start out for one of the larger central villages in a chosen area. Often he pushed his heavily laden wheelbarrow for two days in order to reach his destination.

In the meantime, Martha, along with a Chinese evangelist and Bible woman, gathered together needed supplies for a stay of two to three weeks. Personal items such as a wash basin, thermos, hot water bottle, soap, linens, bread, butter, Bibles, tracts, all were loaded in Frank Connely's car. Everything that could be got on and in the car was packed until the inside was as close as a tin of sardines.

Driving along narrow, unpaved paths, they were surrounded on all sides by beautiful fields carefully manicured. In spring and summer, the fields were green with wheat, millet, and other grains. There were cabbages, greens, onions, garlic, cucumbers, turnips, and sweet potatoes. Fields were fertilized with human excrement, and at times the smell could be almost overwhelming. Missionaries sometimes joked that two things were needed by a missionary to China — a Bible and a clothespin for the nose.

As the missionary crew approached a village, there was quite a stir. Most people had never seen either an automobile or a foreigner. When the car came to a halt, people encircled it, running their hands all round examining everything. Men working in the fields, women cooking, patching, picking worms out of the grain, children running errands or playing games common to children everywhere, all stopped to examine the strange contraption bringing this strange group to their village.

If the village had a church or chapel, that would become the group's headquarters. Most often there was a small house in the native style which provided shelter for them. In the event there was no chapel, they simply arranged to rent a house for their stay.

Those accompanying Martha were tried and true Christians who knew the Lord and had a burning desire to share His message with their people. Both evangelists and Bible women were trained in the Bible schools or seminaries of China. The evangelist was a preacher and Bible teacher who gave much of his personal life to Bible study and prayer. He witnessed to his faith among the villagers, especially the men. The evangelists were men of great faith and deep commitment to Jesus as Lord of their lives. The Bible woman was likewise a person of impeccable credentials as teller of the good news. She was a woman who knew and loved the Lord and His people. She had the gifts of compassion for lost people and for teaching. Her job was to share the gospel story with women and children. Simple stories from the life and teaching of Jesus were accompanied by bright illustrations done on sheets of paper two by three feet in size. On those were pictures and words which the simplest could come to understand as the Bible woman told her story.

Every morning, if weather permitted, Martha, the Bible woman and evangelist packed their personal carry bags with Bibles, posters, flannel graphs, and other illustrative materials and walked two or three miles to one of the numerous villages. They were a happy gospel troupe singing songs as they went. Upon arrival, they set about putting up a few pretty Bible posters and headed for the village's threshing floor. Some one set up an easel for the flannel graph and the group began to sing. Within a matter of minutes, children poured in from every direction. The women taught a few simple choruses and some Bible verses to the eager children who learned them quickly. Those who learned well were often rewarded with pretty Christmas cards which became prized possessions.

Soon mothers came to see what their children were learning. The Bible women and Martha took turns telling the stories of Daniel, or David, or of the sower who went forth to sow the seeds, or the perennial favorite, the Prodigal Son. The women and children watched and listened to the stories of God's love for them. Sometimes, after hearing the stories, a family invited the women to their home to hear more. Martha and the Bible woman joined the women of the house on the kong. Sitting crosslegged, they told the women and children stories of Jesus and of God's love for each of them. The families were always kind and polite in every way. It was an ever-increasing joy for Martha to have the privilege of telling her Chinese friends of God's love for them.

If the villages were close enough, they often visited more than one village in a morning. Sometimes they walked back to their headquarters, eating a simple meal and resting before starting out again. Afternoons were a repeat of the mornings. They never ran out of villages or people and each new day brought new opportunities for telling the gospel story. There was an excitement to the telling because they were keenly aware that most of the people had never before heard the gospel and likely would never hear it again.

To simple, illiterate women, the missionaries taught a prayer on the fingers of their hands. Beginning with the small finger, "I implore you, Jesus,"; finger two, "Save me"; finger three, "Be my surety"; finger four, "and forgive my sins"; and thumb, "In the name of Jesus." The prayer was often set to a familiar Chinese tune. One day an old Chinese woman came from a distant little village which the missionaries had visited several days before. Pointing to her thumb, she said, "I forgot this one."

Martha told of an old woman, whom they named "Pretty Mouth," who came to hear the stories. The old woman had only two teeth in her mouth. These two, one up and one down, were spaced so that "never the twain should meet." When she saw Martha with her full set of beautiful teeth, she immediately called her "pretty mouth." Thereafter when they saw the nearly toothless old woman, they referred to her as "Pretty Mouth."

After a day in the village it was back to headquarters. Despite having walked miles during the day, they were far from finished. At night there were services in the chapel, or sometimes a small house if there were no chapel, or out of doors. There were no pews, so everyone brought a stool or bench on which to sit. Men, women, and children joined in singing songs and choruses, especially "Jesus Loves Me" and "Come to Jesus." Christians took turns telling stories and preaching. They preached against greed and selfishness and from the "Ten Commandments." Evening services began as dark stole the day and lasted until the villagers left for bed.

Following a long day of walking, singing, teaching, and preaching, Martha and her co-workers were happy to set up their cots, unroll their thin mattresses, and lie down for the night. They experienced the truth of the words from the writer of Proverbs who said, "The sleep of a laboring man (and woman) is sweet."

Not long after she began her work in the villages of Tsining, two very special people wrote asking to join Martha there. The two were an evangelist by the name of Pastor Li and a Bible woman named Wang Sue. Long before Martha's arrival in China, Pastor Li had worked with Lottie Moon. He was a dedicated and much respected gentleman who had personally baptized more than 10,000 people. An old man now, he wrote Martha, saying, "I want to work in the country with you." Martha was delighted to have this greatly respected and much loved man of God to join her in Tsining.

Old Pastor Li; led to Christ by Lottie Moon, he personally baptized more than 10,000 people

Pastor Li was a good preacher, often preaching of what God is like. He told of God's love and mercy, but warned also of the need for confession of sins and repentance. He spoke of God's judgement made necessary by man's sin beginning with God's first pair, Adam and Eve. He spoke of the two roads, the one leading upward to life, the other down to hell and destruction. He spoke of the coming of the Savior. Often he talked of the sins of disrespect and neglect of one's parents. He sometimes told of the son, who, when his parents grew old, put them to eating from a large wooden bowl because they were so messy. One day the father came upon his own young son carving a wooden bowl. When he asked his son what the bowl was for, he was told that it would be the father's when he grew old and messy. The audience would weep to hear of such lack of respect on the part of a child.

Another story which greatly moved the Chinese was one which illustrated how Jesus gave Himself on the cross for man's sins. It was of a younger son in a family, who, for some offense, had been condemned to death. The older son, seeing the great grief of his father, arranged with the magistrate to die in his brother's place. The younger son, upon being freed, returned to his father and lived a different life from what he had known before. "That," said Pastor Li, "is what Jesus has done for you. He died in your place. Now, you are free to change your life and live like Him."

When one made a profession of faith in Jesus, he was given further instruction in the Bible and the Christian lifestyle. Later, a group of new converts would come together in Tsining where they would be readied for baptism and church membership. It was a process of study and practice which took a year or more. Real, unqualified commitment was required to take the name Christian. It was not uncommon for one's friends and even family to turn their backs when he accepted Jesus as Lord of his life. But for those who came in faith, there was the greatest joy. It would be hard to know whose joy was greater, that of the teachers and preachers, or those who came to believe the stories of God's love and forgiveness for them.

An amusing story which involves Pastor Li shows the altogether mundane side of the traveling group of Tsining.

Because of the pervasive and bone-penetrating cold of North China, Martha seldom seemed warm enough. She had bought a big English hot water bottle. Every night, just at bedtime, one could hear whistles in the street outside the house; it was the sound of the kettles. Men were selling kettles of hot water for a few coppers. Martha used her hot water to fill the large bottle to warm her cold feet during the night. The same water provided her bath the following morning. One night after filling the bottle, Martha and the others had lain down to sleep. Before her feet had thawed and sleep had come, the bottle burst. With shrieks of surprise, she jumped out of bed, attempting to keep the water from soaking the mattress. All the women jumped up to help and burst into fits of laughter.

The men, sleeping in another rooom, came to see what was the cause of such commotion. Upon learning there was no real problem, they returned to their own room. Martha simply turned the mattress over and lay down again to sleep. In a few minutes there was a halting knock at the door. It was Pastor Li, who had gone out and found a brick which he had heated, wrapped with newspaper, and tied with string. He handed it to Martha so that she might warm her feet.

In addition to Pastor Li, Martha had another dear friend to join her in the work. Not long after Martha made the decision to go to Tsining, a letter arrived from Hwanghsien. It was from Wang Sue, asking to join in the work as Bible Woman. Martha was ecstatic. She and Wang Sue were nearly the same in age and had become fast friends early on in Martha's pilgrimage in China. There was no one with whom she had rather work than Wang Sue.

Wang Sue was from a genteel and most interesting family. At a time when only boys were allowed to go to school, Wang Sue had gone. As a little girl, she was so bright and vivacious that her father had dressed her up like a boy and sent her to school with the other boys. She learned quickly and studied so diligently that soon she held her own in every class. Mrs. Elizabeth Hartwell, recognizing the girl's promise, encouraged her at every opportunity and personally taught her English and music. The other members of her family were also Christian and her brother was a preacher.

Beyond all the rest, Wang Sue was a committed Christian. She loved the Lord and rejoiced to preach the gospel and to teach the Bible. Martha said of Wang Sue that she could preach more forcefully and beautifully than many men she knew.

Early one Sunday morning, Martha and Wang Sue went to the chapel to pray. They asked the Lord to give Wang Sue an illustration to help the people understand God's plan of salvation. That day as they began to talk to the people, Wang Sue brought out three valentine-shaped hearts — a red, a white, and a black one. Placing the white heart on the flannel graph, she asked, "What is this?" After a number of answers, someone said, "It is a heart." Wang Sue then explained that God had given each one a heart which was like that white one — pure, clean, and full of love. "Along the way," she said, "the heart began to get dirty." As she spoke, Wang Sue placed tiny bits of black paper on the white heart until it was almost completely covered. She then placed the black heart over the white to show the result of all those sins compounded. "How do you clean up a black heart?" she asked next. Placing the red heart over the black, she told of God's love for a sinful world. "God loved the world so much that He sent His only Son to die on a cross to cover all sins. His blood cleans even the dirtiest heart and makes it red. In order to get a clean heart, you must reach out in faith. If you will believe that Jesus died for you, then

Martha and Wang Sue in Tsining as evangelist and Bible Woman

140

your heart will be cleaned and made pure again." Wang Sue's illustration often moved her listeners and Martha herself used it hundreds of times in years to come.

After two or three weeks in the villages, the whole entourage packed up their belongings and backtracked to Tsining. The wheelbarrow man packed up everything he could carry and began the return trip. Martha, Wang Sue, and Pastor Li packed their things and made ready for Mr. Connely to come for them in his wonderful car.

Following such a hectic pace and living that primitive life in the village, it was refreshing to get home to her own rooms. Sitting down in a real chair to read mail from home, she sighed a sigh of relief to be back in her own place for a brief respite before beginning again. She really enjoyed the comfort of her own rooms. There was a real American bed, a small German ceramic stove, china, books, a table, and small cupboards, It was a nice, comfortable little house in which she took joy in entertaining some of her new circle of friends. One of the things she most appreciated upon her return was a bath — in a tub — and a shampoo. Weeks of bathing from a small basin left the body sorely in need of a good soaking.

There was a Chinese cook who prepared good meals. He had been taught to set the table formally and to serve accordingly. It was a pleasure to be able to set a nice table in our own house and entertain her friends. The cook daily went to the market to haggle over the price of food. He always managed to have plenty of good food on Martha's table.

In Tsining there was more work to be done. Those people in the villages who had made professions of faith in Jesus were encouraged to come to enquirers' classes which were held at the end of planting or harvest, so that they could leave their work for a few days. In the classes, the instructors made every attempt to give new believers a firm foundation in the scriptures and a sense of a real meaning of following Jesus' example in one's personal life.

There were revival meetings to which new converts from the surrounding villages were invited. Evangelists from several denominations came to preach the gospel. One of the most memorable of those evangelists was John Sung. His love for

God and his relationship with Jesus was so evident in his life that when he preached some said that it seemed as if they could almost hear the angels sing.

The people loved to sing. One chorus and hymn followed another in quick succession. There were testimonies to the saving power of God's love. The preachers preached the gospel in such love and with feelings of joy and expectation such that hardly a meeting passed without someone's being moved to faith as the Holy Spirit did His work among them. At the invitation to faith in Jesus, some came confessing and knelt to pray at the altar. They were lovingly received by the preacher and immediately one of the missionaries or a Bible woman would come to pray with them and talk with them concerning the meaning of being a disciple of Jesus.

In the weeks and months following their initial confessions, each one participated in classes in preparation for baptism. Upon completion of classes, a candidate for church membership stood before the entire congregation to give his testimony and to face examination by the church. "Have you stopped smoking?" "Have you thrown out your idols?" one might ask. "Are your children coming to church?" Confessing Jesus called for a radical commitment of their lives. They had to show evidence of a new lifestyle. One's fellow believers were the examining committee.

Converts did not come in the thousands, not even in the hundreds. They came in one's and two's and sometimes three's — every one of them precious. Every one was evidence of the power of God's Holy Spirit to change the lives of those who came to express their faith in Jesus Christ as God's Son.

In Tsining, Martha and the others of her group of evangelists met daily for prayer and Bible study. They needed spiritual refreshment themselves for the time when they would return to the villages. In the mornings and afternoons, they did house to house visitation, simply knocking on doors. If they got an invitation, they went in gladly to tell the stories of God's love. Often, one of the Christians invited Martha, Wang Sue and the other women to come to her home to share the gospel. Those women would invite their friends and neighbors and relatives, some of whom had never heard of Jesus, to come for those meetings. Together with other missionaries and Chinese Christians, they studied, prayed, laughed often, and sometimes wept when sadness overtook them. Continually, they made plans for other excursions into the villages. There were always so many thousands more who needed to hear the great good news which they had to tell. There were always too few to do the going and telling.

Swiftest horse
Cannot overtake
The word once spoken

During her stay in Tsining, God sent another surprise Martha's way. Her old friend Bertha Smith came to teach for a while and lived in the extra bedroom in Martha's little house. It had been seven years since they met that day in Spartanburg, Bertha returning to China and Martha going for the first time. Martha had grown in seven years into quite a responsible young woman. As different as they were, they nevertheless loved and genuinely respected each other's gifts. Bertha was the scholar, the school marm, the teacher, and preacher. She was a no-nonsense, take-charge person. Bertha could hold her own in any gathering. She came to Tsining to take charge of the mission schools and to teach Bible and English.

So it was that the two women, both major-generals, found themselves living under one roof. When asked how they were able to work together, Bertha answered, "We both loved the Lord and we loved and respected each other. That's all it took."

Each went to her own work during the day. After a busy day, they dined together, studied and prayed together. There were other missions in the city and sometimes Martha and Bertha entertained some of the other single missionaries. The year that Martha returned from her first real furlough, Bertha planned a dinner party to celebrate her return. She had invited two Presbyterian missionaries to dine with them. Martha had "juiced" herself down and was all dressed up in the latest fashions from home. A returning missionary attempted to tell everything she could about current events from home; and, if one had seen the others' family members, one told everything possible concerning the encounter. Martha had, of course, been to visit with Bertha's mother who lived less than fifty miles away from Laurens. Over dinner Martha recalled the visit with Mrs. Smith. Describing every item the woman was wearing, she went on to say of Bertha's mother, "She was pretty as a picture; there was not a grey hair in her head. She was prettier than any one of her daughters. But then she could be that and not be much!" Even before Bertha's mouth had dropped open in disbelief, Martha realized what she had said. She could hardly believe that she had actually said those words. One can only imagine the reaction of their two guests.

Month after month, weather permitting, Martha, and Chinese co-workers visited the villages, telling the people about God's love for them. Every day they were accosted with sights almost too gruesome to endure. Everywhere there were reminders of the power of sin to wreck the bodies and minds of God's marvelous creation. There were those who were blind and deaf. There were twisted bodies which no doctor could cure. Many were addicted to opium, and gambling, and stealing.

Children's Christmas pageant, Hwanghsien

144

Still others were no less ill because of mean, unforgiving spirits. One day Christian friends spoke to Martha and Wang Sue of a country woman who had gone mad because of a dispute with a neighbor over a cow. She was a church member and the other members were concerned. She was like one possessed by a demon. The two women made the long trip out on the Yellow River to visit with her. They spent the day praying with the woman, who was almost consumed with hatred and an unforgiving spirit. Every time she seemed ready to confess, she clapped her hand over her mouth, refusing to say anything. Finally she said, "When he died, I jumped two feet for joy!" They even took her idol and threw it away, but there was no confession and no peace came.

On another occasion, they were asked to pray for a woman who was angry with her husband. In a rainstorm, she had asked her husband to adjust the cover over her precious sitting hen so as to protect her and the eggs. The husband refused and the wife's anger grew until it consumed her every thought and colored her every action. When Martha and the Bible woman arrived, they found the woman rolling on the floor in agony. They prayed for her, spoke words of peace and reassurance, and commanded the demon, in the name of Jesus, to depart. After awhile, they were overjoyed to see the woman get up from the floor and go about her affairs. She was released by the power of God and her faith in Him and resumed her life as a Christian.

The missionaries often visited a large prison in Tsining. Prisons in China were stark, ill-equipped institutions in which the stated aim was punishment and rehabilitation. Food was far inferior to that of even the poorest of the common people. Life was regimented almost beyond belief with every prisoner made to work daily. In the prison, the missionaries and their Chinese co-workers preached the gospel. Someone went weekly passing out tracts or one of the gospels. When one of the prisoners showed any interest, they gave further instruction and left copies of the Bible. Each New Year's celebration brought some of the prisoners to the tennis courts on the mission compound where they gave a magnificent perform-ance. There were jugglers, acrobats, singers, and dancers, using many paper-mache' props, who entertained for two or three hours to the delight of everyone, especially the children.

Life is a dream walking
Death is a going home

It was in Tsining that Martha finally completed her six years of service and made ready for furlough. Much of the joy normally occasioned by furlough was dampened by the news of her mother's critical illness. A cousin, Charlie Bobo, a member of the Foreign Mission Board, arranged for Martha to leave her post a few weeks earlier than originally planned so that she might see her mother once again. Boarding the small steamer for Kobe, Japan, Martha's thoughts were all of her mother. She thought again and again of the four happy months she had spent with her in 1927 after the first two years in China. It was then that the two had got to know each other, and both mother and daughter had experienced unfeigned joy. There was a two-day wait in Kobe, which necessitated Martha's finding a hotel to spend the night. Studying a map of the city, she soon located a church nearby. On Sunday morning, she made her way to the Japanese church, where she was warmly welcomed. When her hosts discovered that she spoke no Japanese, they escorted her to a class being taught in English by an American missionary. She immediately recognized the woman as one who had once spoken in chapel at Winthrop during Martha's student days.

The Sunday was Easter and the scripture lesson included the words, "Grieve not as they who have no hope." The words leaped out at Martha over and over again. "Grieve not as they who have no hope." It was as if the risen Lord Himself were speaking those words to her. Quietly, inaudibly, she responded, "Yes, Lord. Thank you Lord. With your help, I will do as you say." She would grieve for the loss of her mother, but she knew, had always known, the deep faith of her mother. She had the greatest hope, even in her grief. Numberless times she had observed the grief of her beloved Chinese people. It was a

Sept. 14, 1940.

My dearest Dad:

I had everything ready to write you on your birthday but didn't get down to it, but I surely did think of you and wished I could send you a real birthday wish. I think you are a grand and wonderful Daddy and I'm proud to belong to you. I do hope you had a happy birthday and will live to see many more. I thank God for the measure of strength that is yours and for the years He has already given you to us.

School has been in progress for a week and it has been a busy one for me. I am glad though to be back at regular work again. We have a good enrollment — more than last term and they have not all come in yet. I hope we are in for a good year's work. It looks as if we have had a good beginning. I am teaching First Corinthians now and also Personal Work and Bible Geography and one or two classes in English. My Personal Work class also includes methods in working with children.

This afternoon I went to return a book to Mrs. Lide and coming home found two little beggar children at the gate, the youngest was a little boy about four or five. He had on only a short jacket and didn't have a button. He had a rising on his stomach that looked as if it was almost ready to burst — about half as big as my fist. His little legs were so thin and crooked from lack of food. He had runny eyes — his brother said he had had bad eyes since he had the measles. I took him to the hospital and Dr. put a poltice on his tummy then I gave them enough grain for a good supper and told him to come back Monday for some more. It is not always that we can help beggars — some of them, many of them in fact are not worthy of help, but I can't stand to see little children in that fix —there are many, many of them though just in that very condition.

The world situation certainly looks blue, doesn't it? I am glad that we have God's Word for these last days — if we didn't I don't know how we would get through such conditions as we find ourselves in.

Along this line we are grateful every day for the gift from Nat and Preacher. So far everything is Okay. It also gives us much pleasure.

We have had a man here since six o'clock this morning fixing an old organ that looked as if it came out of the ark. I had the carpenter do a day's work on it before this man came. He is a Russian refugee. As far as I can tell he has done a good job on it. We are going to keep this little organ here at our house and use it for a while. I miss a piano so much. This organ will be lots of company for us all. I also had the church organ repaired. That is a very nice instrument but it gets hard use from the students who have their chapel there every morning. He got nearly half a gallon of dust out of it.

Today we had the Cauthens and their two little children for dinner. It was a pretty big order. Lucy got sick on us and the Cauthen children are a team and a half. They do absolutely as they please with never a "don't." It is hard on the people who would otherwise enjoy them.

Mary Herring and Wilma both have birthdays Monday so I baked a cake for them today. Eloise had a birthday this week too so we just put three candles on it and called it a real birthday. Here comes a Seminary student with his family to call.

The call is over and Mary has taken them to the gate, so I don't have to go so I'll get back to my letter. I wonder if I will ever sit down and write a letter right straight through!

I just got that line written and Mrs. Glass came in! Now it is Sunday morning — 7:30. I have just finished my breakfast. Went to prayer meeting at 5:30 and that lasted until nearly seven. I have Sunday School at eight. We have to have the children early so as to clear the church for the next crowd at nine. When the schools get under way we will have about three hundred children in our department and could have more if grief made more severe by its lack of hope.

From that moment, Martha knew in her heart that her mother had died.

On the second day, the steamer, *Empress of Japan,* arrived from Shanghai. The *Empress* made, what was to that time, the fastest crossing ever of the Pacific Ocean. In recognition of her feat, the ship was awarded a blue stripe painted round its entirety. When the ship docked on the West Coast, there was a telegram from her brother, confirming what she had already known in her heart. There remained the long trip by rail across the United States, and Martha was still alone. When the train pulled into the station in Spartanburg, the entire family were there to meet her. The homecoming was filled with great joy and more than a little sadness. Arriving home, Martha was given a little time for freshening up before being taken to visit her mother's grave. Awaiting her there was one of the greatest experiences of her life. As she came near the grave, she saw many flowers still covering a large part of the family burial plot. She had thought that she would be stricken with grief upon seeing the· grave. Instead, she saw a vision of her mother's joy and glory in the presence of God. She felt that there was only the thinnest of veils between them. Her mother had just crossed into God's presence and seemed so very near to Martha at that moment. In the place of her grief, the Lord filled her being with ecstasy and that promised "peace which passes all understanding."

Standing by the grave, Martha's mind raced back to that little mission hospital in Hwanghsien. An old woman was dying and she was helping women of the family as they dressed her in her long-cherished burial clothes. In that part of China, the dying person was dressed before "beginning their long journey." The most elegant, beautifully embroidered dress possible was reserved for that final journey. The woman had bound feet, and it was Martha who placed the pretty hand-made shoes on the dying woman's feet. On the sole of the shoe, there was embroidered a ladder; on either side of the ladder a lighted lantern. The ladder would take her to heaven; the lantern would light the way. On her tongue they placed a piece of jade to enable her to speak eloquent words so that she could get pass all hindrances into the other land. As Martha tried to secure the shoes on those tiny, bound feet, they kept falling off. Reaching for a safety pin on her hospital gown, she took it and fastened the shoes together. Quickly, one of the relatives removed the pin, saying, "Oh no! If you pin them together, she will not be able to walk!"

Standing by her mother's grave, she compared the death of her mother to that of the Chinese woman. Her heart was filled with gratitude to God for the hope and assurance she felt concerning her mother's death. There was another feeling; it was one of urgency. She must hurry back to China to tell Chinese mothers of her Savior, who, when the time comes, sends His angel to take His own by the hand. Holding that hand securely, He leads through the "valley of the shadow of death" and into the presence of God Himself. She could almost have shouted. Her heart did shout, "Hallelujah! What a Savior!"

As the years passed, one quickly succeeding another, there was hardly a day Martha did not think of her mother. She missed her more than she would ever say, but upon every remembrance, she heard the words, "Grieve not as they who have no hope." That "hope" became a soothing balm to her heart. Through all the years in China and Taiwan, her mother's death was the only one of the family at which she was not present. When her father and each of the others died, she was home on furlough.

The clever doctor Never treats himself

After a year at home, Martha made her third trip to China. Her second term soon proved to be more trial than treat. She returned with a new determination to love her people and to share the message of God's love for them at every opportunity. The glowing coals of her joy soon faded and finally grew black as discouragement wrapped its icy fingers round her heart.

Not long after her return, Frank and Mary Connely left for their own much-needed furlough. Bertha moved on to another teaching assignment; and she found herself, a young single American woman along in the Tsining mission. Her joy soon turned to ashes. Despite the many Chinese Christians around her, she felt isolated.

To further complicate matters, a group of Pentecostals had recently moved into the area. Some of the Tsining Christians who were not very secure in their faith had fallen for the teaching of that group whose hallmark was glossolalia, or speaking in tongues. The movement spread like wildfire, and Martha had no idea how to combat it. She became increasingly discouraged. Struggling to continue with her work, she began to feel that she was in a quagmire. The harder she struggled, the deeper she sank.

She had the good sense to realize that unless she got help, her usefulness would soon be gone. Never once doubting that the Lord was with her, Martha needed another like herself. She needed someone whose flesh and blood, like her own, had struggled and overcome. She determined to go to Hwanghsien. There she would find third and fourth generation Christians. They were secure in God's Word—stable, spiritual. There were also her missionary friends who could advise her and encourage her. They would know how to deal with Martha's problem and discouragement. She took the train to Tsinan, another to Wei Hai, and the bus to Hwanghsien. It had taken three days, but Martha was now among friends who welcomed her with wide open arms.

The second morning in Hwanghsien, Florence Lide's co-worker, Mrs. Tzang Pao Chin had the morning free to spend with Martha. The older Chinese woman possessed the strength and wisdom of the Lord. She too had struggled. She too had known discouragement and near despair. She could understand the dilemma of this capable young missionary who now poured out her heart. The older woman knew that unless there were a change, this missionary would be of no further use.

Finding a small room off the rostrum in the seminary's chapel, she allowed Martha to spill all the pent-up feelings which were such a burden for her. After they had talked for a long time, Mrs. Tzang suggested that they kneel to pray. Martha listened as the saintly woman lifted up her face and poured out a steady stream of praise and thanksgiving to the Lord. Her manner was at once both gentle and powerful; her words quiet but firm.

When her own turn came, Martha began with no praise, but instead limped along, a spiritual cripple who felt no joy and saw no hope. She spoke words that sounded only defeat. She whined, complained, and grumbled to the Lord until Mrs. Tzang stopped her. "Miss Franks," she asked gently, "Why do you not praise the Lord?"

Truthfully, Martha answered, "I do not feel like praising the Lord; I am so miserable."

"Is our Lord not worthy of your praise?" asked Mrs. Tzang.

"Oh! Yes, He is worthy!" Martha quickly added.

"Then open your mouth and praise God whether you feel like it or not," Mrs. Tzang admonished her.

Less than half-heartedly, Martha said, "I will." As she

knelt, she could not think of a single thing for which she felt thankful, but she had said "I will" and she had to do it. Martha Franks made a life-saving discovery that day. When one wills to praise the Lord, His Holy Spirit lends assistance; indeed He takes over. It was a great surprise that the first thing the Holy Spirit brought to her mind was her ears. Mrs. Frank Lide had recently returned from furlough with a marvelous orthoponic Victrola and several beautiful recordings. The evening before, they had listened to the records with purest pleasure. It was spring and the birds were singing in the lilacs just outside the window. How sweet had been the sound of Florence Lide's voice speaking to her in her own language. "Oh! Thank God for the gift of hearing!" Martha blurted out, "Thank you, Lord, for ears to hear the sounds you have made!" The Holy Spirit reminded her to praise God for eyes to see the beauty of His creation. In rapid succession they came—all the things for which she was truly grateful, but had too long taken for granted. She remembered an old woman in one of those isolated villages of Tsining who was the only Christian there. She was intelligent, but like most women her age, had never gone to school and could not read. Until her sons learned to read well enough, she would seldom have the joy of hearing the Bible read. Now Martha praised God for the Bible and her ability to read it.

The trickle of praise became a small stream and finally a mighty rushing river as the Holy Spirit reminded Martha of one after another of God's great gifts to His children. For a long time she remained on her knees in prayer to the Lord for all his goodness. As she prayed, depression slowly but surely released his icy grip. After a few days of fellowship with Christian friends, she was ready to return to Tsining. Her faith had been affirmed by others who had struggled with discouragement before her. Martha said that she had learned the great lesson that the best weapon against the demon of discouragement is prayer, especially praise. That experience with Mrs. Tzang marked a turning point in her life.

A good teacher ...
Better than a borrowful
Of books

Prior to the coming of the Shangtung Revival, the number of students at the seminary in Hwanghsien had shrunk to a total of four. The country had suffered an awful turmoil for years. Much of the old had been swept away with the revolution and winds of change blew from every direction. It seemed as though everything nailed down was suddenly coming loose. Everything was in fact being ripped up by Nationalist, Communist and foreigner. The ensuing instability exacted its toll even on God's people. Many young people felt that they had been abandoned by God. Some tended to view Christianity as another example of Western exploitation. Many no longer saw any validity in the Christian message.

**Martha all decked out
in new frock, Tsining**

When the Holy Spirit breathed new life into the hearts of those Christians in North Cina, things began to change. There was evident in the lives of God's people, a pervasive joy that had not been there before. Accompanying that joy was a sense of urgency in sharing the Good News. No longer content just to attend services of worship and Bible study, there was now a compulsion to go out and tell the story of God's love as revealed in the life, death, and resurrection of Jesus Christ.

The Great Awakening was not a movement of the older generation only; the young were also caught up in the moving of God's Spirit. The youth of China began to see in the Christ what all people, young and old alike, want—it was reality. The promises of governments, movements, and ideologies brought no lasting satisfaction to their inner needs. What they could not find in the powers and institutions of this world, they found instead in relationship with Jesus Christ as Lord of their lives. In committing themselves to Jesus, they committed themselves to sharing His message of love with their broken people.

Their new-found faith brought some of them to the seminary in Hwanghsien for training. The first year there were ten of them; the second year more than twenty; by the third year there were fifty students; and to the great joy of everyone, finally a total of one hundred fifty educated men and women came to study so that they might lead their people to the Lord. Everyone involved in those wondrous years of study and training agreed that it was all God's doing. God planned it, and His plan was executed with the cooperation of those who taught. Only a few years would pass before the invasion and occupation of the Japanese, and in rapid succession, the Com munist takeover of the whole of China. Suppression of all things Western, especially the church, forced foreign missionaries out of the country. Depsite all of the devil's best efforts, God's people were prepared, so that for fifty years now, it has been those men and women trained in the seminaries after the Great Revival who have led God's people. For much of that time, they have been forced to lead quietly, surreptitiously. Many have paid the ultimate price of discipleship, as they gave their very lives in witness to their faith. Through it all, God's word is being shared to this very day by those trained in the years following the Revival and by their spiritual heirs. Eventually the communists closed all the churches in China; Christians simply continued their worship in back rooms and private homes; they gained in strength as never before.

One special man of God who helped to prepare the Chinese Christians for those difficult days was Charlie Culpepper. He was perhaps the foremost leader in the Great Awakening in the North China Mission, and the Chinese people honored him as such. Although he did not seek the job, they insisted upon naming Dr. Culpepper president of the North China Seminary.

With the naming of Charlie Culpepper to the presidency of the seminary, there occurred an amazingly unselfish act in the spirit of Jesus Himself. Dr. W. B. Glass had been acting head of theological training and would normally have been named the next president of the seminary. When the Chinese

**Chinese family, Hwanghsien
(woman seated with bound feet)**

insisted that Dr. Culpepper have the position instead, Dr. Glass graciously stepped aside. He was well-trained, experienced, and would have done a good job as president. He did an equally worthy job as teacher and supporter of Charlie Culpepper. He gave his unqualified endorsement to the new president, upholding him in every possible way.

At the time of the new burst of activity at the seminary, it became obvious that additional personnel would be needed to teach those bright, eager men and women who were streaming into the school. Martha was then engaged in the work of country evangelism in Tsining. She was happy in that primitive area of Shantung province far out on the Yellow River. She had come to love those country people. Her quick wit and sensitivity to Chinese ways had gained for her easy entry into the homes and hearts of the people. She loved and respected the Chinese and their culture.

Martha counted it the greatest privilege to go into a village where the name of Jesus had never been spoken before and declare that "name above all names." Living and working in the country were no hardship for her. So-called inconveniences did not lessen her enthusiasm one iota. She saw the so-called hardships of travel and living in such primitive conditions as challenges to be met head on and overcome.

On a day when she was engrossed in her work, trustees from the seminary in Hwanghsien came to Martha inviting her to join the faculty as a teacher. They said to her, "The seminary is filled with young people eager to be trained for full-time work. We believe the Lord would have you come and help us." Martha's reaction was one of disbelief. As she expressed it, she was "dumbfounded!" Not only was her training in elementary education, she was also perfectly content in her work in Tsining.

Martha gave reasons she should not join the seminary to teach. In response, the Chinese trustees said to her, "Miss Franks, what you are doing is addition, one by one. Come and help with the training of national leaders; that is multiplication. We have already prayed. Now you pray and seek God's will." Martha prayed and the Lord revealed to her that the next step in his pilgrimage was to be the seminary in Hwanghsien. She went to her new place of service with fear and trembling. She had been trained to teach kindergarten children; now the trustees were giving her the fearful opportunity of teaching adults who would go out to preach and teach the Gospel. They were young, eager to learn, educated, and filled with enthusiasm to learn how best to share their faith.

Others were equally surprised upon hearing the news of Martha's appointment to the seminary. Bertha Smith, who was herself a scholar, knew that Martha was not. Initially, she was disappointed at the news because she had hoped that the two of them would again find work together. After praying about the matter, God revealed to Bertha that it was His will for Martha to go. She wrote a warm letter to Martha in which she spoke of her initial doubts, but she added, "I now see that this is God's will for you. You will do a good job." Frank Connely, who had come to value Martha's work in Tsining, later wrote a most noble letter to her in which he said in part, "We were happy to stand back and rejoice in your progress as the Lord took you on to higher and more important things."

Florence Lide was assigned the class of college-trained students, and Martha those with high school training only. Having had no experience in what she was now called upon to do, she was forced to study long and hard just to stay ahead. Late into the night she studied, learning one step at the time how to teach the Bible to her eager pupils. They responded with enthusiasm and great joy. She learned to admit honestly and frankly to some of their questions, "I don't know. Let's find out." And she did always try to find out.

Spending hours each day and night studying God's word, Martha discovered some astonishing surprises. From the Psalmist who had discovered it many generations before, she learned "The entrance of thy Word giveth light" (Psalm 119:130) and "Thy Word is a lamp unto my feet and a light unto my pathway." (Psalm 119:105). As a result of her intensive studies of the Bible, Martha made another discovery about herself; it was that God had given her insight, and discernment, and understanding of everyday events and of ordinary things of this world in an extraordinary way. Such things had never been evident to her before. She found that she was able to explain God's Word to the students in a manner that they could understand, but which, at the same time continued to amaze her. God was confirming in her experience what the trustees had articulated from the beginning, "The Lord would have you come and help us." In her new-found joy, Martha wrote the Foreign Mission Board, "I enjoy teaching the Bible so much, I should be paying for the privilege instead of being paid."

Martha spoke of the experience of working under the leadership of Dr. Charlie Culpepper as one of the great opportunities of her life. She said of him, "He was the greatest missionary I have ever know. He combined a deep spiritual nature with practical, common-sense ability." Many times she saw him in his coveralls repairing the sputtering diesel engine which supplied electricity for the hospital. When the time came for leading the seminary in worship, he peeled off his coveralls, put on his stiff collar, and led students and teachers alike to new spiritual heights. The old adage, "Behind every successful

Women's Training Department of North China Baptist Seminary, Hwanghsien, 1930's

159

親愛的父親，

　可惜這幾天未能寫信給你，可是沒有一天我不想你幾次，也沒有一天不是好幾次為你禱告。這幾天我只有一個難過，就是怕你為我掛心。但神這幾天賜我出人意外的平安，深信也必賜給你和全家，請你千萬放心。衣食住及一切需用之物都充足，表哥送我的爐子天天生著也不冷，表哥和牧師送我的小箱子借給別人了。

　我的工作差不多照舊，現在正是考試，三十一號放假，一月九號開學。

　我現在搬到離我本來住的地方有二里遠的一所房子裡，五個朋友同住一起非常快樂。我們得的也感快樂，想多幸虧的朋友的愛心，此意正甜，感謝神，請你放心吧。

　這信請轉給懷路翠護士，請她轉給別的朋友，回信請持給高牧師，他的通信處是（蕫姑娘請你將通信址寫上）我就能接接到了。

你所愛的女兒馬大

一 十二月廿九號

Martha's letter to her father, dictated while she was held captive byu the Japanese, December 1941.

Translation –   Dec. 29th.

Dear Father,

How sorry I am not to have been able to write to you these days, but I have certainly been thinking of you often and praying for you many times each day. My only concern has been lest you should be anxious about me. The Lord has given us peace beyond understanding during this time and I trust this peace has also been in your heart and the hearts of all the family. Please do not be in the least uneasy about me.

Food, clothing, housing — and everything needful – we have. The stove given me by my cousin is keeping me good & warm every day, and the box (or small trunk) that my cousin & the pastor gave me, I have put in the care of others. My work is just about as it was. It is examination time soon and school will be out on the 31st. Seminary reopens on Jan. 9th.

I am now living with the four others in a house about 200 yards from the one was occupying. We are very happy together and have wonderful fellowship & comfort. The local friends are showing a "love that is sweeter than honey." Thanks be to God.

Please send this to Miss Lucy Wright & ask her to give it to other friends. Write to me in the Cauthens care, and they can get it to me.

Love from your daughter,
Martha.

Dear Mr. Franks,

This note was written by one of the girls there for Martha. We shall be so happy to pass your letters to her through Chinese addressed envelopes. They cannot receive mail direct from America. Address us Baptist Mission, Kweilin, Kwangsi, China. Most sincerely, Eloise Glass Cauthen
(Mrs. B. J. Cauthen)

Translation by Mrs. Baker James Cauthen of Chinese letter on preceeding page.

Sunday School Group, Hwanghsien, 1930's

man is a successful woman" was especially true in the case of Charlie and Ola Culpepper. He led and she supported with her love and prayers. Martha happily recalled that they worked together in three seminaries: Hwanghsien until the Japanese got them, Shanghai until communists got them, and Taipei until old age got them.

When the mantis Hunts the locust He forgets the shrike That's hunting him

Historically, Japan has had a burning desire to control East Asia. She had advanced her cause appreciably by the end of the First World War. In addition to loss of territory, China had been forced to pay a large indemnity to Japan. Ever looking for any excuse for broadening her base of activity on the mainland, Japan substantially increased her forces in Manchuria in 1931. Seizing one opportunity after another, Japan, like a hungry pack released from its island, did not delay in gobbling up Manchuria. Using the deposed last Manchu emperor as their pawn, the Japanese set up a government called the state of Manchukuo.

When the League of Nations condemned Japan's actions in 1932, she simply resigned from that body. From that time until her final defeat in 1945, Japan waged a relentless battle for control of the writhing Chinese giant. China's own internal struggles contributed much to Japan's success. The Nationalist Government under Chaing Kai-shek had as much work as it could handle in its ongoing battle with the communists.

Hwanghsien fell to the invading Japanese army without the firing of a single shot. As they had already done in other areas, the army swept through surrounding cities one after the other in rapid succession. There was little resistance because of the lack of arms and leadership and also because of the preoccupation of Nationalists and Communists with each other. There were repeated attempts at reconciling the two for the mutual defense of China, but lack of materiel and means of supply, coupled with mutual distrust, doomed most efforts from the beginning.

It soon became obvious to the American missionaries that Japan intended to take all of China and that a long struggle was inevitable. The mission decided that women with children, elderly missionaries, those whose furloughs were coming due, and any other who so wished, would go home. No one would be compelled to stay.

Those in Hwanghsien felt that war in the area was imminent, but they were shocked both at the rapidity with which it came and with the almost total lack of resistance with which the Chinese met the invaders. With the Japanese army daily moving closer, Martha and other missionaries helped to pack the car owned by Drs. Bryan and Culpepper. They thanked God every day for that car; it was the only one in the entire area. Everything that could be got on the car was loaded, inside and out. The Bryan and Culpepper children were already in Chefoo, at the China Inland Mission School, awaiting their parents. When the day of departure came, Martha watched with mixed emotions as Ola Culpepper, Frances Bryan, Lucy Wright, and Anna Hartwell climbed into the car, waving goodbye as they sped off in a choking cloud of dust.

Had she made the right decision in staying? For a moment she felt her heart sink. Why hadn't she gone with them? No one would have blamed her. She had no idea what awful things might come. They had heard gruesome tales of barbarous acts on the part of Japanese soldiers. Rumors flew concerning atrocities perpetrated by all the armies. She could easily have gone home; what had kept her there? After much prayerful consideration, she firmly believed that it was the Lord's will for her to stay. No other word was needed. She would stay because God wanted her to stay. And she knew that God Himself would be with her whatever came.

Now there were six. In a mission from which, not long before, as many as thirty missionaries had worked to spread the gospel, now only Dr. and Mrs. Glass, Dr. Bryan, Dr. Culpepper, Florence Lide, and Martha remained. Surprisingly, after the Japanese had occupied the country, life continued much as it had before; there was simply a different master in control. One learned how to bow and smile, avoiding any hint of seeming rudeness or arrogance. One also adjusted to filling out multiple forms, waiting interminably for permissions, and carrying on as best he could.

There was one especially important item that proved invaluable to the six missionaries who remained; it was a portable shortwave radio. When Martha was returning from furlough, Dr. and Mrs. Jewel Kyzar (pastor of First Baptist Church Laurens) and Nat and Kat Kennedy (Martha's cousins) had presented her with that wonderful gift. On the return trip, she camouflaged the radio so that it looked very like a lady's small train case. It was covered in black oil cloth with two leather straps and a black leather handle. She prayed the entire trip that she might be able to get the radio through customs without having to tell a lie.

Leaving the trans-Pacific steamer in Japan, Martha boarded a small ship, bound for Lung Ko, which would bring her to within eighteen miles of Hwanghsien. She had with her a small mountain of luggage. There was a huge washing machine for the hospital, one hundred pounds of sugar, a trunk filled with cloth, and all her own trunks, suitcases, and hand luggage.

Fortunately, the Japanese customs officer had only one delcaration form left, so that instead of handing it to Martha to sign, he simply read the questions to her: "Do you have any arms? ammunition? wines? tobacco? etc. etc." He read through the entire list and Martha responded that she had none of the forbidden items. "I have a hundred pounds of sugar. Cloth in the trunk." The official then pointed to the large crates which held the washing machine. "This is too much to examine today. You will have to come back tomorrow!" he ordered.

In an aside to Dr. Culpepper, who was standing next to her, Martha said, "Let's get the hand luggage, especially that little black piece." The precious radio was got through with no one the wiser. In time it proved to be of inestimable value to that isolated sextette, who were sometimes aware of events taking place in China even before their captors.

Every day at noon, there was an English language broadcast which came to them from outside the territory held by Japan. Each day, just before noon, Dr. Bryan started the hospital's diesel-powered generator which provided electricity for the hospital. When Martha heard the engine start, she got out the radio and soaked up the news which she quickly shared with the others in the mission. She quietly passed along to their Chinese leaders any new developments affecting them.

November 1941, the news reported the loss of 30,000 men from the Chinese army as opposed to 10,000 by the Japanese. As Martha reported the figures to the leaders of the high school, the principal shouted, "Good! At that rate, we can still win."

Monday noon, December 7, Martha came home from the seminary for her lunch. She had been teaching all morning in gloves, fur-lined hat and coat, and was chilled to the bone. She crawled under a heavy down comforter, under which hot water bottles had been placed, and hoped to thaw enough to eat a little lunch before returning to school. The radio was beside her bed, and when she heard the putt putt of the hospital's engine, she turned on the radio as usual. The cook had placed a tray containing a bowl of scalding soup and tea on her lap. Suddenly the shocking news came blaring over the air: "Japan has attacked Pearl Harbor!" Tray, food, everything went spilling over the bed. Quickly she put on her thick felt shoes, the long, sheep-skin lined Chinese coat and went as fast as her legs would carry her to Dr. Culpepper's house. The Glasses and Dr. Culpepper were dining when Martha rushed into the room gasping, "The Japanese have attacked Pearl Harbor, and we have declared war!"

They all knew that it would not be long before they saw the Japanese soldiers coming to the mission compound. From that day on which Pearl Harbor was attacked, everything changed. Americans were now the enemy. Japan and the United States were at war. Even missionaries in China were suspect. They began to ask each other how long it would be before soldiers came to arrest them. Plans had to be made for the school and hospital. They wondered where they would be taken and whether they might be forced to walk a long distance. As it happened, they had exactly three days.

The first thing they did was to burn the American flags so that they would not be desecrated. Next, all financial records, both mission and personal, were burned. Each missionary then packed a single bag which could be carried in the event they were forced to walk. Having done all that was considered absolutely vital, the mission carried on with its work with as much semblance of normality as it could muster.

On December 11, Martha was teaching her class on the first floor of the seminary building. She had by her desk the one bag packed and ready for travel, just in case. At about eleven o'clock, a rather large contingent of Japanese soldiers approached the seminary. Quickly surrounding the building, they marched from all sides with bayonets fixed as if going into battle. As Martha and her students watched fascinated, they saw several soldiers drop to the ground, point their guns toward the building, and after a few seconds advance, crawling toward them. The maneuver was repeated until the entire group had reached the building which was quickly and most officiously occupied. Had it not been for her fear, Martha might well have thought it amusing that all those soldiers with bayoneted guns had come to take exactly four American missionaries who hadn't so much as a pocket knife by way of arms.

No one knew quite what to expect. There was a tenseness caused by fear of the unknown, as they heard the cleated boots of the soldiers stomping down the halls of the building. Upon entering the classroom, one of the soldiers told Martha in a very loud voice that she was now a prisoner of the Great Imperial Army of Japan. She and the others were marched off to the Culpepper house while soldiers conducted a thorough search of all the buildings. Locked doors were kicked open by the soldiers and anything which looked in any way suspicious was summarily confiscated.

Opposite Martha's classroom, there was a small storage room which was somehow, miraculously overlooked by the soldiers. The student food committee had bought wheat at harvest time directly from local farmers. They had piled enough wheat in that room to last the students for the entire school year. They had, rarely, a little fish and a few fresh vegetables, and meat twice a year. That grain was the mainstay of their diet. If the soldiers had found the wheat, they certainly would have confiscated it, thus depriving the students of their chief food stuff. Every other room in the building was closely searched. That one small room with its precious hoard was somehow overlooked. Once again they observed the hand of God lifted in their behalf. The students, one and all, thanked God for His miraculous protection of their lives and of their food.

In short order, all six missionaries were ordered to the Culpepper house. The men were required to accompany the soldiers to every building in the compound. A strip of paper, on which was written in Chinese "Controlled by the Great Imperial Army of Japan," was pasted on every object in every house—even their toothbrushes were so labeled. Finally the doors of all unoccupied homes had large strips of paper with the same message pasted across them. It took all day for the itemizing of every single object. Martha and each of the others were required to list every article in their houses without being allowed to enter them. Each piece of furniture, every piece of

Chapel, Mission Compound, Hwanghsien (It was here missionaries were confined by Japanese, December 1941.) Straw refugee huts in foreground.

cutlery, linens, everything had to be listed. It was almost night before the men returned to the house.

After some time, the others were terribly distressed when Dr. Bryan was suddenly seized by the soldiers and marched off to a filthy, freezing prison with no bed nor toilet facilities of any kind. The only cover he had against the bitter cold was a nasty dog skin, until a kindly Chinese Christian woman took him a warm cotton quilt. The Japanese were out to prove Dr. Bryan a spy and questioned him for several days before moving him to Chefoo. The others who had prayed for his protection were anxious because they all knew of his quick temper which might get him into trouble with his captors. After a few weeks, the Japanese concluded that he was not a spy after all, and allowed him to return to the mission.

There were several bands of Chinese guerillas operating in the area, and the Japanese soldiers were anxious to get back behind the city walls of Hwanghsien before dark. Leaving behind a couple of dozen soldiers, the main body of troops then left for the protection of the city.

Those soldiers who remained ordered the five missionaries upstairs while they occupied the first floor. The Japanese allowed the Chinese cook to remain the entire time of their internment. They permitted him to bring scalding tea and hot food, which were sorely needed since they had been under intense pressure all day and had no heat in any of the rooms on the second floor. In Dr. Culpepper's bedroom there was a small metal grate about one foot square which was directly above the large stove in the dining room. The captives took turns lying on the floor watching the soldiers. Each soldier had a saucer containing a spoonful of sugar from the kitchen larder. As they talked and laughed, the men dipped their fingers into the sugar, licked them and dipped again. They laughed a raucous laughter and spoke loudly in Japanese, making the group upstairs increasingly anxious to know what might happen next.

They did not have long to wait. One of the soliders came to the foot of the stairs and called in Chinese, "Send the young woman down!" Martha was the only young one among them. What should they do? What could they do? There was no recourse but to do as they had been ordered and pray God's protection for her as she went. As the other missionaries knelt to pray for her safety, Martha started down the stairs. She felt as if God were walking beside her. Hadn't He promised to be with His own each step of the way? Martha knew that someone must be in charge. Silently, Martha prayed to God, "Lord, someone has to be in charge; let it be me. Show me what I should do."

With a firm grip on herself, Martha opened the door, stepping into the dining room filled with Japanese soldiers. She smiled broadly and bowed as politely as she had ever done in her life. At once she looked at the piano and, without having planned it, walked over, sat down and began to play. She played every kindergarten march, chorus, and tune she could recall. Having exhausted her repertoire of children's music, she played "Silent Night." As the strains of that beautiful carol of our Saviour's birth filled the room, some of the soliders hummed the tune with her. When she had finished playing "Silent Night," Martha got up from the piano, bowed very low to the soldiers, all of whom stood bowing to her in return. Without a word, she turned and left the room and walked back up the stairs. The others surrounded her, thanking the Lord for His love and mercy.

Believing them to be spies, the soldiers searched what they thought was every inch of the Culpepper house. Every drawer was opened and emptied of its contents. Every visible closet was ransacked. Again, the hand of God was lifted in their behalf.

Each summer the Culpeppers canned as much food as they could store. They placed the food in a closet under the stairs to await the coming winter. (Mason fruit jars were valuable possessions.) As the soldiers searched the house, they inadvertently placed a piece of furniture in front of the small door behind which the food was stored. Throughout the six months of their internment, that cache of food provided much more than they could ever have had from the market.

After satisfying themselves that the missionaries were not spies and presented no real threat to them, the Japanese moved back into Hwanghsien, leaving behind a large group of Chinese puppet soldiers.

The missionaries were then left in the home alone and allowed to resume their routine of study, prayer, and recreation within the confines of the house and its walled compound. The soldiers surrounded the entire compound with barbed wire and were always popping up at the most unexpected moments so that there was always a tension about the mission. The winter was bitterly cold, freezing solid the water in the pitchers in their bedrooms every night. They were blessed with good beds and plenty of cover to keep them warm. Every morning the cook came with a kettle of hot water for bathing.

Having nothing but the clothing she wore, Martha, after several days, approached the officer in charge to ask for permission to visit her house in order to retrieve some much-needed personal articles. Knowing almost no Japanese, she bowed low, and speaking politely, said, "A re ga to go tsai a mas" (Thank you very much); "A re ga to go tsai a mas—toothbrush"; "A re ga to go tsai a mas—soap". Grasping her collar, she said "kimono." After she stammered for several

Dr. Charlie Culpepper, Taiwan

seconds, the officer, standing with a bemused and condescending smile, said in perfectly good Chinese, "After awhile." Martha thanked the man and, a day or two later, was ushered to her house where she hurridly snatched up as much as she could carry of her personal things—clothing, toilet articles, and others, including Chinese checkers. She had been allowed twenty minutes in her house. The soldier who had watched as she gathered the things then escorted her back to the Culpepper house. She was never allowed to enter her own house again. Chinese friends afterward told her that her books, furniture, and all other items were sold in the local markets.

One of the first things the soldiers took was Dr. Culpepper's motor bike. Each day the Japanese officer in charge rode that motor bike to the mission compound to check on his prisoners. The sound of the approaching motor bike was a warning to them to hide any item they did not wish him to take and to cease any suspicious activity. Upon every occasion, the prisoners were ready to face inspection with never a question raised.

On the day of their arrest, the soldiers took away all of their money. Both their personal funds and mission money were gone. Each week the Japanese authorities gave Dr. Culpepper a meager amount of money for the purchase of food and other necessities. The faithful cook every few days put a large market basket on his arm and walked into the city to buy food. As he made his way round the market, haggling over the price of an egg, a piece of pork, or a bunch of carrots, Christian friends surreptitiously slipped other items not easily purchased into his basket. Those Christian friends, knowing that the missionaries were under house arrest, provided luxuries that they could never have purchased.

The father of one young man whom Martha had taught in kindergarten operated a candy store. Refined sugar was a rare commodity, which he was able to get only because of his business. As the mission cook walked by, the candy man dropped in two precious bags from his own small store of sugar. On another day someone dropped in a lemon. It was a beautiful lemon which had been lovingly tended and grown inside the house. When Martha saw the lemon she took a small rosewood stand and placed a few lumps of coal on it with the single lemon on top. She set the arrangement on the dining table for a centerpiece. It was a reminder of the kindness of their Chinese friends. The real treat came when Mrs. Glass took the lemon and made a pie for their dessert.

Martha said that she had never seen a cup of coffee in a Chinese home in all of her experience in North China. But one day, upon his return from the market, they discovered in the cook's basket two bags of coffee beans. Martha and Dr. Bryan were the only two of the six who drank coffee. They set about teaching the cook how to roast the beans. As Martha went rummaging through the attic, lo and behold, a coffee mill! Every morning, for as long as it lasted, she and Dr. Bryan had a single cup of fresh roasted, ground coffee for breakfast.

And they had meat! The Culpeppers and Bryans had kept cows so that the children might have fresh milk. With the listing of every single item, soldiers had likewise numbered and recorded each animal. There were five cattle, one of which was a young calf not yet a year old. One cold winter's night a calf was born, making six. Quickly they decided to butcher young Ferdinand, hoping that before they were caught, the new calf would have grown sufficiently to take his place. If they were counted, there would still be five head of cattle. At midnight the entire mission slaughtered the calf, hanging the meat in the attic where it was frozen solid by morning. When the cow man came to milk the cows as usual, there was no mention of a new calf. He simply took the required supply of milk to the Japanese within the city.

Each day the cook climbed into the attic, sawing off enough meat for dinner and soup for supper. As the weather grew warmer, there was still a good supply of meat hanging in the attic. They faced the problem of saving the meat for future use. No one had any idea how long they would be confined, and the meat might be a lifesaver in the months to come. There was a pressure cooker, but no one knew how to can meat. Martha suggested cutting steaks to fit inside the mason jars in the pantry. All the remaining meat was duly cut, cooked, packed inside the jars, covered with broth, and placed in the cooker. As Martha was busy frying the little steaks for preserving, a Japanese soldier suddenly apeared in the kitchen door. "Ah, Yo!" he said as he sniffed the aroma of those frying steaks. "You are cooking beef. Where did you get it?" Before Martha had presence of mind enough to answer, the cook, who was drying a bowl, without so much as a flicker of his eyelid, said, "If you go to Lung Ko on a market day, you can sometimes find beef to buy." Nothing further was said concerning the beef, which was soon hidden under the stair with the rest of their supply of food.

The days ran together. They stretched on—one coming fast on top of another. Among that little group there was no time for self-pity. God had preserved their lives. Their "stuff" was gone. Martha's Matthew Henry (Bible Commentary) had likely been used as fuel to cook someone's garlic, but she thanked God for His gracious mercy. "Things" could be got again. For the present, they had work to do. God's Chinese people were suffering. They had no idea how long they would be there. Their task now was to continue in study and prayer until God brought a change in their status for better or worse.

There was a daily regimen of study, prayer, exercise, and work. While the yard had been fenced with barbed wire, they had a place in which to walk. With the coming of spring, they could hear the singing of the birds and smell the fragrances of roses, lilacs, and wisteria in the garden. Each sound, each smell, each kind act of a friend was a reminder of the goodness of God. They missed the trees in the backyard. They had been forced to cut them down for fuel during the winter. It was not hard to cut them up, because they had no coal; and it was their only resource for cooking and for heat during that bitterly cold winter of their imprisonment. Martha and the other women gladly took their turns helping saw the wood from those beautiful trees which had stood so many years on the mission grounds. Work helped—there was cleaning, washing, mending to be done. Life goes on, as so many were to learn during those awful years of World War II. Life goes on whether behind a barbed wire fence, a stone wall, or in the open.

Despite the fact that they were not allowed to attend church services in the city, they could worship inside the house. On Sundays as they knelt to pray in thanksgiving to God, they had especial reason to rejoice. Barbed wire was no barrier to the strains of music coming from the Chinese chapel near the Culpepper house. God's people in Hwanghsien sang his praises whether foreign missionaries were present or not. The little group who gathered in the mission house to worship knew that the church were praying for them, even as they prayed. They prayed that God would protect His Chinese children and strengthen their faith. Time would reveal that the Heavenly Father heard every prayer and answered as Jesus had promised.

When they had exhausted all their resources for work, recreation, study, and worship, they sometimes resorted to such wicked games as Chinese checkers. Dr. Glass had a copy of Merle D'Aubigne's *History of the Reformation*. A worm had eaten through the middle, but there was a reading round the worm hole each night before checkers. Forty years later some of them spoke of the absolute boredom of that game. There they sat, each struggling to get his marble from one triangle to the one opposite before his opponent could do likewise, a reversing of the board and back again. Dumb! Dumb! Dumb! But it helped sometimes to have something different to do after supper and a worm-eaten history of the Reformation. After all, no one played cards.

One of their treasures was the piano. They could still sing. The songs of faith which had sometimes been mere words on their lips became now real statements of faith and prayers. When they sang "Savior, Like a Shepherd Lead Us" and "I Will Guide Thee With Mine Eye," their hearts were warmed and their spirits lifted. God was still in charge and he was ever present with them. Behind that barbed wire fence, surrounded by a sea of soldiers who had no sympathy for their faith, they firmly believed that the Lord would see them through.

One of Martha's greatest concerns was that her family know of her safety. She well knew that they would be greatly distressed knowing as they did of the Japanese occupation of Hwanghsien and all of North China. How could she get word to them? It seemed that any communication was out of the question, but God provided a way as He had done so many

times before. A former seminarian and student of Martha's by
the name of Rose Dong had gone to the far west of China as a
frontier missionary. Martha dictated a letter to one of the
young girls in the seminary who wrote it in Chinese characters.
The letter, intended for her family, was addressed to Rose
Dong. Rose had no idea of the family's address, but she did
know the address of the Foreign Mission Board. When the
letter arrived in Richmond, Virginia, it was immediately
forwarded to the Franks family in Laurens. The letter with the
notation "Translation" at the top reads as follows:

Dear Father,

*How sorry I am not to have been able to write to you these
days, but I have certainly been thinking of you often and
praying for you many times each day. My only concern has
been lest you should be anxious about me. The Lord had given
me peace beyond understanding this time and I trust this peace
has also been in your heart and the hearts of all the family.
Please do not be in the least uneasy about me.*

*Good clothing, housing—and everything needful—we
have. The stove given me by my cousin is keeping me good and
warm every day, and the box (or small trunk) that my cousin
and the pastor gave me I have put in the care of others. My
work is just about as it was. It is examination time soon and
school will be out on the 31st. Seminary reopens on
January 9th.*

*I am now living with the four others in a home about 200
yards from the one I was occupying. We are very happy
together and have wonderful fellowship and comfort. The local
friends are showing a "love that is sweeter than honey."
Thanks be to God.*

*Please send this to Miss Lucy Wright and ask her to give
it to other friends. Write me in the Cauthen's care, and they
can get it to me.*

Love from your daughter,
Martha

There was great rejoicing in Laurens that Martha was safe—under house arrest and surrounded by Japanese soldiers and their stooges the Chinese puppets, but she was safe—if she could only get home!

Early in their internment, the Japanese authorities gave each missionary a questionnaire which they completed and returned. One of the questions was, "Do you want to go home?" Dr. Culpepper, Dr. Bryan, and Martha responded with a "Yes." Dr. and Mrs. Glass and Florence Lide, who had no immediate family awaiting them, responded with "No."

It was the first week of April that an officer arrived one morning to announce that they would soon be leaving Hwanghsien. The soldiers took out those inventory lists made several months before and checked every item. "Culpepper—five cows." Down the entire list for Culpepper, Bryan, the Glasses, Florence Lide, they read off every item and checked to see that it was there. When Martha's turn came, there was a hitch. "Franks—one camera." The camera was a good one and, having realized that she would probably not be able to keep it, Martha had given it to one of the teachers at the seminary. There were some tense moments as the soldiers waited for Martha to produce her camera. Once again, the attic, with its heap of ancient pieces, proved to be of great benefit to them.

One day Dr. Glass had discovered there an old folding Kodak. This old camera he now presented to the officer for inspection.

After checking every article, the soldiers gave them a few minutes to pack their bags before leaving the mission for the last time. They boarded a bus bound for Chefoo. Upon their arrival in Chefoo, a Japanese official informed them that Culpepper, Bryan, and Franks would be repatriated to America. Dr. and Mrs. Glass and Florence Lide would remain in China. Upon realizing that she would be alone (as a single person) Florence Lide wanted desperately to go with them. Dr. Culpepper approached the authorities to see whether Miss Lide might be included in the repatriation list, but he was unable to persuade them to let her go. Martha then offered to remain in her place, allowing Florence to leave. The Japanese would not give an inch. Florence Lide and Dr. and Mrs. Glass were taken to an internment camp in Wei Hai where they remained for the duration of the war.

After tearful and anxious farewells, Drs. Culpepper, Bryan, and Martha boarded a small Japanese steamer bound for Shanghai; there on the ship they were given the one and only stateroom. The trip round the Shangtung Promentory is always a rough voyage. The Chinese call it "turning the corner of the sea." As they entered the "turning of the corner of the sea," Martha, who was subject to seasickness, knew that she would not be able to stay up. There was only one thing for her to do—she would be forced to go to bed in order to keep from being disgustingly ill. How was a single lady to manage that in the presence of two gentlemen? Knowing that something had to be done in short order, Martha said, "You boys give me a few minutes. When I'm in my bunk, I'll pull the curtain and whistle for you." Quickly, she undressed, got into her bed clothes, jumped into the bunk, and, pulling the curtain, whistled for the men to return to the room. The sea churned, pitching the ship one way and rolling it another. The trio in their stateroom, thoroughly exhausted from months of strain and travel, slept until morning brought sunshine and calmer waters. Martha was still sick in the morning. Dr. Culpepper came to the door asking whether she would like breakfast. "No," she answered, "Go away!"

"What about some fat meat?" he teased; but Martha for once was in no mood for teasing.

Upon their arrival in Shanghai, they were escorted by the Japanese soldiers to the Old Country Club. There they joined other Americans, being repatriated from all over China. They were happy to see friends from other missions and to meet a large number of people from other walks of life. The Old Country Club provided them a small measure of semi-comfort, but mosquitoes were ferocious. Had it not been for netting over the cots, they never would have got any restful sleep.

They waited in Shanghai for several days while scores of forms and mounds of paperwork were processed. Near the Country Club was a home for girls called the *Door of Hope.* Before the coming of the modern revolution after the war, families frequently sold girls into prostitution. If there were too many girls in a family, the cost of keeping them was a burden on the family. Selling the poor girls provided a little money for the rest of the family. A kind and gentle Austrian woman by the name of Gladys Dieterly had established a home for saving some of those girls. Sometimes, she paid the price asked by the families, while the courts gave her other girls. Miss Dieterly gave the girls a home and taught them so that they might eventually go to work supporting themselves. Her goal was to save them from prostitution, and to introduce them to the Savior.

At the end of a refreshing visit with that Godly woman, Gladys Dieterly prayed God's blessing upon Martha and the others in her group. Pausing in the middle of her prayer as if listening, she sat silent for a few seconds before continuing, "He shall cover thee with His feathers, and under His wings shalt thou trust." There was another pause—"Now Lord, what does this mean? You don't have feathers." Another pause—"I see your ship sailing through dangerous, mine-infested waters. Above you, hovering as a bird, your Heavenly Father's protection as the feathers and wings of a bird protects its young."

Later, as they entered those mine-infested waters between Shanghai and Mozambique, passengers were ordered not to strike so much as a match to light a cigarette on deck. There must be total darkness. Naturally, there was great tension on the ship. Many were afraid that they would never make it through without being blown to bits. For those who knew of the protecting wings and feathers of God, there was a calm assurance that he was present all the way. They simply went below, climbed into their bunks, and slept the restful sleep of all those who are assured of God's protection. Many others were so frightened that they could not bring themselves to leave the deck.

The Lord accompanied them every league of the way. Day after day of calm sea and rough, they kept to a schedule of study, prayer, and recreation. The ship's crew took no pains for their comfort. One of the worst features of all was the food. It was both scarce and of the meanest quality. Going down to breakfast one morning, Martha met Susan Eames just returning from her own. "Good morning, Susan," she said, "the early bird gets the worm." Without even pausing, Susan retorted, "I did! The cereal was full of them—I fished them out and ate every bite."

After what seemed an almost interminable voyage, the repatriates finally reached Mozambique. The site of that Swedish ship *Gripsholm* was almost breathtaking! She lay in dock with 1500 Japanese prisoners of war from the United States. Their own ship docked next to the *Gripsholm*, and the Japanese were soon exchanged for Americans. They watched as crewmen brought baggage from the *Gripsholm*. The Japanese transported enormous amounts of luggage. There were washing machines, sewing machines, food stuffs, and large carts containing a great variety of goods. Finally, the ship's officials allowed the Japanese prisoners aboard as prisoners were exchanged one for one.

The 1500 Americans then picked up their own baggage (most had been allowed a single carrying bag) and walked off the Italian ship and on to the *Gripsholm*. They had little in their hands; there was much in their hearts. As they descended the gang plank, they could see high on a hill nearby the American consulate. The American flag floated proudly in a stiff breeze. The stars and strips on that piece of cloth had never looked more beautiful to them. They had not seen the flag since burning those of the mission months before. A shout of joy rose from the whole entourage followed by many tears of relief. Leaving their Japanese masters behind, they repeated, again and again, "Free! Free! to be an American and free! What a privilege and joy to be a citizen of the United States of America!" The Apostle Paul had expressed similar sentiment at being able to claim Roman citizenship almost 1900 years before.

The welcome awaiting them on the *Gripsholm* was overwhelming! As they climbed the gangplank to the spacious deck of the ship, an orchestra began to play "The Star Spangled Banner," which was followed by a long list of beautiful familiar tunes, all refreshing to their weary spirits. The deck itself was lined with numerous tables of food. The crew had laid beautiful tables, covered with snow-white linen cloths, with what seemed to be every good thing one could imagine to eat. There was a large table of salads, another held cold cuts—turkey, ham, beef; tables of hot foods of even greater variety; on still others— desserts. It looked as if some great potentate had ordered a banquet just for them. After that wormy cereal, insipid gruel, and Italian pasta, it was heavenly. One can hardly imagine their thoughts as they made their way from table to table while the orchestra played in the background.

At that first meal, Martha stood by Dr. Theron Rankin. He was wearing a pair of pants made from a flour sack which had been hand stitched by Auris Pender. He was able to eat very little of the great abundance of food. Having been in a real prisoner-of-war camp where food was extremely scarce, he had little nourishment; his stomach had shrunk so that it was a long time before he could eat normally again. For those who could eat, it was glorious.

From Mozambique the happy travelers set sail for Rio de Janeiro. There was still a great deal of anticipation, but they felt that they were really heading home. They were in what seemed their own territory; this was their part of the world. The Far East with all its troubles was fading behind them. The war was yet a long way from finish, and there were dangers on all the seas; but they were headed for the Americas. They would make it now, by God's grace.

Again they spent the long days in study, prayer, recreation, and entertainment. The respite was a welcome one. Surrounded by friendly faces, with good food and luxurious accommodations (as compared to that other ship) they really enjoyed the trip across the Atlantic Ocean. Martha recalled that she and Bertha sat on steamer chairs on deck, memorizing Psalms; they enjoyed concerts and games together.

Rio welcomed the weary travelers with wide-open arms. Missionaries in Rio took those Chinese missionaries into their home for the brief stay. After the drudgery and sameness of the long trek from Chefoo to Mozambique, the sights, sounds and smells were wonderful. They had Brazilian coffee, orange juice squeezed from fruit just off the tree; and to delight the eye and make glad the heart, orchids. They grew everywhere even from utility poles.

The Baptist mission treasurer in Rio gave each of the repatriating missionaries a small amount of money. One of the three in Martha's group bought oranges; another bought coconuts; Martha spent hers on a great handful of orchids. As their ship sailed out of the harbor in Rio for New York, the three of them sat in their deck chairs eating coconuts and oranges, while admiring the orchids for which Martha had paid fifty cents.

The trip from Rio to New York was a happy one, but there was a shadow cast over the whole because of the necessary work of several government agencies. Masses of returning Americans stood in long lines for interrogation by agents of the Federal Bureau of Investigation and Central Intelligence Agency. Every day while en route they lined up alphabetically to answer questions. Tiring of the long lines, Bertha Smith quipped, "If ever I marry, I am going to marry a man with the name Aaron Adams."

When the ship docked in New York, Myra Scovill, a Presbyterian missionary, who had also been stationed in Tsining, experienced labor pains. Her doctor summoned an ambulance; and with sirens screaming, it sped Mrs. Scovill from ship to hospital. The other missionaries took charge of the Scovill children, who lodged in the same hotel. As they sat down to dinner, a dignitary who had come to greet them sat at the same table as the Scovill children. When the waiters brought the food to the table, the dignitary objected that the plate was not what he had ordered. One of the Scovill children said, "It's food! Eat it!"

New York was American soil, but it was not home. After all the anxious moments, the dangers, the transfers from one ship to another, they had still to get out of New York to various points called home. Because of all the transporting of troops criss-crossing the country, train passage was at a premium. At the depot, Martha begged, "Please put me on—I'll ride the whistle." She got on and was soon stepping down from the train and onto the platform in Clinton. It seemed this time that there were as many people to greet her as when all those Smiths had seen Bertha off on their first trip together in 1925. She was home again. The family were all there to greet her with words of joy and a great flood of tears of relief. They had wondered whether they would ever see her again. Now she really was home. Martha was glad for this relief after all their worries and sleepless nights for her. The fire engine was not there to greet her, but she had never had a warmer welcome before in all her life.

Who rules by cruelty
Must sleep lightly
Or sleep long

The war years (1942-1945) were a forced respite for many missionaries driven from their fields of mission. Martha spent a part of her time traveling to various cities to share the gospel. She was often asked to visit one of the churches or speak at a conference, telling of her work.

Because there were hundreds of families working in the shipyards in Charleston, Martha wrote the pastor of First Baptist Church, North Charleston, asking if there were some service she might give in exchange for room and board. Martha was soon settled into the apartment of a woman who was away

Baptist Compound
Pao Shing Road
Shanghai
Jan. 25, 1949--

Dear Friends,

Your beautifully packed parcel of lovely things arrived a few days ago and when I went to the Post Office to get them out the customs examiner said, "But those can't be for relief, they are too nice"—I said, "Of course they are nice, they are from nice people!"—When I showed him the declaration tag and the return address as proof they were from a church, he finally agreed that they could be for relief! I suppose it is unthinkable to any one except an American that people could give away good clothes!

I have them ready to give to the Jews here—They are in need and I have talked already to a lovely Christian Jewish friend of mine who works with the refugee European Jews in Shanghai—She will be so happy to have them—So, a thousand thanks to you all! I appreciate so very much your love and interest—

We are beginning to get clothing thru the New Orleans center now—Our first bundles came this week—

Our war news today is bad—things are tense here again. The communists here have had an overwhelming victory and it is just a matter of time before Nanking and Shanghai fall— Perhaps we will not be so far behind the iron curtain that we can't get in touch with each other. We hope to be able to stay on and to carry on our work. The communists won't surely have time to screw us down within the next few years and maybe by then they will have hanged themselves by their own cruelty— we'll wait and see!

Thanking you again for your love and generosity.
Sincerely yours
Martha Linda Franks

Baptist Compound
Pao Shing Road
Shanghai
January 25, 1949

Emba darling,

The lovely things from the Hazel Todd Circle have come and so I am writing them and saying hey to you too—It was so good to have your after Christmas letter. Just buy a whole package of those air letter things and keep them at your elbow— then you'll write often which will do me good and help me too.

Things are getting tense again—The communists do not really need to talk peace they've laready won, so they can demand surrender. My own hope is that now since they have won, just as soon as possible they will hang themselves by overdoing their bolshevism—and it is real sure enough Red Russia communism with its anti-God and therefore anti-Christian ideas—We are going to try to hold on and I think we can stay on for a spell—maybe even years. Just wait and see.

I am dickering with a landscape architect to draw us a plan for our campus. If we can strike a deal that will give me something completely absorbing to do so I won't have time to get tense—won't it be fun? Half a dozen coolies, a perfectly empty campus and a plan to create—(If you are reading aloud to preacher <u>STOP</u> here) More fun than the woman in Vogue who said she wished she were naked with a check book. O green light.

Chinese New Year comes Saturday—I was downtown yes-terday and all 540,000,000 of China's entire population plus me and Sugar Lump were on Nanking Road at the same time.

The Culpeppers leave for furlough in April—I've tried so hard to get you salt dishes but they are behind the iron curtain. Maybe I'll soon be there too—then I can get them—maybe! Anything else on your mind?

Olive Lawton and Marie Conner are with me in my little apartment—we have a gay time in spite of all that's going on.

My goodest love to you and Preacher,

Marnie

Seminary Group, Shanghai, About 1950

for a long stay in another part of the country. Martha had wanted to make her own contribution to the war effort and was able to minister to the families of soldiers in the ports. She prayed with the people and for them, she worshipped with them, and she sometimes helped with things like finding a place to spend the night or a way home after their men had shipped out.

A happy pair by the name of Tommie and Sadie Turner took Martha under their wings during her sojourn in North Charleston. She spent many joyous hours in their presence and in their home. They had no child, and Martha prayed God to send them one. After she was gone, the Turners' child was born and named Martha. That Martha is now happily married to a preacher.

All the while she thought of China, prayed for her, and longed for the day when she might return to her own work. To Martha's complete surprise, in the spring of 1946, a telegram arrived from the All-China Baptist Seminary in Shanghai informing her that the trustees had elected her Dean of Women. In the autumn she sailed for China. Little did she know that it would be her last trip to that land in which she had spent almost half her life.

The Foreign Mission Board gave great freedom to missionary personnel in their work. The area of the country, the type of work, and decisions as to when to leave, were left largely to the missionaries themselves. Martha felt that it made one feel much more responsible to one's colleagues. Each wanted his work to be of the highest quality. She and her own group were returning to China with the knowledge that much had changed since their departure in 1942. They realized also that the future was less than certain. They would work as long as God gave them opportunity and strength to do. The Lord had led in the past; He would continue to be their guide and stay.

Martha returned to China with the title Dean of Women in the All-China Seminary. The wonder, the honor was the fact that she was a teacher in the seminary. She, who had gone to China to teach choruses, marches, Bible verses, letters, and numbers to Chinese pre-schoolers, was now teaching the Old Testament to future preachers and teachers and evangelists.

In the missionaries' absence, all of North China had fallen under control of the communists led by Mao Tse-tung. The provence of Shantung would never be open to them again as paid missionaries. God provided another place and other people with whom to labor and love. They resumed their work in Shanghai.

The missionaries returned to a devastated and increasingly demoralized China. The "seminary" when they arrived to begin, was nothing more than four walls shot through with bomb shells and a roof ruptured by the war's destruction. They found that little can be much when the need is urgent. A little patching all round and the word *seminary* becomes reality. No need for fancy buildings nor furnishings. The only ingredients necessary are willing students and able teachers. Both were present. It was not long before twenty-five men and women were studying on Pao Shing Road in Shanghai at the All-China Seminary. By the beginning of the new term in 1947, there would be forty.

What in the world could forty people or a hundred and forty do in a sea of millions? Could forty life-boats rescue a sea of drowning people? In a short time all of the "foreign" missionaries would be gone. But those who had come to faith in Jesus Christ as Lord of their lives would become missionaries to their own people. And they would do good work. They and all those who came to believe would continue to spread the glorious news, "Jesus Christ is Lord!" They would go as shining lights into the darkness of China.

One of the most inspiring stories of those shining lights is that of the Wang family. Mrs. Wang, the mother, was one of those sad women who had the misfortune to bear several children who did not survive infancy. In her own simple belief, the cause lay in spirits who did not want her to have a child. Each time she bore, the spirits came to steal her child. When Della was born, her mother took the child, laying her in the middle of the road in front of the house. She went to a neighbor, saying, "Take my baby and keep her for a while. When the spirits see she is not mine, then I'll get her back." After keeping the baby for a few days, the neighbor returned

Della to her mother. The family named her "Received from the Road."

The spirits' will had been thwarted, and other children came to the Wang household and survived to adulthood. More than that, they came to faith in Jesus Christ. Della's sister taught in the seminary; a brother went to Nepal as an agriculturalist; one brother became a preacher of the gospel.

When the communists had taken control of the country, they soon proved how fearful they are of education and free expression of opposing thought. As the authorities dismissed teachers and preachers from their posts, they snatched Pastor Wang from his congregation and family and sent him to the coal mines in the far west of China. After twenty years, the overseers called Pastor Wang to meet with local authorities concerning his forced exile. They informed him that his arrest had all been a mistake. Intellectuals, they said, should not be there. By that time, Mr. Wang was pastor of three churches in the region. To this day it is the Pastor Wangs and other disciples who hold the key to China. Della herself had three opportunities to leave China. Committed to telling the story of Jesus despite the dangers, she chose to stay and spread the Word.

As China plummeted ever deeper into chaos, rampant inflation led to such outrageous sights as a pair of shoes advertised for 20,000 Chinese dollars and a can of salmon went for a million dollars. The seminary announced for a replacement for its music teacher and found a Russian woman who offered to teach ten pupils in one day for five million dollars per week. One U.S. dollar was then worth thirty eight thousand in Chinese dollars. With all the resulting poverty, it was amazing to see expensive cars on the streets and furs and imported designer clothes in the shops of Shanghai. The day the missionaries received their monthly checks, they rushed to the bank with a gunny sack and then to the market to spend the money as quickly as possible.

Amidst all the turmoil, the Russian presence was soon evident everywhere. They opened shops, brought in supplies, and generally infiltrated the country, aiding and abetting those officials who spread the lie of relief to a beleaguered people.

Even as thousands fled communist-held territories, one heard praises for the "liberators" of China: "They're not so bad. After the fighting, they will bring peace and prosperity to China; and the people will be free."

Increasingly, their deeds gave the lie to all their words. As civil war raged, the resulting devastation surpassed anything done by the Japanese occupation. News arrived of intense fighting in Tsining. There were sad tales of the deaths of many whose only crime was their commitment to the Christ. Communist "liberators" robbed, tortured, and killed those called Christian in vain attempts to obliterate the faith from China. The communists burned to death one whom the missionaries had known and loved as a friend. In Pingtu, they tortured to death dear old Pastor Kuan, a gentle, quiet man of faith. They closed all churches as freedom became a vanishing memory.

From Hwanghsien there was news that the government had driven Christians from their homes and confiscated all their property. Pastor Tzang, who had labored alongside Baptist missionaries in the years before the war, was among those driven at the age of eighty-eight, from his home into the street. Authorities continued to arrest individuals with threats to wipe out the entire Christian community. Despite the threats, students eagerly sought places at the seminary, committing themselves to study, prayer, and witnessing.

Happiness and sorrow Flow along The same river

In late summer 1947, Martha and Olive left the seminary for a brief stay at the Lawton summer home in Kuling. It was to be the last trip they would make there. None of the other members of the Lawton family ever saw the house again. Despite the evidences of unrest in the country, the physical rest and spiritual renewal were a much-needed change. That late-summer trip was like the proverbial calm before the storm. It was a magnificent change of pace and of scenery. As they reached the mountains, the cool, clean air, huge ferns and beautiful lilies were like a salve to their sore and hungry spirits. Everywhere they looked there was green; beautiful, cool green met the eye in a wide expanse of God's garden in Kuling. The lofty mountain vistas greeted them at every turn with ever-increasing examples of the glory of God's handiwork.

Reaching the foot of the mountain on which the Lawtons' summer home sat, they began to dicker with the coolie chair bearers who would carry them up the thousand narrow winding steps to the house. Olive was never very large, but Martha had tended to put on weight over the years. As they made arrangements for the ascent, the man in charge looking at Olive said, "This missy allight. Four-piece coolie can do." Looking askance at Martha, he continued, "This missy too fat, too heavy, must take six coolie." Martha agreed, paying the difference; and soon she and Olive were in the chairs riding up the mountain.

The house they found in good repair although the Japanese had stolen the furnishings. They had their cots, and Chinese neighbors lent other furnishings needed for their stay. That last summer in the mountains was a happy one with war and conflict far away. They walked along the mountain paths, listened to the singing of the birds, watched the water cascade down the rocks; they picked beautiful wild flowers and pic-nicked by the crystal-clear pools. They talked of China's troubles and prayed for her people. There was no fear, no whining to God. They knew that it was He and not the opposing forces in China, who would carry the day in the end.

On the third of September, they participated in a service of Thanksgiving attended by President Chiang Kai Shek, who graciously came and greeted them. His announcement several years before, that he had himself become a Christian, had been a great boon to their work and that of all missionaries in China.

When their vacation ended (much too soon, it seemed) they engaged the coolie bearers for the trip down those same steps they had climbed several weeks before. There was a breathtaking view of the Yangtze Valley, but Martha was afraid to look for fear at the treacherous path they trod. One can hardly imagine sitting on a chair atop the shoulders of six men, all running (yes, literally running) down a thousand narrow, winding steps with a fearful drop on one side. The view was indeed breathtaking, but her breath was taken more than once at the narrow twists and turns along the way. Several times she closed her eyes, gripping the arms of the chair as the coolies deftly maneuvered the hairpin curves. All her fear was for nothing, as the entire entourage arrived with not so much as a scratch.

Arriving back in Shanghai, they found Charlie Culpepper and Baker James Cauthen just back from a trip to the Frontier Mission Station. They brought the most encouraging news of ten years of God's work by Dr. Abraham Hsu, a physician, in the only hospital west of Lanchow. Dr. Hsu had very little equipment, but the lack was more than compensated by his faith and hard work, improvising with what was available. People by the hundreds flowed into the hospital for medical attention. Some of them left with a knowledge of the *Great Physician*. Dr. Culpepper had baptized five new converts while there, bringing the total congregation to seventy-seven. Seventy-seven among millions! One might ask, "What is that?" until one remembers that Jesus left twelve to spread the good news to the whole world.

Summer in the mountains had been a refreshing experience. Shanghai presented the same problems *and* challenges they had left behind. Martha was ready for school to begin. She was teaching Genesis to an eager group of China's bright young men and women. The need was almost overwhelming with thousands of students just emerging from the tragedy of war past and battle to come. All wanted to attend university. Many gladly received the gospel. There were so many who needed to hear, so few to tell the story.

Repeatedly, Martha met young men and women hungering for a chance at education. She talked with a group of four who had come to Shanghai with a hoard of ten thousands to stand entrance examinations for the few places at the national universities of China. All four had failed and were on the way home in despair. At the Eliza Yates Mission School of the Baptist Mission in Shanghai, four hundred had applied for the one hundred thirty places available. Illustrative of their openness to the gospel message is the fact that Dr. Baker James Cauthen had preached for ten days in May and one hundred forty students professed faith in Jesus as Savior and Lord. In a short time, the foreign missionaries would be gone. Home missionaries, many of them having come to faith in Jesus after the Second World War, would continue to tell the story to their people.

Martha herself sometimes became God's latter day "pied piper," going into the street with her accordion. Many of the children attended no school, had no playground on which to play, and simply hungered for some diversion, some attention. Sometimes crowds of fifty boys followed her back to Pao Shing Road where they played ball with seminary students.

On Sunday mornings when Martha stood to teach the University Sunday School Class, it was not to a handful of sleepy students, but to a roomful of seventy-five and more who came to hear of a Savior who offered peace and hope. Martha declared that those young people emerging from the horrors of war were more eager to learn, than any she had ever encountered. As fighting raged on between Nationalist and Communist both vying for the people's allegiance, by God's grace, some came to declare their loyalty to a higher authority. It is they who, to this day, hold high the shining light of the risen Christ in China's darkness.

*Clear conscience
Never fears
Midnight knocking*

With unrelenting violence and cruelty, the struggle for China continued until Mao Tse-tung's army held undisputed control. Chiang's lack in bringing inflation under control, ever-increasing anarchy in every segment of society, and the promises of Mao to bring order and prosperity finally led to the defeat of the Nationalist government. It had been a long, costly, bitter struggle in which the people had suffered untold loss of life and property. Many were glad just to hear of a cessation of war and fighting. They never dreamed of the nightmare to come.

Whereas before they had gained control of the country, the soldiers of Mao had been on their best behavior; once the communists held undisputed dominion, they proved how ruthless they could be in stifling dissent. First they grabbed control of all forms of communication. Next they began the elimination of all free expression of thought and learning. University people were arrested, imprisoned, and many killed. They set out to erase all things Western. Foreigners were again suspect. Again and again the screws were tightened, one turn at the time until an icy grip of fear settled like a dark cloud over the vastness of China. Through a process of "re-education," they sought to mold a nation's thinking to conform to their own evil design.

As Chiang and his Nationalist army fled, communists filled every place voided. They invaded every crack and crevice like lecherous hands of a parasite preying on the people after pretending for so long to be their savior. One cannot dispute the elimination of many criminals, prostitutes, addicts and other undesirables — the government simply shot them. Like a giant, long-armed, hungry octopus, communism, long having pretended to be the people's friend, became their spy, their policeman, their judge, jury, and executioner. That hydra sought to control every facet of life by controlling first their minds. Daily bombarded with thoughts of Chairman Mao, many succumbed. Impressionable children and youth fell into the trap and were soon spouting the Communist line, even to their teachers. Olive Lawton recalled the last examination she gave in China with the communists fast closing in. The school had decided to give examinations early because of the uncertainty of their situation. Her twelfth grade English class memorized some piece of classical poetry for recitation before their peers. One bright and handsome young fellow stood, quoting in a strong and steady voice from Tennyson's "The Idylls of the King:"

'The old order changeth, yielding place to the new, and God fulfils Himself in many ways . . . .'

Increasingly, there were subtle and sometimes not so subtle signs all pointing to "go." Baptists had been in China for one hundred years. The opening of China's doors had been a slow and laborious process. The door so reluctantly opened, had been shut again. This time the door was slammed and locked tight; so tight, in fact, that thirty years would pass before those who had served there were to learn the fate of the ones left behind. Time would reveal that the seeds sown by those missionaries, and others like them, had been good seeds planted in fertile soil. But their exodus in 1950 was a heart-rending move.

Olive spoke of her final encounter with an official of the government before their exodus. He said, "The American government told you to go home."

Olive asserted, "I am not under orders to the American government, but to God Almighty!"

Quietly, politely, the official asked, "And what did God Almighty say to you?"

Martha said of the years following the Second World War that they were the most difficult of all her years in China. In fact, they were the most difficult period of her life as a missionary. The times of uncertainty in the early years and life under the Japanese paled in comparison to the unrelenting harassment and ever-increasing cruelty of the communists. A communist soldier stood at her door night and day. Every week a member of the government police visited every house and interrogated each missionary in attempts to trap them into some word that might be interpreted as a threat to the country. The periods of questioning were lengthy harangues in which no answer ever appeared satisfactory.

The pressure increased from outside the Christian circle, but it was Martha's own dear friend and pastor, who convinced her of the absolute need to go. His words were, "Don't come to church anymore, and please don't speak to me when we meet in the street. It is too dangerous for us all." Even though she knew that he loved her, the words stung like the sharp snap of a whip touching her face. She knew that the time had come to go when her staying endangered the lives of those whom she loved and with whom she had labored for half her life.

Authorities made the leaving as difficult as possible. Martha was forced to fill out forms until she lost count of them. She had to take stacks of forms in multiple copies from one agency to another. The rounds to one office after another got to be like a merry-go-round which stopped too often, but never allowed one to get off and offered no assurance that one would be allowed to continue. It seemed that final exit permits were never granted until the last measure of patience had been wrung from the applicant. Martha's own permits came as a welcome relief.

The task had been a joyous one. The struggle had been long and difficult. The better part of valor was now, indeed, discretion. They would trust the Lord and go on to do His work as doors opened in other places. One by one the exit permits were granted to the missionaries. Pearl Johnson's was the last. All got out except one — Bill Wallace, a quiet, kindly doctor who was tortured and killed.

Man has A thousand plans . . . Heaven but one

By April 1950, Chiang Kai-Shek controlled nothing but Taiwan. It was a great reversal for one who had fought more than thirty years in vain attempts to govern that ancient giant, China. Taiwan is a tiny speck of a place (when compared to the mainland). Resembling one of the jots in a Chinese character, it lies just one hundred miles off the coast southeast of Foochow. The land mass is a little less than 14,000 square miles, roughly the size of the states of Delaware and Maryland. Running down the center of the island like an exposed backbone, a chain of mountains splits the island as it rises to heights of as much of 14,000 feet. Indeed, along the chain, there are seventy peaks rising to heights of over 10,000 feet. The climate is semitropical with good rainfall which enables the land to produce a wide range of excellent crops of all kinds, including two crops

196

Baptist Compound
Pao Shing Rd
Shanghai
Sept. 10

Dear Miss Alleene:

I betcha your school has already started and mine starts Monday. I have been trying to get all of my running around done and my ducks in a row. This afternoon I ripped up this dress that just doesn't fit and tried to re cut it but there isn't enough material. Do you think you might find some like it? I got it at that place where they had lots of cotton goods. I think you go out the side door of that store near Meyers Arnold — coming down the street and it is just opposite — a sort of dime store I can't think of the name of it. I need enough to cut back and front waist — skirt and sleeves are OK. If you can't okay I'll pass it on to someone who is smaller than I.

This morning I went to a part of town I haven't been around very much and it is just like being in Russia or Paris or somewhere. I am having the fur coat Mrs. Spooner gave me repaired and was just browsing around in that neighborhood — I guess there are hundreds of white Russians in Shanghai and some of them have opened very swank salons and shops in this section — I looked at some of the things in the windows and went in one shop and asked how much they charge to make a dress — $20.00 U.S. money! One of the shops had American shoes — I looked at a pair of I Miller suede pumps, low heel in the window and they were darling — I tried them on, they fit and I asked how much and the reply was $40.00 U.S. Of course I bought two pairs!! It was just like being in Europe. It is quite a way from where we live and entirely out of our reach and our domain so therefore I didn't tarry long, but I enjoyed looking around and it was nice to see a part of the city I didn't know. I don't know who buys this stuff. In a cloth shop I priced voile — $5.00 a yard . . . .

Good letter from you yesterday — One from Corrie the day before. We heard yesterday that Bertha's passport had been held up. Tsining has been so disturbed that they would not grant it for there. I expect it is too late for them to get another passport or rather a passport for another place and still get her on that boat —

Our house is still a lively place. We all revolve around the baby. They will be going back to Peking in about two weeks. Ola has already started school. Our students are beginning to arrive — by this time next year I hope we will have some permanent buildings and get into them. Makeshift gets a little wearing and tiring after so long a time.

Am getting my glasses Saturday. It has been awful trying to wear these bifocals — I am just not ready for them!

Heaps of love to all of you — remember me to all the folks especially Lide and Ruth and Aunt Mattie, May and Nelle, Nat and Kat, etc.

Love,
Marnie

of rice a year. In addition, there is a good supply of valuable minerals of great variety.

Because of its wealth of natural resources, many countries have looked with greedy eyes upon those riches. At the end of the first Sino-Japanese War in 1895, the Treaty of Shimoneseki gave Taiwan (Formosa) to Japan. Japan eagerly exploited the island, building an excellent network of railroads to facilitate transportation of her newly acquired wealth.

With the defeat of Japan in 1945, Taiwan was restored to China. When Chiang Kai-shek lost all control on the mainland, he and his Nationalist army, along with all their dependents, retreated to Taiwan. One could not begin to imagine the turmoil resulting from the influx of many hundreds of thousands of people into such a small place. The wealthy and educated were among the first targets of the communists who had wrested control of China from Chiang; they too fled to Taiwan. In addition to the humiliation of their loss, the masses of people suffered overwhelming feelings of abandonment by much of the world. Chiang and his government believed themselves to be the rightful rulers of China even though they had failed to master the art of governing her. The people were demoralized — afraid for their lives, homeless, many penniless — cut off from the past, they despaired for the future. They were not welcomed by the native Taiwanese.

Little did those servants of God know what lay before them with the group of exiles on the island of Taiwan. They had been scattered over a land so vast that one could hardly comprehend its length and breadth; now they were squeezed together almost in a closet. If the soil had been fertile in China, it now proved to be richer and more productive than any field they had ever worked. Martha explained it thus: "They had nothing. Homeless, abandoned, poor, grief-stricken, strangers in a strange land. All they had known and loved, including their families, had been left behind." Most of them would never go home again. Many never again saw or heard from parents and children. For those who got any word at all, it was often nothing except a notice of death, imprisonment, or dismissal from a valued station. Having lost everything else, many found new reason for hope as they came to faith in Jesus Christ.

Following so many years of continued upheaval in China, the missionaries who came to serve in Taiwan felt that they were experiencing the proverbial "calm after the storm." The tensions between mainland China and Taiwan were real enough, often with threats of invasion, but they were free to preach the gospel with no fear of reprisal from government sources.

Martha's part in that agonizing retreat to Taiwan began not long after the exit permits were granted for Shanghai. The board informed her that she had been assigned to Taiwan. She was overjoyed. Her facility with the language and experience of twenty-five years among the Chinese would not come to an end.

Before going on to Taiwan, Martha returned home for a brief furlough. There had never been any question in her own mind; she would serve the Chinese people wherever God allowed. The communists closed the door to the mainland, but as God had opened for the missionaries the door to Taiwan, their part was to step through and continue His work.

As she made ready for the move to Taiwan, probably the most generous gift anyone ever gave Martha for her work came during that furlough in 1950. God led several women of First Baptist Church in Laurens to raise funds to provide for Martha a panel truck for use on Taiwan. It was beautiful, more so perhaps for its potential usefulness than aesthetically. It was almost a dream come true to have a means of transportation for people and goods. Martha could hardly contain her joy in that beautiful blue van. Before departure, she filled every nook and cranny of the van with a large variety of things for Taiwan. She packed personal items such as books, bedding, kitchen utensils, linens, and clothing tighter than one could possibly imagine. It was like getting ready for a trip to grandmother's house for Christmas as they wedged and stacked everything to capacity. The only free spaces were those for three people on the large bench seat. Martha's brother and sister, Clyde and

Martha's "blue panel truck"

Alleene, planned to accompany her to the West Coast, returning by train once they had seen her aboard the ship for Taiwan. On the day before their departure, Western Union delivered a telegram from the Foreign Mission Board in Richmond. Wondering what could possibly be so urgent, Martha privately opened the telegram which said, "You cannot take panel truck to Taiwan. The government will not allow it in." In all of Asia, fuel was in short supply. Gasoline for private cars was so severely restricted that the government had issued a ban on their importation. She read the words again almost in disbelief, folded the telegram, and without a word to anyone, put the message in her pocket. The packing continued as if nothing out of the ordinary had occurred as Martha made ready for another long trip. On the day of their departure, many came to wish them a bon voyage. Not one ever suspected the contents of a telegram in Martha's pocket.

The trip across the United States was the first in which Martha had driven. It was made more pleasant by the presence of Clyde and Alleene who helped with driving. The trio laughed, joked, looked, and enjoyed being together. They were almost like young children again. Martha silently prayed often, "Lord, you know how we need this truck. You know what a great help it will be in your work in Taiwan. Provide a way for us to have it there." There was no crying, no misery on the trip for Martha. The Lord had provided a way out for her before; he could take care of so small a matter as a panel truck into Taiwan. The same God who had given the truck would certainly make a way for it to be delivered. With that confidence, she "hilariously" traveled on toward San Francisco. Only one question was raised on the entire trip: Authorities at the California border examining the contents of the truck wanted to know about the roots she carried. They were sassafras roots from South Carolina which were good for making tea.

Arriving in San Francisco, they immediately made their way down to the freight company so as to get the truck on board ship as had been arranged many weeks before arrival of that telegram from Richmond. The man in charge threw up his hands, saying, "No way! It cannot be done!" Thus the word from the freighting company echoed that from Richmond: "You cannot take the truck into Taiwan." They refused to ship it. With nothing more than a polite "Thank you," Martha simply walked down the wharf looking for offices of other shipping companies. The first door she saw was that of a Scandanavian firm. Martha walked in, introduced herself, asking matter-of-factly, whether the firm could transport her van to Taiwan. The man replied, "Yes, of course. We're leaving in the morning. Bring it down for steam cleaning and we'll load it today." Martha asked, "Should I unpack the van for cleaning?" The answer was, "No. You may simply lock it and it will go as it is." And so the truck was steam-cleaned and loaded for Taiwan.

Martha, Clyde, and Alleene went to a hotel, had dinner, and slept the sleep of those who rest in peace. A few days of sightseeing followed, after which they soon parted company: Martha for the other side of the world, and they for Laurens by way of that northern train route which took them back through Canada and the United States.

When the family learned of the telegram from Richmond, they were not terribly surprised at Martha's response to it. They had seen her act in similar fashion a hundred times before. One can only wonder whether Clyde and Alleene would have had half so good a trip had they known. Many a person might have said, "Well, that is that. Nothing can be done. You can't fight government." Martha saw every such challenge as an obstacle to be overcome. It was like a game to her, a game of which the outcome was serious business. This was the work of the Lord. Whenever an unexpected turn appeared in the road, one had simply to be ready to maneuver so as to stay on track. The road was there; it was passable, sometimes treacherous, and the view not always clear; but the outcome was certain for one willing to persevere. Martha was ever a persevering one. It took a month jockeying from one agency to another in Taipei and a mound of paperwork, but the van was finally got into the country.

When the melon ripens
It will fall of itself

The work was already underway when Martha arrived in Taiwan. At the first mission meeting she attended, Martha was elected to chair the committee which would plan and direct summer conferences. She called her committee to a planning meeting, loaded them into the Laurens panel truck, and drove to the top of the mountain. In a little Japanese inn, the committee spent the day in fasting, prayer, and planning. From that meeting was born a dream, not just for a summer conference, but for a summer conference center of their own. The Lord planted an idea in Martha's heart that they might really have their own place. The Lord gave a vision of a place where people might withdraw from the everyday demands of life to concentrate on feeding and refreshing the spiritual self. They would then be better prepared to continue as witnesses to their faith in Jesus Christ as Lord. There would be conferences for all age groups, running all summer long. The leaders would emphasize "spiritual growth." There would be a place for spiritual refreshment, a time and place for deepening awareness of God at work in one's personal life. Those attending would concentrate on relationships with God and their fellows, both believers and non-believers. The inspiration for such a conference center had come to Martha as a result of her own experience at Ben Lippen in North Carolina.

The vision was a bold one. The mission had said nothing of establishing a conference center. There was no money; they had no land, and land was worth its weight in gold. With no more than their vision from the Lord, the committee set out to find a site for the center. It must be accessible, a place with a view, and one that could be bought. For days, while others kept their eyes and ears open, Martha rode up and down the mountain looking for the place. Every time she saw one that seemed aesthetically pleasing, she asked, "Lord, is this it?" There were dozens of places, all magnificently beautiful on the road up Yang Ming San, but none had proved to be *the* one.

Finally, a friend came to the group with news that there was a place available. It was just fifteen minutes up the mountain at a bus stop called Ling Toe (Crest of the Hill). Immediately, as she drove on the property, Martha knew, "This is it!" The location was perfect, the price was possible, and it had potential for beauty. It looked out over a valley so grand as to fill the senses with wonder at God's creation. This was it!

The committee took the project, plans, papers, and many good words to the next mission meeting, asking for funds to buy the small piece of property at Ling Toe. They presented the needed items one after another to the gathering, who discussed, and accepted or rejected them. The list seemed endless. Martha had difficulty maintaining any semblance of patience; she squirmed and twisted; she discussed the merits of other projects, voted, and waited her turn. She waited for what grew from long hours to longer days. On the final day of the meeting, the moderator presented the matter of a conference center as the last item for discussion. It was approved! They too had caught the vision. They would buy the property; and by God's grace, they would build a center. If the others had noticed her impatience before, they certainly were aware of her eagerness to be done now. She hardly heard the *"amen's"* and *"goodbye's."* Jumping into the panel truck which God had given and got into the country, she drove as fast as she dared to Ling Toe. Walking on to that property, she thanked God for His provision and laid down the "Key Money" for a conference center for the Baptists of Taiwan.

The property which was sold by the ping (a mat six feet by three feet for sleeping) was a series of rice paddies cut into the side of the mountain. Terraces were narrow, and wider spaces were necessary for any building they might do. Wider spaces were easily accomplished simply by moving soil from the uppermost terrace, filling in the third, thus creating a single terrace where there had been three. There were so many people and so little work that labor was not hard to find. Men, women, and children were happy to work for a few coins a day. Coolies came, mostly women and by sheer muscle power, moved the mountain. At least they moved that part which the mission had bought. Each came with a shoulder pole, on either end of which was a basket which they loaded with soil. They made hundreds, and thousands, and hundreds of thousands of trips until the upper terraces were stripped away, filling terraces below. And so it was done. The land was made ready for the building of a conference center.

Bamboo grew profusely over the property, providing homes for snakes, especially a bright green one called the bamboo snake. In one of the encyclopedias, Martha read in the first line of the entry on Taiwan, "It is an island with many poisonous vipers." Because of the danger from so many snakes, Martha offered a bounty of five Taiwan dollars for each snake killed. One of the young mountain-moving coolies came with a long piece of grass tied round the neck of a snake he had killed. "Is that a very poisonous one?" Martha asked. His answer was, "No'm, not too poisonous — you could walk a hundred steps after a bite from this one." It was called the *"hundred paces snake."* The missionaries were never able to equal St. Patrick's accomplishment in Ireland, but they made the snakes scarce on their new property.

"Pig Pen" house at little Ridgecrest where Martha lived the first summer

They had got the property, rearranged the soil, and killed snakes, but what of buildings for meetings, dormitories, kitchen, and necessaries. There were precisely two small buildings on the place: the one a farmer's house, the other a pigsty. Martha had been reared to believe, "Where there's a will, there's a way." The first item was a large tent for meetings. Next on the agenda was a dormitory for boys; it was of the *"facing difficulty"* variety (as simple as could be). The girls slept on kongs in the farmer's house. Mary Simpson, Lorene Tilford, and Martha got the pig pen. After removing about a foot of soil, cleaning the walls, and repairing the thatched roof, they put fresh gravel on the floor, hung mosquito nets, set up army cots, and the center was almost ready to open for business. The one absolute necessity lacking was a kitchen. They set four poles in the ground, placed cross poles atop them and a piece of straw matting for the roof. They brought in two large iron woks for cooking and boiling water, and *voilá* — a kitchen. A large open air pavilion served as dining room, recreation hall, and class room.

By the time summer came round, the center was ready for the first youth conference on the mission's property. The vision had come from the Holy Spirit. The missionaries and fellow Christians saturated the project in prayer from first thought through first sight; through hauling of soil, cleaning of buildings, and planning of program. God had led each step of the way, providing more, much more, than any one of them had ever dared dream possible.

When summer number two rolled around, there was an "air-conditioned" meeting house. Air flowed through when the walls of doors were folded back, allowing the air to flow through from all sides. There was nothing plush, but all adequate. Everything gave cause for rejoicing which was an essential element of the atmosphere at Ling Toe, which came to be called Little Ridgecrest after the Southern Baptist conference center at Ridgecrest, North Carolina. God's people were learning. They were growing in "nurture and admonition of the Lord." The "Good News" spread in ever widening circles as a result of those experiences at Ling Toe.

Mosquitoes proved to be a hateful annoyance from the first. As darkness fell, the mosquitoes dropped in swarms, attacking every living piece of flesh available. There was such a resulting slapping of legs and flapping of fans that it was sometimes impossible to concentrate on anything except avoiding as many bites as one could manage. They resorted to placing coils of incense-burning repellents under the benches on saucers.

To be happy for an hour . . . roast a pig
To be happy for a year . . . take a wife
To be happy for a lifetime . . . plant a garden

Martha had always had an affinity for beautiful things. She feasted her senses on the magnificence of God's world. In every place she ever lived, she set about surrounding herself with that beauty. She cultivated it, enhanced it, and sometimes rearranged it, bringing it closer to herself and in her line of vision. Much of what was done at Little Ridgecrest was sheer hard work. The fun came in making it pretty. Azaleas, which were native to the island, were plentiful and cheap. The large

Laurens Dormitory for women, Little Ridgecrest, Taiwan

magenta variety, called by the Portugese Formosa (as was their name for the island), was most prolific. Martha almost went broke saving money, buying dozens and dozens of those large azaleas which grew in such profusion on the grounds. A pond was needed to serve as a reservoir. Taking her inspiration from the Japanese, who are especially adept at the art of making pools, Martha had stones arranged to make a garden pool. The first two trials were unsatisfactory. The third attempt achieved the desired effect. The coolies dug the pond, laid out the stones, planted azaleas; and thus added another element to the beauty of that mountainside retreat.

Little Ridgecrest had such appeal that Martha decided that she would live there all year round. She and Bertha Smith, together again, built a small cottage at the top of the grounds in which they lived happily for a number of years. Across the entire length of the house, facing the beauty of the valley, they built a screened porch. A fellow Chinese craftsmen built a large dining table for the porch to accommodate the numbers of guests who continually streamed through the grounds. Visitors came all year round. There were mission meetings, dinners, conferences, and simple, much-needed private retreats, many of which they held on their porch. As she surrounded the house with azaleas and poinsettas on the outside, Martha sought to bring beauty inside also. On the porch she hung three hand-made cages, inside which, three lovely canaries sang every day. Each day the ah ma (cleaning woman) gathered huge hibiscus blossoms, which she placed on the cages, tables, and mantle of the house.

Among ten matchmakers
Only nine will lie

Bay Woo facilitated the entertaining of so many friends and guests. He was a hard-working and talented Christian gentleman who had accompanied Bertha from the mainland as she came to work in Taiwan. He was cook, gardener, keeper, all rolled into one. Every house should be so blessed as to have its own Bay Woo. On his rounds, he visited non-Christian neighbors, befriending them in such a way that it was said of him that "Bay Woo is the best missionary on the mountain."

Each morning before leaving for the fifteen-mile trip to Taiwan Baptist Seminary where they taught, Martha and Bertha simply reminded Bay Woo of the number of guests expected for supper. Whether six or twenty-six, nothing was ever left to chance. Without a single disappointment or surprise, Bay Woo had good dinners, all prepared and served to perfection. Year round they had fresh fruits — bananas, pineapples, watermelons, papayas, and, in season — oranges, pumalo, and a large variety of other fruits and vegetables.

In the beginning, the two women had dedicated their house to the Lord, and He took them at their word. They had available to them a row of guest rooms on the conference grounds. Through those rooms paraded a line of men and women whose lives had been lived in service to God. Saints of many persuasions came to recuperate, to rest, to enjoy the warmth, beauty, and hospitality of that mountain retreat. The "Small Woman" whose story was told in *Inn of the Sixth Happiness* stayed for several months; a Presbyterian missionary recovering from surgery spent several weeks there; Gladys Dieterly

Martha's Porch, Little Ridgecrest, Taiwan

(who had prayed for safe passage as they left China in 1942) and two Presbyterian co-workers stopped for several weeks while locating a house for their own mission. Each guest proved to be, rather than a burden, a blessing sent from God. Entertaining would have been of a much leaner sort without Bay Woo.

When Bay Woo had come with Bertha from the mainland, it was with the plan that as soon as he found housing, his family would follow. Not long after, the so-called Bamboo Curtain fell, practically severing communication with family and friends. One of the saddest and most heart-wrenching results of the flight to Taiwan was the wrecking of families. Cut off from home, in a strange land, isolated from all they had ever known and loved, many of them never again saw husbands, wives, children, or parents. After several years, news reached Bay Woo of the death of his wife several months before. Not long after the news of his wife's death, a parade of Middle Men began approaching Bay Woo with proposals of marriage. The word was about that a man was available. He was gainfully employed, of good reputation, kind, generous, and of good disposition — he was an excellent prospect for some woman needing a husband.

Martha was Bay Woo's Middle Man. She proved to be too particular, so much so that tongues began to wag. The other mission cooks were heard to say, "If it weren't for Miss Franks, Bay Woo could have married long ago." Perhaps Martha had been overly selective. The time had come to get down to serious business. She could not allow it to be said that she stood in the way of Bay Woo's happiness. Martha and Bay Woo prayed earnestly that the right woman might soon come his way. She was not long in coming. Sallie was (after 13 proposals) a small, lively widow with a ready laugh, good health, intelligence, and energy. While she was not exactly easy on the eyes, neither was she hard on the eyes. Martha agreed with her Middle Man and they set a date for the wedding.

Bay Woo wanted a proper Chinese wedding. He planned for ten tables for guests, chopping documents, speeches, congratulations from guests, formal bows to each other, and to the Middle Men. Martha insisted on a proper Christian wedding, as all the parties were Christian. It proved to be an eclectic mix of the two. The day of the wedding found all the preachers away attending a conference on another part of the island. Martha then played the two parts of Middle Man and preacher. They set ten tables for eight guests each in the Conference Dining Pavilion. They dressed the tables beautifully; there was a profusion of potted palms and fresh flowers, and the marriage duly done. Bay Woo's and Sally's wedding was a beautiful one and their marriage equally so. In the course of time, a baby was born to that happy union. She was given the name Sue Ling. No grandparent has ever been prouder than was Martha Franks at the sight of Sue Ling.

Peace and tranquility . . .
A thousand gold-pieces

Each summer brought new faces, new experiences, and greater joy in discipleship for those attending conferences at Little Ridgecrest. Martha and others were ever alert to ways for improving the facilities, each added feature an enhancement of their purpose in strengthening and deepening the spiritual self. After a few summers, they felt the need for an outdoor place for vespers. It should be different from the main service of the evening, providing a quiet place for individual reflection. Thus was born the idea for an ampitheater. The contour of the land lent itself naturally to the building of such a theater. By moving a little soil and building up other places, it could easily be done. The beauty of the place would likewise lend itself to meditation on the goodness of God as seen in His handiwork in nature. The site looked down over a plain through which meandered a sparkling river; beyond, rising in the background, was a stately ridge row of mountains, one of which was called Kwan Yin (Goddess of Mercy).

Visions were long, budgets short. Billeted at the foot of the mountain was a small contingent of soldiers. There was no law dictating separation of church and state. The soldiers appeared to have plenty of time on their hands; perhaps they could help with the work. She asked and got it.

Leading the borrowed soldiers to the site, Martha took a bamboo pole and long string with which she determined the center of the amphitheater. Here the soldiers would build a raised platform, she indicated. Moving up the hill, she circled the design of tiers of seats. The soldiers then set about the task of moving soil and in a few days had raised a platform for speakers, cutting seats for worshippers in the process. They bricked in the platform and seats and soon all was ready for use. It was practical and pretty.

Martha found great joy in introducing those Chinese boys and girls to the sights and sounds of nature. They were not naturally inclined to stop, look, and listen to the natural world. Perhaps it was because of the necessity of always being at the business of providing necessities for life. The intent of vespers was something other than a mini-worship service. The idea was not preaching, but a deepening awareness of other avenues of experiencing fellowship with God. The first night five minutes of silence was set aside for looking and listening to the beauty around them. The result was a joyful surprise to those who came. They tuned their senses to the trees, flowers, and birds surrounding them, watching as the sunset colors grew in

Reservoir pool at Little Ridgecrest

intensity and variety. Likewise the sounds of crickets, cicadas and birds all singing their *"end-of-the-day-go-to-sleep"* sounds were awe-inspiring. Before the end of the first week, five minutes had grown to fifteen and more. The amphitheater proved to be a source of spiritual refreshment to many.

A typical day at Little Ridgecrest began with *Morning Watch*, a time for individual prayer and reflection. Each morning the youths scattered all over the grounds with Bibles opened, kneeling in prayer. Next came *Bible Study* done in groups. The best teachers available came to lead in those studies and were themselves inspired by the enthusiastic response of their students. After Bible Study, there was a time for testimonies. Often, the students stood in quick succession to share personal relationships with the Lord. They spoke of successes and failures in their own lives and in their churches. Everyone looked forward to break time, the time for tea and cookies and relaxing. *Morning Preaching* was designed to encourage participants in their personal walks with the Christ. Preachers for those services were not limited to denominational affiliation. The best came to preach God's Word. Lunch came at midday with a time for rest after. The afternoon was open for group meetings, nature hikes, and a great variety of games. Supper was not long in coming, followed by *Vespers*. Last on the agenda, and the day's culmination, was *Evening Worship*. At the end of such a day, teachers and students both gladly lay down for a night of rest before beginning again.

As has been said of other outstanding edifices, Little Ridgecrest was always under construction. The kitchen, which was four poles sunk into the ground, seemed hardly adequate for the feeding of two hundred people. But the two huge iron woks under that simple shelter did just that. Participants ate numberless tons of *ta chia fu* (everybody's happy), which included a little of everything — vegetables, meat, and almost anything in good supply. In addition to cooking, those woks boiled all drinking water for the center.

Three feet of ice . . .
Not frozen in one day

For seven consecutive years, Martha asked for two or three thousand dollars to construct a proper kitchen. Annually, the mission stations met to plan work and budgets for the entire island. They then submitted those requests to the Foreign Mission Board. Every budget had of necessity ·to be trimmed to the limit. No fat ever got into any of the budgets, and often lean was cut away. For six years running, the request for a kitchen on Ling Toe never got on the mission's budget request. The conference center could make do, and there were other requests which were far more pressing than that for a kitchen. In the seventh year, the request for a kitchen was finally approved and forwarded to Richmond for an allocation from the Lottie Moon Christmas Offering; Martha knew that it would come through. A contractor approved plans and Martha initiated discussions with him and the builders. A dear friend, Leo Lau Ban (a contractor), located sand, bricks, cement,

Martha, entrance to Little Ridgecrest

and steel needed for the long-awaited kitchen. Believing all along that the funds would materialize, Martha begged for money to do the work before the rainy season began so that the next summer's camp might have use of the new kitchen. "No!" the answer came; a firm "no." "You cannot do anything until the money is in hand." All the missionaries always prayed for the success of the Lottie Moon Offering. That year, they prayed as they had never done before. Finally, the long-awaited cable-gram arrived: "Money available for kitchen at Little Ridgecrest!" Martha immediately jumped into her panel truck, drove to the contractor's and before dark, his trucks were delivering such treasures as bricks, sand and cement. It was years later that refrigeration and natural gas came to Ling Toe, but in Martha's time nothing was prized more than that little kitchen. It was possible because of gifts from caring Christians back home who gave gifts at Christmastime. Lottie Moon had first articulated her dream, and Baptist women all over the land were determined to keep it alive. As the contractor's trucks crept up the mountain near the close of that day, Martha again bowed her head and her heart to thank God for His provision.

All the while Little Ridgecrest was being built and conferences were being conducted, Martha was working every day as a teacher in the seminary. When their own little house on the

Little mountain girl with her first pair of socks and a new dress, Taiwan

crest of the hill had been completed, the seminary sent a student to assist with upkeep of the grounds. Wang Hsu, a graduate of the college of agriculture, was a great help in beautifying and maintaining the entire center. He was married to a tribal woman who was intelligent and eager to learn. She wanted desperately to attend classes for wives at the seminary but was prevented from doing so because she could not afford to pay a sitter for her small baby. They finally decided to send to her tribe in the mountain asking that a "little sister" (cousin) be allowed to come and care for the baby.

The "little sister" who came was a ten-year-old girl totally deaf. She had never before been out of the mountains and was as skittish as a deer. Her parents were happy to have her come for nothing more than her food. She came completely empty-handed, wearing only a pair of underpants and a worn dress. The baby, then about ten months old, was tied to her back in the fashion of the native Taiwanese. "Little sister" was a pitiful sight with the baby tied to her back, the child's feet reaching almost to her knees.

Martha attempted repeatedly to approach the girl, only to meet with a frightened face and a hasty retreat to other

Martha's blind children, Taiwan

216

quarters. She could not accustom herself to that strange looking woman with white skin, white hair, and not brown eyes. She was happy as a baby sitter, but she was not at all sure of the "all white" woman.

One afternoon Martha came home early from the seminary to work on the grounds of Little Ridge Crest. Hurriedly she donned her gardening togs, placed a large coolie hat on her head, and picked up her hoe. Chombo, her pet monkey, looked at her as if to say, "I'm so bored; please take me along." Chombo had been a gift from a friend who said, "Monkeys will keep the snakes away." Martha succombed to Chombo's pleading look and started down the hill to work in the chapel area with her pet riding on her hip.

In no time, Martha, several coolies, and Chombo were chopping away at the weeds surrounding the azaleas. Chombo climbed on to Martha's shoulder in order to get a better view and liked it so much that he moved on up to her head. As Lu Te came along, baby on her back, she looked up to see the "all white" woman wearing a coolie hat with a small monkey sitting atop her head. The little deaf girl dropped to her knees, doubling up with laughter. She continued rocking back and forth, unable to believe such a sight. The ice was broken. Lu Te could see that there was nothing to fear from Martha, and it was not long before the two were the best of friends.

Martha grew to love Lu Te and out of that love came an interest in the plight of the deaf. Near the seminary there was a large school for the deaf and blind run by the government. Martha made arrangements for Lu Te to enter the school for the fall term. The Wongs had also moved to the seminary where child care was available for their baby. Everyone was set to go to school — both the Wongs to seminary, and Lu Te to school for the deaf. For her first year of school, the children of the Sunday School of First Baptist Church Laurens sent a package of underclothing, dresses, book satchel, crayons, pencils, clips for her hair, and a pair of socks. She had never before had a pair of socks in her life. She felt like a princess. All she owned when she came to Little Ridgecrest was a pair of panties and a very worn dress. Now it seemed she had everything!

Soon after the opening of school, one Sunday morning, Lu Te and several other deaf children came to True Light Church where the seminary was housed. Martha was delighted, but had no idea where to turn to help them in Sunday School. The Junior Department was under the guidance of Mrs. Chang whose father had once been Premier of China. Her twelve-year-old son, who had lost his hearing as a result of a high fever when he was an infant, assisted her. Teddy and his mother made a good pair of Christians as they led in Sunday School. Martha quickly sent out an S.O.S. and in a matter of minutes, a Department for the Deaf was born.

Lu Te and the other children advertised, and the following Sunday there were twice as many children; the third Sunday saw the group double again. Soon, there were more than one hundred deaf children of all ages coming to Sunday School. How could they possibly handle so many? Martha was certain that the Lord had sent the children to them. They were eager to learn, but what could she do? She felt a special bond with them, undertaking the task of teaching the older ones herself even though she signed not a word. While they could not hear, they could read Chinese. Christian friends provided a Bible for

Miss Alleene, Taiwan

each of them.

Additional help came from a family of dear friends, the Kus. Martha had approached the lovely and talented young daughter of the Kus, inviting her to join in helping to teach the deaf children. Alice graciously accepted the challenge. At the time, Martha was teaching a course in visual aids in the seminary and had many Bible stories in Ka M. Shi bi (a dozen or so pictures on a single story which could be flipped on a chart or arranged on a flannel board). It was just about the most fun of anything Martha had ever done. In the door of the room was a small window. Every Sunday, one after another amused face looked in at her class. They peeped in, saying to each other, "Miss Franks and her deaf class — signs and wonders. She signs and they wonder!"

Long after, Martha remembered the joy she shared with her deaf children. They wanted to learn, were grateful to be taught, and desperately in need of someone to love and care for them. Family and friends often shunned and rejected them until they came to Sunday School at True Light Church. They went to Ling Toe for picnics. In the summer, some of the older ones came to Little Ridgecrest for a conference planned just for them.

When the number of deaf (and a few blind) children had reached one hundred fifty, two sisters of the Camp family from Franklin, Virginia, who had long taken a keen interest in Martha's work, each contributed three hundred dollars for that work. Martha invested the money and used the interest to charter a bus for transporting the children to church and employing an interpreter.

Not long after the Sunday School for the deaf was in full swing, on a Sunday morning, God sent a Japanese deaf preacher to the front gate of the church. He appeared from nowhere, without an invitation, thus the conclusion, "God sent him." Martha and her co-workers welcomed him with wide-open arms. No one had any idea of his theology nor anything else about him, but could he ever sign! Japanese and Taiwanese sign language are the same, and he was wonderful with the children. They loved him. Their "God sent" preacher remained several months, teaching the children each Sunday.

When their Japanese preacher returned to Japan, Martha was once again faced with the task of finding help with her children. Ever on the alert for possibles, she had already observed in the School for the Deaf, a Taiwanese teacher who signed so beautifully; her movements were like a ballerina's. Martha's friend Mrs. Lu invited her to come and interpret on Sundays as a paid assistant. Even though the young lady was from a devout Buddhist family and not herself a Christian, she accepted Martha's offer, and the two soon became good friends. They stood together on Sunday mornings, having come from two very different worlds. Martha, an American, a Christian, speaking in Chinese to those deaf children; her interpreter a native of Taiwan, devotee of Buddha, signing the language of the deaf. As funds were added to the endowment for the deaf, the young lady was asked to sign for worship services and again accepted.

The time came for Martha's furlough, and she returned to the United States, leaving behind for a time her teaching at the seminary and Sunday School. When she returned to Taiwan, she brought with her a very special person known by all the family as "Miss Alleene." Alleene and Martha had grown closer with each passing year as they wrote long letters sharing many spiritual experiences. Alleene had recently retired from a long career of public school teaching. She came, having planned to spend four months with Martha in Taiwan. Those planned four months eventually grew to four happy years for the two sisters who had seen too little of each other for most of their adult lives. Alleene assumed most responsibilities of running their busy house and greatly added to the beauty of Little Ridge Crest as she rooted hundreds of poinsettas each year, thus surrounding the place with vidid colors when the azaleas were not in bloom.

Mrs. Lu, the Taiwanese interpreter for the deaf, wanted to learn English. Miss Alleene became her happy teacher. Every Tuesday afternoon, Mrs. Lu arranged to get away from her school duties, taking the bus to Ling Toe. The two women spent the afternoon studying English. Alleene used as her text *The Simplified Bible.* Mrs. Lu was an apt student. Soon, she knew English *and* Jesus Christ as Lord. It was "Miss Alleene," retired first grade teacher who introduced her to the Savior. Not only had many of the deaf students come to faith in Jesus, their interpreter also professed him as Lord of her life.

In the beginning of her work with the deaf children in Sunday School, it was only the deaf who came. Knowing that there were a number of children who were blind, Martha wondered why none of them ventured to attend. With only a little encouragement, where the deaf led, the blind were sure to follow. Little by little, almost timidly, the blind children made their way to the church. In order to best meet their needs, Martha arranged to accommodate the deaf children on Sunday mornings and the blind in the afternoon. The children loved to sing. One of their favorite songs was "This Is My Father's World." Listening to those children who could see nothing of this world singing God's praises for the earth's beauty brought tears to Martha's eyes.

One Sunday afternoon a tiny six-year-old boy groped his way in with the other children and straight into Martha's heart. It was his first year in school. Life was most difficult because he had no one to help him bathe and wash his clothes.

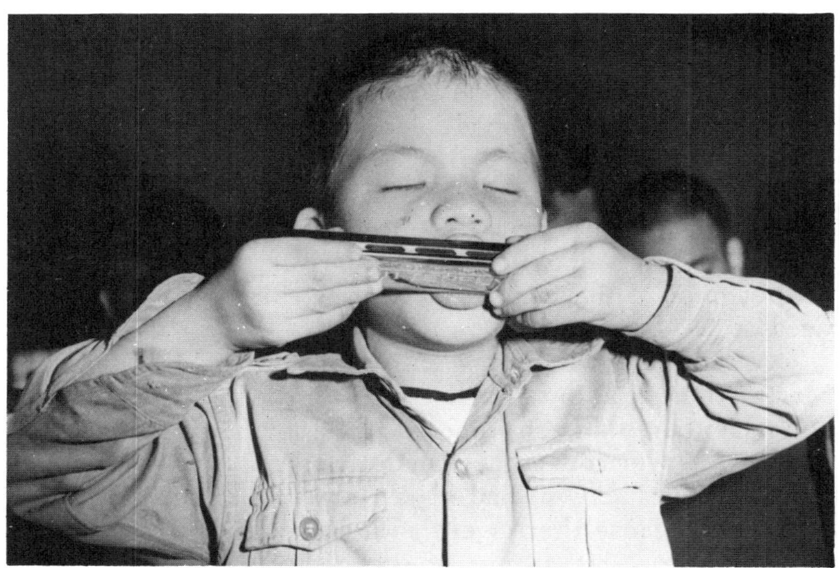

Martha's "Heart Strings" with his Christmas harmonica

Accompanying the smaller boy was another of about the same age whose eyes were terribly red and in constant pain. Martha engaged an elderly woman living near the school to go each Saturday to bathe the boys. She purchased two changes of clothing for each boy, and the old woman took one change home each Saturday where she washed and pressed the pieces before returning them to the boys on the following Saturday. Each little boy had two cotton underpants and shirts, two outer shirts, and two pairs of pants, which were the sum total of their possessions. While the deaf could take care of their possessions, anything that the blind did not have on their bodies was quickly stolen from them.

The months January and February bring the rainy season to Taiwan, and the normally good weather often turns a bone-chilling cold. Sometimes the clouds are so heavy that the sun is not seen for a month. As the rainy season approached, wives of the United States military stationed on the island assisted in collecting sweaters and jackets for the blind children. After Sunday School one Sunday, the children were "warmed," each with a heavy shirt, sweater, or jacket. Until that day, none of them had owned more than a cotton shirt.

Martha's "Heart Strings," so named by Jennie Alderman, came into her office for his "warming." When Martha told "Heart Strings" that she had a warm sweater for him, he said, "Isn't there someone who is colder than I?" The only sweater left that would fit Heart Strings was a girl's pullover. Martha decided to put the sweater under his shirt so that no one could see that it was a girl's sweater. She had pulled the sweater over his head and was about to put his shirt on top, when he said, "Never mind. This is enough. Give the shirt to someone who needs it."

At the time of her work with the blind and deaf children, Martha came to know Ai Mei, a young girl who was a victim of polio. Her parents were students at the seminary and the poor mother was worn out from so many children. Ai Mei, paralyzed from the waist down, had little training and received scant attention because there were so many other children in the family. There was a tiny house at Little Ridgecrest near Martha's own, which was made available to Ai Mei so that she might have some independence. One of the seminarians taught the girl how to care for herself and soon she was an amazement to everyone. One of the military wives gave Martha a beautiful Easter dress which was about Ai Mei's size. Hanging the dress on one end of her long porch, Martha told her, "When you can walk the length of the porch on your crutches, the dress is yours." Before summer's end, Ai Mei claimed her prize. The dress was the only beautiful thing she had ever owned in her life.

The house in which Ai Mei lived had two rooms and when summer came, Heart Strings took up residence in the other room. Martha had engaged another seminary student to tutor Ai Mei and Heart Strings. The girl proved to be an excellent tutor and companion for the two and the trio spent a happy summer together on Ling Toe.

Despite his intelligence, Heart Strings had made little progress in learning to read Braille. The little "humps" on the paper meant nothing to him. He could make no sense of what his teachers attempted to teach him by having him feel the paper. In an attempt to help him get the feel of it, Martha took a tin tray in which she poured sand about an inch deep. Taking

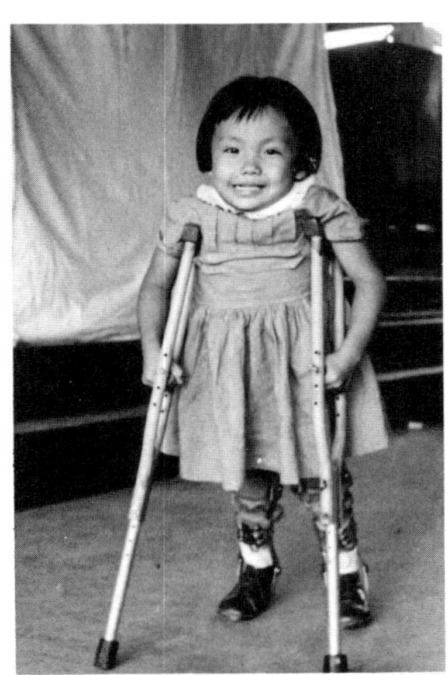

Ai Mei finally got her dress

then a handful of marbles, she positioned them in the sand to approximate the Braille "humps" on the page. Heart Strings soon got the idea and in a short time was matching marbles on the tray with the Braille in his books.

Martha spent the summer directing conferences at Little Ridgecrest. She looked forward to getting home at break time and the end of the day, especially her own private time with Heart Strings. They walked hand in hand and talked of the world and of God's love for all his children. As they strolled about the grounds, Heart Strings asked about the panel truck. Martha described the truck in detail — color of blue, windows, lights, and mirrors. He was so fascinated that he spent more than fifteen minutes examining every inch of that marvelous machine. He ran his fingers over the sides, lights, bumpers, doors, windows, mirrors, and tires until he had felt to his heart's satisfaction exactly what the truck was like. Having temporarily exhausted his curiosity with the truck, the two of them continued down the path bordered in azaleas, then in full bloom. Martha guided Heart Strings to an especially lovely plant. Taking his hand, she encouraged him to feel the leaves and blossoms, attempting to see its beauty for him. The leaves and blossoms were not nearly so interesting as the truck had been, but knowing how she wanted him to see, he said, "Fan Chao Shih (Miss Franks), you are a good woman."

A well-known European eye surgeon visited Taiwan for several days in an attempt to determine whether he could help any of the blind children to see. Heart Strings and his red-eyed companion were taken to the clinic with a large group of the children. Upon examining Heart Strings, the doctor found that his blindness was congenital and could not be helped at all. His companion suffered from inverted eyelashes, which could be altered by a relatively simple surgical procedure. While the damage to his eyes could not be undone, the pain was alleviated and a part of his sight restored. Heart Strings could not understand why his friend could be helped to see, while he was left out. Hearing that his friend was going to be helped, he begged of Martha, "Won't you ask him to help me — just so I can see a tiny bit?" Taking the little boy in her arms, Fan Chao Shih blinked back the tears which he could not see.

P.O. Box 427
Taipeh, Taiwan
Sept. 20, 1960

Dear Friends:

Back to school!! It gives me a roll-up-your-sleeves-and-get-to-work-feeling. I hope it lasts until I catch up with all of the letter writing I didn't do during the summer filled with typhoons, summer conferences, conventions, clinics, etc.

We seem to be off to a good start in the seminary with some very good prospective "Gospel Proclaimers" in our first year class. We urgently need your prayers as "line upon line" we attempt to guide them in their preparation for this part of the vineyard where the opportunities are so great, the fields so white, and the harvesters so few.

Guess who is in the office next to mine? Juliette Mather!! We are so grateful that she consented to stay over to help us this year as we found ourselves in an acute emergency caused by the loss of two professors. Pearl Johnson is also coming two days a week to put her shoulder to the wheel.

Thank you for your prayer help that pulled us through the summer of "blood, sweat and tears" required for the production of summer conferences. Our weariness was forgotten in the summit experiences of "Say So" meetings at the close of each conference. There were from thirty to eighty professions of faith in each conference, as well as many who publicly professed their dedication to the Lord. Not a few acknowledged their answer to the call for full time Christian Service.

My greatest thrill came the last night of the conference for young people when thirty or more of our "silent" young people made professions of faith in the Lord Jesus as their Savior. Three made dedication for life service, and already one of them is "preaching" every Sunday night in our church to the deaf. During this conference, Mrs. Wang, who has worked with

Pearl Johnson with the deaf in Tainan, interpreted. An American college president who does not know the sign language, said, "Her interpretations are more beautiful than a ballet."

For recreation, our silent young people made stamp albums. They could hardly believe that the albums were to be their very own. Thank you for the used postage stamps you sent. We will be wanting some more for next summer (please!). The five blind young people took your beautiful Christmas cards, wrote Bible verses in Braille on them and sold more than two hundred of them to help a deaf evangelist from Japan with his hospital expenses.

Another great joy Miss Alleene, Olive and I had this summer was our five week camp for five handicapped children — two blind, two deaf, one polio victim. Ai Jen, the five-year-old polio child, made the most evident progress. When she came to us, she was so shy, she would wail if you looked at her. She could not walk or take care of herself. She is now "getting around" with braces and crutches. The day she climbed on her little toilet by herself was a hilarious victory for the entire group!! To see her emerge from her little shell into a beautiful, happy, independent child was a most rewarding experience.

Da Cheng, the seven-year-old blind boy, they called my "Heart Strings." He came to us, a lovable, affectionate child, chock full of questions. Although he had been in the school for the blind for a year, he had not learned one single Braille character. We used every method we could think of to help him "see" those tiny dots. Finally, I got a tray of sand and some marbles to try to teach him how to place those dots to say the first character "be." He just could not get it! Why should dots or marbles placed in a certain position, say "be"??? And what does said "be" mean to me???? After trying to teach him how to place those three marbles without success, I said, "Tomorrow when you start your lesson, ask Jesus to help you learn to read." He did just that, and in one day, learned four characters! Prayer and the things of the spirit are very real to him.

I could go on forever about our children, but I am afraid someone would say I am like you "S.O.G.'s" — Silly Old Grandmas.

Please keep us, these children, the seminary, and next year's camps in your love and prayers. It seems that Miss Alleene and I may be coming home next summer. Gladys Hopewell, who did such a grand job helping me this summer, will be "toting heavy." Pray for her! We are already making plans and inviting speakers for next summer.

May your heart be filled with joy and peace as you serve and love Him in your part of the vineyard.

Lovingly and gratefully yours,
Martha Linda Franks

As she remembered her work with the blind, Martha had one good word to say of the Japanese. They took much from Taiwan and one of the few gifts the Japanese left with the Taiwanese was the art of massage. While "masseuse" and "masseur" have sometimes a bad name in the United States, it was not so among the Chinese. At the end of the day, one could hear coming down the street the masseur and masseuse. Each was recognized by his own tune of four or five notes played on a little flute. If one wished a massage, he simply opened the door, inviting a particular practitioner in. For a few cents, one could rid one's body of a great deal of tension through the hands of a skilled craftsperson. Massage provided a living for many blind persons so that they were not reduced to begging.

The peony is beautiful
Yet it is supported
By a stalk

Martha spent fifteen years in Taiwan. She played the accordian on the streets of towns and villages and told the old, old gospel story to any who stopped to listen. She helped organize churches; she worked with women, encouraging them to realize their own worth as God's servants alongside the men. She realized the dream of a summer conference center as she personally oversaw the planning, building, and operating of Little Ridgecrest. She learned sign language (a little) and worked with the blind children because of a special love God had planted in her heart for them, many of whom had been rejected and abandoned first by their families and then by almost everyone else; Martha took them up. She was invited to give English lessons on the largest radio station in Taiwan. The government informed her that she could also preach the gospel if she were willing to teach the people to speak English. Martha

Martha preaching, Taiwan

was eager to have the radio opportunity because she was aware that people on the mainland would also hear her messages of the love of God. All the while, she taught classes in the seminary. The men and women she taught are themselves this day teaching and preaching the gospel. The message continues as our Lord admonished "To the end of the world."

The last speaking engagement for Martha prior to her retirement was on the occasion of an annual associational meeting of Women's Missionary Union in Taipei. There were several hundred women in attendance from churches in Taipei and surrounding areas. Her assigned subject was *Witnessing*. Martha arrived early and randomly invited five women to help her with the subject. At the time designated in her notes, she asked each in turn, "How did you first hear about Jesus?" The answers sounded like many recorded in the Bible. The first woman said, "I was walking to market one morning when rain began to fall and I had no umbrella. Another woman on the crowded street was also headed for the market. She asked me to share her umbrella and as we walked together she told me about Jesus."

The second said, "I was a patient in the hospital. Some ladies from Women's Missionary Union of Jen Ai church came to visit. They stopped at my bed, talked to me about Jesus and left some tracts."

The third woman said, "My child went to a Baptist chapel near our house. A nurse gave her a beautiful Christmas card from America. On the card was a Bible verse in Chinese. It told me about Jesus."

The fourth woman said, "A neighbor invited me to go to church with her and there I heard about Jesus."

The fifth said, "My husband died and in my great distress, I went to a nearby church to see if they could help me. They did. They told me about Jesus."

Each one had been introduced to the Lord Jesus by another Baptist woman. Here they were at the annual women's meeting, having come from different towns and villages to serve the Lord. In the beginning, it had been the Women's Missionary Union of Grove Avenue Baptist Church of Richmond, Virginia who raised the funds to send Martha to China. For forty years they paid her salary. The very first letter Martha received as a missionary in China was written by a Sunbeam girl from Chester, South Carolina. Through all the years, it was primarily efforts of women that provided the means for her and others to serve round the world as messengers of God's love.

No road to happiness
Or sorrow . . .
Find them in yourself

How does one come to the end, or better perhaps to a new beginning? Martha had once had the sad experience of watching a close friend leave China most unhappily. War was imminent, and one of the missionaries who was in failing health and advancing in years, was told she could not be approved for another country. She had done a good job sharing God's word among the Chinese people. She loved them and they loved her. Now it was time to leave. Martha watched the woman go unwillingly. Later she concluded that she never drew another happy breath as long as she lived.

One thing Martha determined was to go with some semblance of dignity and grace. She prayed to God that when her time came, her superiors would not drag her kicking and screaming to the boat. She took the approach that one phase of her life was finished. It had been a happy, glorious experience made possible by God's grace. She had loved the work and the people and was grateful for every day of it. Inevitably there comes another turn in the road of life which brings a parting of good company who must take their separate paths. Rather than a dark foreboding, she wondered excitedly what God was planning for her in America. She thought of how as a college freshmen she had asked the Lord to plan her life. He had done so wonderfully through almost fifty years. There was no reason to doubt that he would continue to "Silently plan for [her] in love" as the prophet Jeremiah says. God's plans exceeded her best dreams.

The first surprise was a place to live. Her very own house! All the years home away from home, she never really had a place to call her own. Martha's brother Clyde told her she could choose any spot on his seventy-acre estate. That seventy acres is a beautiful piece of wooded land miraculously preserved in the heart of the city of Laurens. Martha chose what to her was the loveliest spot on the grounds. Her house would sit on the side of a hill looking out over a pretty valley. A hundred years before it had been a deer park when Colonel John Drayton Williams built his magnificent Italianate villa. The "Villa" which Clyde had restored and in which he then lived, sat not far away from the house he would build for her.

Clyde arranged with a contractor to build Martha's house before she came home, but before the plans were finished, the contractor died. Two long-time family friends, the brothers C.D. and Garfield Beasely approached Clyde, offering to build Martha's house. So it was that those two dear black friends came to build the house in which she lived upon her retirement. Clyde began the planning and overseeing of every aspect of this project of love for Martha. He cut timber from his property and took other steps to cut the cost to the barest minimum. He was never happier than when engaged in the construction or renovation of some building. He had begun as a young boy, building a playhouse back of the family's home. Years later he bought and restored Rose Hill, the Governor Gist mansion in Union County. Clyde was as excited about Martha's house as she.

Martha's retirement homecoming was a joyous occasion. There were family gatherings, dinners, parties, speeches, words of love, expressions of appreciation. For years she had been collecting and sending back precious parcels to Laurens. Now she came home bringing a mountain of stuff for her own house. Clyde, too, had been busy in that regard. There was a great antique poster bed for Martha's comfort and many other pieces collected from all over. His daughter Sadie said of her father, "He thought if one of something was good, a dozen of the same would be wonderful."

Her sister Rosalie, now a widow, had a spacious house and invited Martha to come and live with her. Another sister Alleene was already living there and the three of them could have had a happy time living together. The offer was tempting, but the thought of her own place was even more so.

Construction on her house was well under way with windows, some flooring, water, and electricity, but no doors. Martha moved in. She thrilled to see each nail driven. For more than forty years she had lived with necessities, sometimes barely so, and now she could wait for the luxuries. And watch! She enjoyed watching as cabinets were built, moldings fitted, doors hung, painting done. And changes made! After all, it was her house.

Along the back of the house, overlooking the wooded valley, she had planned for a porch to run the length of the house like the one she had at Ling Toe. The one under construction was too narrow for the entertainment to which she had been accustomed. Just because she had retired from China, it need not follow that she would not continue to entertain. The porch was widened to allow for much informal entertaining. Women's groups, Sunbeams by the score, VIP's, friends, and family ate on that porch. The first year of their return, Olive Lawton came to live with her. Olive kept a record of the guests in that one year and found that more than one thousand people enjoyed Martha's porch.

Every Sunday that Martha was not away speaking to some church group the entire Franks family came for lunch. Sisters, brothers, nieces, nephews, all came for a time of fun, food, and fellowship. After more than forty years of separation, it was good to be together again.

On a Sunday afternoon Clyde stood on the lawn by the porch waiting for dinner to be served. Looking round at the beauty of the place, he said aloud to himself, "I don't understand it. I just don't understand it."

Martha had overheard him talking to no one and asked, "What don't you understand?"

"How this place in the heart of Laurens has been left intact — virgin forest — untouched all these years," he answered.

Martha replied, "I understand it. The Lord left it intact, untouched for a retirement center he is going to build." The Lord had already given her that vision. She and others were in the process of moving under God's guidance to make the dream reality. A group of women had begun to pray, and God was listening to their prayers.

Pure gold
Does not fear
The smelter

It took almost twenty years of praying, working, believing, before the dream became reality. One remembers the twenty years Marie Monson prayed before she saw revival come to China. How long is twenty years with God? Prayer, work — the two are an unbeatable combination. Dreaming all the while, Martha worked. She traveled all over the country telling of God's grace in her work in China. She led prayer retreats from coast to coast. Her little Volkswagen Rabbits were a familiar sight to many; she wore out thirteen of them, six "bugs" and seven "Rabbits".

A perusal of Martha's engagement calendar for 1967 impresses one with the grueling pace which she set for herself upon "retirement." She was engaged in churches forty Sundays, participated in six conferences, ten prayer retreats, two crusades, and one hundred fifty week-day meetings. She drove to Florida (and flew down twice), Georgia, North Carolina, Virginia, and Tennessee.

The book is filled with notes of letters to write, and scores of recipes for the entertaining she did in her own home. With such a demanding schedule, she took time to enjoy the height of the azalea season at Magnolia Gardens and a Fall Foilage Tour.

Martha continued a similar routine until well past her eightieth birthday. Even though she had long since reduced the load, it was not until she was in her ninetieth year that she finally retired from speaking engagements. In late summer 1989, as she drove back from a conference at Ridgecrest in North Carolina, she heard the Lord say to her, "Martha, this is a part of your life that is coming to an end." Her response was, "Yes, Lord. Thank you for all of it."

In the spring of 1967, Martha and Olive traveled to Richmond by bus. They had several speaking engagements and loose ends to tie up at the Foreign Mission Board. Martha consulted with attorneys at the Board who helped her to draw up a will stipulating that all her worldly possessions would go to the envisioned Christian Retirement Center in the case of her death. She felt better having disposed of that matter. Now to see how the Lord would lead.

The afternoon just prior to their evening departure from Richmond, several old friends invited Martha and Olive to dine with them at Miller and Rhodes Department Store. Martha finished off her meal with strawberries and chocolate silk pie. It was to be a long and sleepless night! But not a fruitless one.

As the bus bounced down the road bound for Laurens, Olive curled up and went into a restful sleep. For Martha, the combination of berries, chocolate, and that ride, all served to make her too uncomfortable to sleep. She was carsick much of the night. Realizing that there would be little sleep for her, she refused to waste an entire night just being sick. As she had learned to do so many years before in China, Martha began to pray. Prayer had proven to be a warm companion on many a cold and agonizing night before. Now, as on those other occasions, she found the Lord wide awake and listening. The Psalmist had declared that truth thousands of years before, "Behold, He that keepeth Israel shall neither slumber nor sleep" (Psalm 124:4).

Between the bouts of sickness she prayed. "Lord, where do we begin?" she asked. "What do we do?" Building was nothing new to her; she had personally directed the construction of Little Ridgecrest and her own house on Ling Toe in Taiwan. A retirement center is something altogether different, however. It was a great unknown for her. How does one go about building something as complex as a retirement center? What about laws, zoning, sewerage, permits, and a thousand other requirements?

The Lord answered simply, "Begin where you are with what you have." Thinking then of what they had Martha quickly totaled it up. There was exactly $55.00 in the sugar bowl in the kitchen cabinet. Mary Hayes Owens had sent

$50.00 earned from tutoring, and Olive's niece, Gwyn, had spent a few days, leaving $5.00 as a parting gift. Resources which seemed meager in the extreme were not so with God. "Begin where you are with what you have;" that is what God had said.

Later in the night as the bus rolled along the road, and strawberries and chocolate rolled in her stomach, she had the idea for a Thrift and Gift Shop. Now she was really getting excited! She had always loved flea markets and second-time-around shops. There were few things more fun to Martha than going into some dusty little shop and finding an unexpected treasure. In China, she had sometimes had the experience of discovering some exquisite piece which turned out to be priceless. In the early days, some of those treasures could be had for a few dollars. All kinds of things could be got for the "thrift" side. For the "gift" side, there would be beautiful Chinese things which could be purchased in Hong Kong and Taiwan. Bargains on the one side would be balanced by really good and lovely items on the other. The long night on the bus was well-spent in conversation with God. Fairly dancing in her seat, Martha was glad that she had been unable to sleep.

The next day, Martha was in Belks Department Store in Laurens when she saw the manager approaching. "Miss Martha, we have several boxes of stuff here. I wonder if you could use it?" The manager of the store had no way of knowing that God was working through him to help confirm the vision of a thrift shop. Here it was — the "thrift" for the shop. Martha's heart leaped at the confirmation of last night's dream.

Leaving the store with praises to the Lord as she drove from the square onto Main Street, she could hardly believe her eyes! One block from the square was an old house unoccupied for years. The house had originally been the family home of her late brother-in-law. It took no time at all to gain permission from the present owners to use the house for a Thrift and Gift Shop. The four rooms on the ground floor would be just right for the shop. Hurriedly she called an electrician who met her at the house within the hour.

The first seeming hurdle soon appeared as the electrician told her that it would be necessary to rewire the house. He would have to begin upstairs and put new wiring down the walls, as the old had worn out long ago. Martha had assumed it would be the simplest matter of connecting a few wires and pushing a button. In her naviete she was almost afraid to ask, "How much will it cost?" The electrician replied that he had recently done a similar job for $250.00. There was only $55.00 in the sugar bowl.

"You poke around some more," Martha said, "and give me a little more time." Going into a back room for consultation with a Higher Authority, she asked, "Lord, what shall we do?" From the Lord there came a word as clear as crystal: "If you will make this whole project — shop, center, everything — a place of prayer, you may trust me for the necessary finances." Having got her answer from God, she returned to the electrician. "It is not necessary to conceal the wires and I have some wire in the truck and fixtures which I will give you," he said. She accepted. They were in business. The wiring was done for a few dollars.

There was the thrift, there was a house, now to spread the word. She got into the car and drove directly to the office of the *Advertiser*. She placed a notice in the paper announcing a prayer meeting in the Anderson house for Thursday night at 7:00. Anyone who had a desire to pray for the matter of the shop and a retirement center, or any other concern, was welcome to attend. Almost twenty came to that first prayer meeting. They had made a beginning. God was at work as He had promised, as she had known He would be.

Shop fever was contagious. Ladies come to scrape the walls and to paint. Paint donated was of several different colors, but there was nothing to do except mix it all together in order to have enough to cover the walls. The color came out just right (so everyone agreed) for the walls of their shop. Other women went to work on the floors. From various and sundry places, they had obtained many small squares of carpeting which they laid to form a most interesting psychodelic covering. They hung curtains and the old Anderson house made a first-rate thrift shop (the gift was yet to come). The thrift stuff began to pour in. There was no shortage of volunteers to mind the shop. For several years Elsie Sims managed the shop, doing a superb job throughout.

There was one person who proved to be a God-send indeed. Ruby Todd set up a model set of books which proved to be invaluable later on. An unknown informer reported to the Internal Revenue Service that Martha was benefitting personally from the sale of those hand-me-down items. She was dumbfounded to open a letter instructing her to come to Spartanburg for an interview with the IRS. Upon talking with her, the man was convinced that there was no irregularity. The man took one look at Ruby Todd's bookkeeping and was gone. No one had reason to think anyone involved in that shop had any but the highest motives.

The Professional Women of Laurens sponsored a bake sale; another group sold dogwood tress. Nell Kendrick suggested collecting glass for recycling at the Laurens Glass Factory. Abe and Ike Smith gave a nice red truck which they parked just outside the house, near enough to the sidewalk that people could bring their glass for recycling. Each week, Curtis Sims drove the week's collection to the factory. The average weekly income from glass alone was $50.00.

Ever alert to the possibilities of teaching along the way, Martha and Olive organized a noon Bible class for business women. It caught up nicely, sputtered, smoked, and died out. But how those women would work. Ruth Roper invited a professional teacher of decoupage to teach ten selected women the art. It was such a success that on the day of their first big sale, decoupage alone made a thousand dollars.

Miss Alleene, upon seeing some of the stuff that had been donated to the shop, observed that it was some of the "thriftiest" stuff she had ever seen. She said to Martha, "I think people are getting the wrong image." Martha replied, "Just wait until we go to China and bring back the 'gift stuff.' That will put us in the high brow category." And it did.

The Lord provided money for a trip to China and for buying. One summer, years before, when Martha was home from Winthrop, she and several friends went to the country club to swim. A cousin, B. Duckett, got cramps, and was going under. Martha had had Red Cross rescue lessons and jumped in, pulling B. to safety. When the Mr. Duckett died, he left Martha twelve thousand dollars. She felt it belonged to God and used it to buy goods in China for the shop.

In 1972, Olive, Ruth Roper, Edna Foy, and Ruby Todd accompanied Martha to Hong Kong and Taiwan for a shopping spree most people only dream of. Mainland China was not then open to most foreigners, but there were good buys of first quality porcelains, silks, brasses, cloisonné, water colors, and many others of endless variety. Martha knew all about packing and shipping, and the business was concluded with no hitches at all. On a return trip a few years later, they found that the prices of everything had skyrocketed.

On the day before their departure from Hong Kong, a school friend of Olive, a Mr. Bartell, invited the women to the Penninsular Hotel for dinner. Their schedule was crowded, and Martha was not inclined to go. They finally settled on snacks at ten o'clock in the evening. As they visited, Mr. Bartell, a Swedish Baptist, reared in China, told of a wonderful experience some years before. When the communists occupied Shantung, and missionaries were ordered out of the country, he chose to stay without the title missionary. During the terribly destructive reign of the notorious Red Guards, they forced their way into every house, destroying anything considered anti-revolutionary. Books printed in foreign languages were special targets. When the Red Guards reached the Bartell house, they burst through the door, grabbing every book and paper, especially Bibles. All were thrown into a heap in the yard and set afire. When the ruffians had gone from his street, Mr. Bartell went out to look at his treasures, now reduced to a pile of ashes. With the toe of his shoe, he kicked randomly, sadly at the pile. There was one small piece of paper left unharmed. Taking that piece lovingly in his hands, he read the words, "My church and the gates of hell shall not prevail against it." Martha thanked the Lord that she had gone to meet Mr. Bartell.

Returning to Laurens with a great load of treasure, they found people eager to buy every item. Martha held the first big sale at McAlister Square in Greenville where she and volunteers sold three truck loads of Chinese and other hand made American pieces. Rosalie, Alleene, and others continued to pray for the center, for hurting people, and for missions. Martha and her group continued to work. She traveled, spoke, prayed, studied, and dreamed of the day when the Christian Retirement Center would become a reality. Continually, there were roadblocks: legal questions concerning the land; engineering problems — water and sewerage. She never knew that there could be so much to building a place for old Christians to live out their final days. Never once did she doubt that it would be done.

During one of those periods when roadblocks arose everywhere, Dr. Signe Berg came for a visit. Dr. Berg and her husband, missionaries from Sweden, had also served in China. After the coming of the communists, they had continued their work as physicians. While on a bus trip in the interior, Dr. Berg, the husband, was ordered off the bus by soldiers. They then shot and killed him and every person aboard. Dr. Signe Berg, (the widow) soon thereafter came to work in Taiwan and became a favorite speaker at Little Ridgecrest. On a beautiful morning, Dr. Berg sat on Martha's porch in Laurens reading the Bible and praying. She later said to Martha and Olive, "The Lord has given me a verse for the center: 'God, who quickened the dead, and calleth those things which be not as though they were,' " (Romans 4:17).

If I keep a green bough In my heart . . . The singing bird will come

Dr. Tom Garrett, Director of South Carolina Baptist Homes for the Aging, outlined the marriage of Martha's dream and Baptists' recognition of the need for a new home for the aging. Long having recognized that Bethea Home in Darlington was woefully inadequate to meet the ever-increasing demands of an aging population, the South Carolina Baptist Convention at its annual session November 1977, approved a committee to study the matter. In 1978, trustees of South Carolina Baptist Homes for the Aging recommended to the convention the building of a home in the Piedmont region of the state. The convention approved and appointed a site committee. Dr. Garrett as Director surveyed numerous sites, being pressured from many sides to move quickly in making a decision.

In February 1979, Mr. Jim Ferguson of Laurens advised Dr. Garrett of what Martha was attempting to do. Mr. Ferguson then arranged a meeting between Martha and her committee, and Dr. Garrett and his site committee. After general discussion and a viewing of the site, it seemed to both parties that a home in Laurens might become reality. Several meetings followed with a formal decision in June 1979 to build a new home in Laurens.

Martha and the Christian Retirement Center Committee handed Baptists several hundred thousand dollars raised over a dozen years, and eleven acres of land. She had never dreamed that the home would come in this manner; she simply accepted the reality as God's will.

Martha, Olive, Dina Hair (Director of Social Activities), and Lottie Moon's dressing mirror

After approval by South Carolina Baptists and a successful fund-raising campaign under the leadership of Dr. S. George Lovell, Jr., who served as Director of Development from 1981-85, architects Neal, Pierce, and Brownings of Greenville, taking their inspiration from the 130 year old "Villa," designed the magnificent edifice which was named the Martha Franks Baptist Retirement Center. The fully-equipped home, complete with long-term nursing facility and adjacent apartments, is designed to accommodate 160 people.

On February 4, 1985, Martha, her sister Rosalie, Olive, and a host of others moved into the newly completed home. In every public area, there are reminders of the years spent in China. The wall hangings, screens, porcelains, carvings, Miss Lottie Moon's dressing mirror — all add to the beauty of this place conceived by Martha as a final home and . . . 'House of Prayer' for all people.

Upon entering the retirement center, Martha had no thoughts of sitting down to await the *last call*. She began the work of beautification of the grounds. In addition to those professionals who are universally employed to plant their plastic-looking sameness encircling every building, Martha personally oversaw the planting of rose gardens, hundreds of irises, and thousands of bulbs. But her greatest love was azaleas. For years she had busied herself rooting hundreds of the varieties with which she had beautified Little Ridgecrest.

One day in 1986, finding herself with seven hundred plants and no one to do the planting, Martha drove down to the city jail to ask whether two or three people might be available to do the work.

Sure enough, there were three men in jail for driving while under the influence of alcohol. If they were willing to work, it could be arranged. The men were willing. For a day's wages and lunch, they would work. But none of them had a license to drive. Martha, at 85, drove the truck herself. Three jail-birds and one old white-haired long-retired missionary planted seven hundred azaleas. One man did such good work that the residents took a collection and paid his fine so that he could remain with the center.

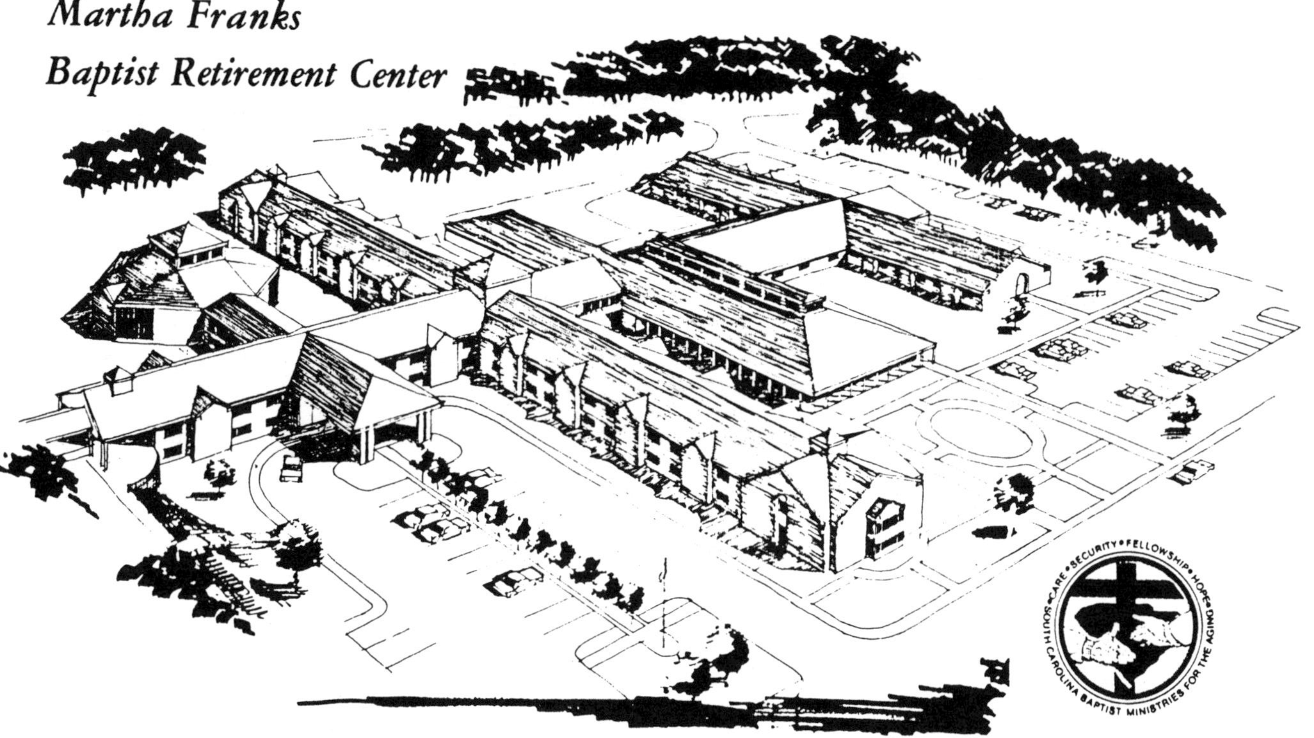

Martha Franks
Baptist Retirement Center

Martha, now well into her ninetieth year, spends her days in reading, study, and prayer. She receives and entertains scores of guests and continues to lead an active, happy life that inspires those who fall under her spell.

As with her Chinese checkers so long ago, she has moved her marbles back and forth, and will continue to do so until the Lord makes his final move in her behalf.

If in the dark
He kneels to pray
He really prays

It was not until the decade of the nineteen eighties that authorities allowed churches to reopen in China. More than a decade had passed since the reign of terror of the notorious Red Guards. The Red Guards had been masters refined in the black arts of destruction, intimidation, and humiliation. They had the huge Baptist church in Canton closed after destroying its contents.

When word came that the people might re-open the church, they anxiously cleaned the building and made ready for worship. On the Sunday before Christmas 1981, the faithful filled every seat, all the aisles, even wall spaces, and hundreds more stood in the street to be a part of that first open service in many years.

Where had they come from? The official line that the world had heard repeatedly was that communism had supplanted outdated religious beliefs.

On that Sunday morning, the pastor who stood to lead the service was one of those seminarians trained by Baptist missionaries just prior to their expulsion from China. As the pastor announced the first hymn, there was a noticeable nervousness on the part of the congregation. Many of them wondered if all of this might be a trap set by the authorities to flush them out as Christians. As the organist began to play, the people stood to sing "Holy, Holy, Holy." On the third "Holy," the entire congregation burst into tears. It had been thirty years since they had heard the organ and almost as long since some of them had felt secure in singing aloud of their faith. It was several minutes before they could continue the song of praise to God.

Estimates vary greatly, but indications are that there were four to five million Chinese Christians when the *foreign* missionaries left. Many people believe that today there are fifty to one hundred million, and perhaps many more.

"The old order changeth, yielding place to the new: and God fulfils Himself in many ways."

The Beginning

Yellow gold
Plentiful compared to
White-haired friends

Martha at 88 years of age